OSCAR WILDE

Edouard Roditi

Oscar Wilde

A New Directions Book

Acknowledgements are due to *Poetry: A Magazine of Verse* (Chicago) and to *Chimera*, which have printed certain chapters of this book as separate essays; to the William Andrews Clark Memorial Library, in Los Angeles, for permission to consult their unique collection of Wilde manuscripts and documents; to my friends in Los Angeles, and especially to Charles Aufderheide, Sam From, and David Sachs, for constant encouragement and assistance.—Edouard Roditi

Manufactured in the United States of America
Originally published clothbound by New Directions in 1947; reissued in a revised, enlarged edition as New Directions Paperbook 624 in 1986
Published simultaneously in Canada by Penguin Books Canada Limited

Library of Congress Cataloging-in-Publication Data
Roditi, Edouard.
    Oscar Wilde.
    A New Directions Book
    (New Directions paperbook; 624)
    Bibliography: p.
    1. Wilde, Oscar, 1854–1900—Criticism and
interpretation. I. Title.
PR5824.R6   1986   828'.809   86-8578
ISBN 0-8112-0995-4 (pbk.)

New Directions Books are published for James Laughlin
by New Directions Publishing Corporation,
80 Eighth Avenue, New York 10011

Contents

Author's Note for the Revised, Enlarged Edition

To the present reprint of the original edition of this book, I have added three new chapters, now published here for the first time— "Wilde's Life and Writings in the Perspective of History," "Was Oscar Wilde a 'Shy Pornographer'?" and "Wilde's Art in His Life." They are justified, I feel, by the publication of so much important new material, concerning Wilde's life or his writings, that was not available to me in 1945, when I undertook to write this critical study. These more recent publications include, in addition to some previously unpublished writings of Wilde, two volumes of his collected letters and a number of new books on his life or his trials or of memoirs of contemporaries who knew him personally.

A particularly interesting such publication is Martin Fido's *Oscar Wilde, an Illustrated Biography*, first published in 1973 by Hamlyn Publishing Group Limited and reprinted in New York in 1985 by Peter Bedrick Books. In addition to a fascinatingly varied iconography, it includes at the end, among the acknowledgements, a very ample critical bibliography, which neglects, however, to mention the original edition of the present volume.

Although my style as a writer has, quite understandably, undergone a considerable evolution since this book was originally written in 1945, I feel justified in now refraining from making a great number of minor corrections where I might today express more or less the same thoughts in somewhat different terms.

A German translation of the original edition of this book was published in Munich as early as 1947 by Herbert Kluger Verlag and was sold out within a few months. Later, this book was also extensively quoted in French in Philippe Jullian's biography of Oscar

Wilde as well as elsewhere. Together with George Woodcock's excellent *The Paradox of Oscar Wilde,* published in London in 1949 and never reprinted, it thus appears to have remained for many years a pioneer attempt to evaluate Wilde's importance as a thinker and a critical theoretician rather than to gloat over or to minimize the more scandalous aspects of his private life and of his unfortunate trials.

E.R.

OSCAR WILDE

Introduction

The fate that proverbially awaits the prophet in his own land is amply illustrated in English and American criticism of the last few decades. Of all the great nineteenth-century innovators in our poetry, but two have obtained direct recognition from our critics: Whitman, whose complex thought is erroneously believed to be fully accessible to the common reader and whose poetic style has been cheaply imitated by some of our least intelligent and most journalistic poets, and Gerard Manley Hopkins, the elucidation and imitation of whose art has become the lifework of a specialized élite.

We had to discover Baudelaire and Mallarmé before we could learn to love our own Poe; and an appreciation of his poetry is still considered, in some quarters, the shibboleth of a high-brow cult rather than an indication of average understanding of, and normal respect for, one of our major classics. Of Byron, who inspired Lautréamont, little is known or appreciated by those who admire *Maldoror*, though French Surrealists again praise *Manfred*. Of Browning, whose acrobatically rhymed and often jocular poetry, with its quaint plots and topics derived from such varied readings, sometimes offers striking similarities to that of Guillaume Apollinaire, not a word in whole collections of our advanced magazines which now fuss over Aragon, Apollinaire's cheap and easy imitator. Of Coventry Patmore, whom Claudel translated into French, little is said except by Catholic critics or students of Hopkins. For Swinburne, whose *Poems and Ballads* involved the author, in 1866, in a criminal prosecution similar to that provoked, in France, by the publication of Baudelaire's *Les Fleurs du Mal*, we hear but contempt, since Eliot's essay on him, in quarters where Verlaine, who would deserve to be condemned on the same principles, is still admired. Tennyson, greatest of all innovators in English metrics, is

1

beginning to be appreciated again, in a tentative manner, since the publication of Eliot's and Auden's essays on his poetry. But Beddoes is scarcely ever mentioned, though the somber soliloquies of *Death's Jest-book* have much in common, in both their neo-gothic diction and in their thought, with those of Melville's much-admired Ahab; and John Davidson's *Thirty Bob a Week* is never read by our younger critics who are now so busy discovering a similar poetry of despair in the works of Tristan Corbière. Finally, little but unsavory gossip is now remembered of Oscar Wilde by many English and American critics who praise Gide and Stefan George, both of whom acclaimed Wilde as one of their masters.

It can be argued that few of these nineteenth-century innovators have contributed directly to what we now call modern literature. But French critics all agree that the modern movement in poetry begins with Baudelaire, from whose work a tradition can be traced which leads directly to Surrealism. English and American critics might likewise begin their histories of our modern poetry with Poe, who was Baudelaire's master, and include in them both Rossetti, who was inspired by *The Raven* to write *The Blessed Damozel*, and Swinburne and Wilde, Baudelaire's earliest disciples in our language. But curious high-brow prejudices make many of us neglect our good writers who have gained popularity with bad readers. Malcolm Cowley has observed that Poe, though known and admired amongst the poets of the Caucasus, was long neglected by our best poets and critics; and this, in spite of the fact that Poe's works had been reprinted more often and more carelessly, and read in America more widely and by less discriminating readers, than those of any other American poet. The same might be said of Oscar Wilde, some of whose poems, in excellent translations, are widely known and admired in France or Germany, and whose works are constantly being reprinted, here and in England, though generally with very little care, and being read by large numbers of adolescent or semi-literate readers. It would indeed be difficult to find a writer whose works have suffered more, at the hands of hasty editors, than those of Wilde. A majority of the editions which pretend to be *Complete Works* fail to include, for instance, his verse-drama, *A Florentine Tragedy*; many of them print, in various places, "Castilian" instead of "Castalian" or "symbols" instead of "cymbals," and most of them also skip a word in one of the opening lines of *The Harlot's House*, offering us a badly limping verse, "The *Treues Liebes* of Strauss" instead of *"The Treues Liebes Herz* of Strauss."

And other editions of the complete works still include, without any editorial comment, *The Priest and the Acolyte*, a semi-pornographic tale which was proved at the time of Wilde's trial to have been written by a vague disciple whom he had never met.

Intellectual lethargy or a weirdly technological esthetics of material progress which somehow confuses art with washing-machines or radio-sets likewise makes many of us think of modern poetry almost exclusively in terms of new forms and devices which can easily be detected and defined, perhaps even patented, and rarely in terms of new ideas which must be carefully traced and analyzed. And Wilde's modernism was of ideas now wide-spread rather than of forms that were adapted or imitated by later writers. Formal innovations, in modern English and American poetry, came somewhat earlier, in the *vers libre* of Whitman, in the metrics of Tennyson, in the Anglo-Saxon alliterations and assonances and rhythms of William Morris, systematized and perfected later by Hopkins, in the various innovations of Rossetti or of Browning; or else, they came after Wilde's time, in a second and more critically discerning wave of enthusiasm for French modernism, when Rimbaud and Laforgue were discovered and their techniques appreciated and imitated as much as the ideas of Baudelaire or Huysmans had been some decades earlier. Though Wilde already wrote prose poems in English, more after the manner of Baudelaire or Pierre Louÿs than after that of Rimbaud, his formal innovations, both in this prose poetry and. in that of his lyrical drama, *Salome*, were perhaps premature; and our literature has now adopted the more complex forms of innovators who came later and whose experience included a knowledge of the *Illuminations en Prose* and of the lyrical dramas of Claudel.

Wilde does not seem to have believed, moreover, that only new and confused art-forms could express the novelty and confusion of modern life. Like Baudelaire, he tended to adhere to traditional forms, even to revive them; he is more neo-classical, closer to Byron or even Pope, especially in his orderly handling of narrative, than Tennyson or Browning, much as Baudelaire was closer to Racine or

Malherbe than to Victor Hugo or Musset. And this very art involves a complex body of critical beliefs which it illustrates more or less clearly. It is thus for his criticism that Wilde deserves most certainly to be honored as a master of modern literature. Here, his ideas are clearly and fully expounded, in all their novelty. Two or three generations of writers have now been influenced by them, directly or indirectly, either by reading Wilde or by inheriting various concepts of his esthetics from such disciples as Stefan George or André Gide. And to realize Wilde's stature as a critic, we need but return, from his dialogues, to the work of some other critics of his generation or of the next two decades. Saintsbury is but a reliable and sensible scholar; Charles Whibley, a charming enthusiast with exquisite taste but vague principles; Sir Edmund Gosse, a first-class columnist for the Sunday supplements; Sir Arthur Quiller-Couch, an unbelievably sentimental fuddy-duddy who is content to state that a poem is good because, after twenty or more years of knowing it, he is still moved to tears by its beauty.

Matthew Arnold had indeed laid the foundations of a serious and academically sound tradition of English Romantic criticism which became the heritage, in the Universities, of a number of competent scholars and was kept alive, in literary journals, by a few more scholarly critics among whom the most brilliant was perhaps Walter Bagehot. But Ruskin's followers, almost without exception, had become either sentimental moralizers whose taste rapidly degenerated into a vague socialism of arts and crafts, or equally vague esthetes who gasped before Gothic or Renaissance monuments as, Baedeker in hand, they wandered from Amiens to Venice or from Florence to Chartres. Most of Pater's followers too, inspired by his tastes rather than by his few principles, had become archaeologists or classical scholars, or else rather hedonistic or intellectually irresponsible decadents and impressionists. In all the confusion of late Victorian criticism, where the soundest sought refuge in mere scholarship and the most perceptive, such as Arthur Symons, often seemed content with a sort of spinelessly enthusiastic literary journalism, Oscar Wilde's ingenious, imaginative, and vigorous dialectical thought appears monumental. Few critics in our own more critical age are gifted with his scholarship, his acumen, his stylistic brilliance, his masterful authority that never condescends to the coy false modesty which mars much of Eliot's criticism, and especially with Wilde's sense of philosophical structure, which places him at once in the same class as Matthew Arnold and Coleridge.

The purpose of the present study is to indicate the central position that Wilde's works and ideas occupy in the thought and art of his age, and in the shift of English and American literature from established and aging Romanticism to what we now call modernism. To prove conclusively Wilde's equality with Coleridge or Arnold would require as varied and detailed a comparative analysis of their ideas and methods as of Wilde's; and this, like several other suggested comparisons, would lead far beyond the necessary limitations of this book. It is to be hoped, however, that some of these comparisons, though not fully documented, will be found fruitful, if not entirely acceptable; and that the range and variety of considerations that an analysis of Wilde's works and ideas can suggest will convince the reader of their historical importance and lasting value.

Poetry and Art-History

For the discriminating reader, a careful examination of Oscar
Wilde's poetical works now raises many problems of taste and
criticism. Wilde is still, to some extent, popularly remembered as a
poet, as the author of *The Ballad of Reading Gaol*, of *The Picture of
Dorian Gray*, a poetical novel, and of *Salome*, a dramatic poem, a
play in lyrical prose; nor has it been forgotten that Wilde was, in his
day, a champion of poetry as the supreme art and a leader of the
movement of art for art's sake. Yet few types of poetry can now seem
quite so alien to our stricter conceptions of pure poetry than most of
Wilde's, with its traditional forms and ornate descriptive manner. It
is even difficult for us, at times, to remember that Wilde's lush art
once blossomed from the same roots of Pre-Raphaelitism as did the
starker poetry of Gerard Manley Hopkins; and that our whole
modern movement, in English and American literature, has been to
a great extent facilitated by the activities of the Pre-Raphaelite
Brotherhood and of the later Aesthetes who, in spite of their doomed
tastes, at least helped save our literature from being completely
drowned in the triumphant tide of nineteenth-century argumentativeness, sentimentality, and commercialism.

Oscar Wilde's poetry, including the *Poems in Prose* and the prose
poetry of his fairy tales or of such lyrical dramas as *Vera*, *The
Duchess of Padua*, and *Salome*, can be classified according to three
distinct manners which correspond to the three major periods of his
life as an artist, to the more unsophisticated youth that lasted until
his trip to America, to the brilliant heyday of success in London and
Paris that greeted him on his return, then to the devastating prison-
years and the listless aftermath that dragged on until his painful
death. The manner of Wilde's first period, illustrated chiefly in his
poems and in the two earlier lyrical dramas which, if not yet

completed, had at least been conceived before his American tour, is still loftily Pre-Raphaelistic or neo-antique in the poems, somewhat gothically neo-Elizabethan in the dramas. The manner of the middle period, of the fairy-tales, the *Poems in Prose*, the few more mature poems such as *The Sphinx* or *The Harlot's House* and the later lyrical dramas, *Salome* and *La Sainte Courtisane*, is much more personal and original, though still, at times, very ornate; and it corresponds closely to our generally accepted notions of the decadent and *fin-de-siècle* style, which Wilde helped, in these works whose manner was so much inspired by French models, to establish in English and American art and literature.

The manner of Wilde's last period, that of *The Ballad of Reading Gaol*, is both intimately devotional in its display of emotions and openly rhetorical in its somewhat loosely emphatic handling of a poetic form which has purported, ever since Wordsworth and Coleridge or Thomas Hood, to be more popular or traditional than learned or inventive. Wilde's shattering experiences seemed to have stripped him of his faith in most of the artifices of his earlier poetry; and he was thus forced to rely, in his last poem, on a disarming candor or sincerity, as a mode of persuasion, and on a much cruder or more direct rhetoric and esthetic. This harsh blending of conflicting tones corresponds, moreover, rather closely to the poet's ultimate doctrine. At the level of essayistic prose, Wilde expressed his new outlook similarly in the devotional and apologetic manner of *De Profundis*, which constantly shifts from the very intimate whisper of the private confessional to the more oratorical tone of a public testament such as *The Confessions of an English Opium Eater* or Cardinal Newman's *Apologia*.

Foretastes of a later manner can, of course, be discovered in works of each earlier period, just as echoes of an earlier manner often persist in work of a later period. But each one of Wilde's three manners illustrates a somewhat different conception of poetry and especially, in their author, different tastes or notions of the beautiful or the sublime. In the early poems, the intellectual devices of poetry, as distinguished from its more formal techniques, are not yet very clearly separated from those of other arts, especially those of painting or of sculpture. Form seems to be, to a great extent, confused with mere scanned and rhymed description of things whose shape

would appeal immediately to the eye, as in *Charmides*; and ornament is not of an exclusively poetic nature, as in some of the
conceits of the metaphysical poets or in the more traditional devices
of a neo-classical poet, but consists rather in verbal description, in a
subject-matter that emulates the book-illustrator's art:

> We two will sit upon a throne of pearl,
> And a blue wave will be our canopy,
> And at our feet the water-snakes will curl
> In all their amethystine panoply.

Form and ornament, in such an art, are indeed to a great extent
extraneous, merely reflected, in the mirror of poetic diction, from
the world of nature or the other arts.

In the poems of the middle period that are not merely occasional,
this descriptive art of poetry gradually becomes informed with a
symbolic or personal meaning which transmutes it into something
more purely poetic. It frequently imitates the art-styles of decadent
or hybrid periods or cultures for which Wilde felt an ever greater
affinity: Hellenistic Greece, a syncretistic Orient or Renaissance
Spain, for instance, rather than the Golden Ages of Athens, Imperial
Rome or Florence. In *The Harlot's House*, the contemporary scene
is thus sometimes described in archaic symbols which suggest, as if
in a dialectic of repeated historical cycles such as those of Vico,
Hegel or Croce, the terms of a Hellenistic decadence. In the "danc-
ing feet" and "Harlot's house" and "house of lust," the age of
Salome, of Herod and the Gospels appears beyond the symbols and
terms of mere nineteenth-century decadence, beyond "the *Treues
Liebes Herz* of Strauss," the violins and cigarettes, until an absolute
decadence is expressed rather than the relative decadence of
Wilde's own age. The imitation of visual arts or of the forms of
subject-matter is moreover integrated into the very forms of this
later poetry whose syntax, in a curiously mimetic pattern of involu-
tions and repetitions, follows the arabesques of the dancers that it
describes:

> The dead are dancing with the dead,
> The dust is whirling with the dust.

Conversely, in *The Sphinx*, the props of Ptolemaic Egypt have
acquired a macabre meaning as symbols of bestial passions which

Christianity and traditional morals repressed in Wilde's own age. The "beautiful and silent Sphinx" of the opening lines becomes, towards the end of the poem, a "songless, tongueless ghost of sin" that has "crept through the curtains of the night" to tempt the poet with visions of an awful past; and the very diction in which these visions are described, with its hieroglyphs and obelisks and basilisks and hippogriffs, imposes on the poem a hauntingly foreign rhythm, with rhymes that sound both modern and archaic.

Finally, in the only poem of Wilde's last period, *The Ballad of Reading Gaol*, the subject-matter, structure and manner all indicate, as indeed they had already done in some poems of the middle period, that the artist had been acquiring an ever greater ability to integrate the raw material of individual experience into literature and poetry:

> The warders strutted up and down,
> And watched their herd of brutes,
> Their uniforms were spick and span,
> And they wore their Sunday suits,
> But we knew the work they had been at,
> By the quicklime on their boots.

Here, the emotional significance of descriptive detail, of the Sunday suits and the quicklime, is not to be sought beyond the context of the poem, in any memories of art, of history or of literature: it has been established within the poem itself, by the descriptions of prison routine and of the hanged man's burial.

Slowly, Wilde had thus developed forms, a manner and a diction which were better suited to his peculiar experiences, thoughts and emotions, and expressed them more concisely or in less elaborately ornate and impersonal symbols. From a sometimes absurdly self-assured loftiness such as that which had once riled Heinrich Heine in the poetry of August Graf von Platen, Wilde's German counterpart for neo-antique, italianate and oriental enthusiasms as well as for other passions, the poet had progressed to a far more lyrical and intimately symbolic art where experience of his own life rather than of traditional art was his true subject-matter, and where the analysis of his own emotions, if at times diffuse, had replaced the description of objects which constitute a sort of common and traditional language of poetic emotion.

Wilde once said that he gave his talent to his writings, but kept his genius for his conversation. This may indeed be true of much of the poetry of his earlier period, which was scholarly enough to satisfy his Oxford classical masters, lofty enough to please his gushing and histrionic mother, and ornate enough to impress the unreading public of socialite lion-hunters whose invitations he sought. Oscar Wilde, in those days, was posing as a poet, as many young writers have done during their apprenticeship, when their borrowed skills and tastes were not yet fitted to their true temperament and talents. But his later poetry, ever less decoratively talented but more immediately related to his individual genius, indicates that his progress, in spite of beginnings no more inauspicious than those of Tennyson or Yeats, might have led him to emerge as a major poet, had not the accidents of his life involved him in so many other kinds of writing before, in his last period, he abandoned writing much as Rimbaud had done, and for analogous reasons.

Wilde's gradual abandonment of poetry illustrates moreover a symptomatic trend in the literature of Romanticism and of the schools which followed in its path. When poets identify their art too exclusively with the sublime rather than with given topics which must be handled according to given techniques and rules, the pursuit of the sublime becomes in itself a life's work. As the transitions to poetry from other kinds of writing appear ever more difficult or hazardous, the poet gradually abandons poetry in favor of genres which do not aim exclusively at the sublime, unless he devotes himself exclusively to poetry and the sublime as Mallarmé did. Society makes many other demands on the poet, often expecting him to express himself in prose or forcing him to write all kinds of literature to earn an adequate living; and the poet finds it ever more difficult to return, from these forays in parts that gradually cease to be strange, to the Holy of Holies of poetry. Finally, he is often tempted to abandon completely, in his religion of art, the pursuit of the pure sublime, much as the habitual sinner gradually loses all hope of achieving salvation by leading the good life; and of this defeatism and its aftermath, *Léthargie de la muse*, one of the last poems of Petrus Borel, the French Romantic, is a striking and pathetic illustration.

In acquiring experience of communicating his doctrine in modes less mythical than the poetry where he had first sought to initiate his readers to a better or more beautiful life, the poet who is dedicated to the sublime indeed faces a curious dilemma. Either he must conclude that poetry, as a medium, is proper only to topics in which the sublime manifests itself most immediately, and that less sublime thoughts or experiences are better communicated in the more rational or expository medium of prose; or he must assume, as the "pure" poets Mallarmé and Valéry have done, that there is an element of the sublime in everything and that the poet's task is to discover it and communicate only this aspect of things, so that all topics remain proper to poetry, though only when they are viewed *sub specie eternitatis* or handled in a sublime manner, whether in poetry or in prose.

Oscar Wilde chose, at first, the former course, when he found that he could expound more effectively or to larger audiences in lectures, articles or book reviews the doctrine of his "New Hellenism" which he had previously illustrated in poetry, in such myths as *Charmides* or *The Burden of Itys*. But he soon began to illustrate his more mature doctrines in prose too, though now in prose myths whose appeal was more popular than that of his earlier poetic myths, in fiction, drama or critical dialogue. In the more productive years of his middle period, Wilde thus seems to have shifted to the second course, and to have again pursued the sublime in almost all that he wrote, in the poetical prose of his fairy-tales, of his *Poems in Prose*, of his later lyrical dramas, of his novel and of his dialogues. And during these years, he returned to more traditionally poetic forms only when his experience of the sublime, as in *The Sphinx, The Harlot's House* or *The New Remorse*, seemed to him so immediate or so absolute that it could be communicated as absolutely or imme- diately only in the forms in which, as a young man, he had once communicated it, when he experienced it more often if not as poignantly. Finally, Wilde's experience of the horrors of prison was so shattering that he seemed able to communicate it only in poetry, in *The Ballad of Reading Gaol*; yet many poets, without direct experience of his anguish and pain, would have found in his topic, far from an absolute sublime, but the material of a story or an essay.

Wilde's earlier manner, when poetry still seemed an adequate medium for most of his thought, is illustrated in the poems which constitute the major part of his poetical work: in *Ravenna*, which won him the Oxford Newdigate Prize in 1878, in the poems of the volume which he published in 1881 and which earned him his reputation as a poet, and in his two earlier poetical dramas, *Vera or The Nihilists* and *The Duchess of Padua*, the first written in 1881, the second completed in 1883 but conceived before the poet's trip to America. The manner and style of these earlier works are often humorless or inflated; they fail curiously to reveal many of the qualities of vivid insight and intellect which earned Wilde his fame as wit and critic among his contemporaries and which still shine in the dialogue of his comedies, in much of his fiction, in his critical work, and in some of the poems of his later periods. These early poems are indeed, to a great extent, the product of Wilde's education rather than of his individual experience. They seem so traditional in form and descriptive in manner that, had they been written by a French poet of the same period, they would now be called "Parnassian"; and they illustrate the techniques, tastes, and thoughts of the more sedate later generation of Romantic artists who reverted, from the passions and innovations of the age when Byron or Victor Hugo or the beauties of gothic art had first become known, to an ornate historical poetry which sought to reflect the various glories of the past in an attempt to escape from an age of drab industrialization. In *Theoretikos*, Wilde himself thus declared that his soul was not fit for nineteenth-century England:

> For this vile traffic-house, where day by day
>   Wisdom and reverence are sold at mart,
>   And the rude people rage with ignorant cries
> Against an heritage of centuries.
>   It mars my calm: wherefore in dreams of Art
>   And loftiest culture I would stand apart.

First and foremost among the loftier cultures where young Wilde sought refuge came that of Greco-Roman antiquity. But this culture was, in Wilde's poetry, artificially pastoral and somewhat Alexandrine or Sicilian, that of a Silver Age such as Bion, Moschus, Theocritus, Lucian or Longus invented, or such as Virgil in his Eclogues Ovid and the Elegiac poets of Rome imitated, rather than that of a truly Periclean or Augustan Golden Age whose genius expressed itself more sternly in Sophoclean tragedies, in the *Aeneid* or in the lyrics of Horace. Its Arcady is the setting of Wilde's *The*

Garden of Eros, The Burden of Itys, Panthea, and *Charmides,* which the poet pronounced in 1882, to a reporter of the *San Francisco Examiner,* his "most finished and perfect poem"; and other glimpses of this setting for nymphs and fauns are offered in many of the shorter poems of Wilde's earlier period.

Refurbished by the Humanist enthusiasms of Renaissance poets from Politan to Tasso and Guarini and from Spenser to Milton, the flowery luxuriance of an imagined Arcady which had once beguiled the spleen of citified Ptolemaic Egypt thus continued to blossom through the ages, though each generation in turn colored it with some of its nostalgia and idealism. Surviving the rococo affectations of eighteenth-century Trianons, with their periwigged shepherds and shepherdesses, it had returned in the more archaeologically correct fantasies of Victorian poets and artists such as Pater and Swinburne, Sir Lawrence Alma-Tadema and Lord Leighton; and a typical example of its appearance, in this last avatar, is to be found in Wilde's *Charmides,* a poem whose theme, probably derived from one of Lucian's tales, is the story of a boy who fell in love with a goddess, ravished her statue, and was punished by her with death:

> And when at dawn the wood-nymphs, hand-in-hand,
>   Threaded the bosky dell, their satyr spied
> The boy's pale body stretched upon the sand,
>   And feared Poseidon's treachery, and cried,
> And like bright sunbeams flitting through a glade,
> Each startled Dryad sought some safe and leafy ambuscade.

Hostile critics objected that nature, in Wilde's ideal world, often ignored the cycle of the seasons and seemed to give birth to all their various blossoms in one eternal moment. But this might be said of almost any pastoral poet except Milton; and E. K. Chambers pointed out in 1895, in *The English Pastoral,* that nature, for the pastoral poets, "was a thing only to be felt, not studied," and that "emotion was its interpreter and not science." In the eternal present of their Golden Age, death comes, as in the beliefs of some primitive tribes, only as a tragic accident, and the cycle of the seasons, with its grim recurrence of birth and decay, has not yet been noticed.

Another loftier culture where young Wilde sometimes sought refuge, in his earlier poetry, was a somewhat neo-gothic or Pre-

Raphaelitic reconstruction of the chivalrous Middle Ages. He describes this world in such poems as *Ballade de Marguerite* and *The Dole of the King's Daughter*; its landscape, like the background of an old tapestry, is also mainly pastoral, and Wilde offers us glimpses of its morris-dance mummery in occasional echoes of Chaucerian diction in other poems too, in *Ravenna*, for instance:

> And small birds sang on every twining spray. . . .
> Some goat-foot Pan make merry minstrelsy. . . .

A flamboyant vision of the Renaissance, from the age of Dante to that of Milton, offered a third avenue of escape. Wilde reveals it more fully in *The Duchess of Padua*, so melodramatically reminiscent of the horrors and rantings of the "gothic" dramas of his mother's uncle, Robert Maturin. And he turns to it more nostalgically in such sonnets as *To Milton, On the Massacre of the Christians in Bulgaria, A Vision, Quantum Mutata,* and *Ave Maria Gratia Plena,* or in *Ravenna's* visions of the past:

> And at his feet I marked a broken stone
> Which sent up lilies, dove-like, to his knees.
> Now at their sight, my heart being lit with flame
> I cried to Beatrice, "Who are these?"

Antiquity, the Middle Ages and the Renaissance had long been the haunts, in Victorian art and literature, of Tennyson, Arnold and Browning, then of the Pre-Raphaelite Brotherhood and of the schools of Ruskin and of Walter Pater. And Wilde acknowledges his great debt to some of his masters among these painters and poets when, in *The Garden of Eros,* he lists the few nineteenth-century votaries of the "Spirit of Beauty" whom he wishes to emulate: Keats, Shelley and Byron, "Morris, our sweet and simple Chaucer's child, Dear heritor of Spenser's tuneful reed," the poet-painter Dante Gabriel Rossetti, "Whose double laurels burn with deathless flame," and the painter Burne-Jones, "Who saw old Merlin lured in Vivien's snare And the white feet of angels coming down the golden stair." To discussion of the virtues of these six masters, and of Elizabeth Barrett Browning too, Wilde constantly returns, in his critical writings; and much of his earlier poetry is indeed so Pre-Raphaelitic, in its sense of pictorial style and ornament, ' ~+ it instantly suggests, as his sonnet *Madonna Mia* does, both Rossetti's style as a painter and his poetic devices of description as they are illustrated in his sonnet in Giorgione's *Venetian Pastoral*:

> A lily-girl, not made for this world's pain,
>> With brown, soft hair close braided by her ears,
>> And longing eyes half veiled by slumb'rous tears
> Like bluest water seen through mists of rain:
> Pale cheeks whereon no love hath left its stain,
>> Red underlip drawn in for fear of love,
>> And white throat, whiter than the silvered dove,
> Through whose wan marble creeps one purple vein.
> Yet, though my lips shall praise her without cease,
>> Even to kiss her feet I am not bold,
>> Being o'ershadowed by the wings of awe,
> Like Dante, when he stood with Beatrice
>> Beneath the flaming Lion's breast, and saw
>> The seventh Crystal, and the Stair of Gold.

In a preface to Wilde's fairy tales of *The Happy Prince* and *The House of Pomegranates*, W. B. Yeats once discussed the passion and sensuality with which writers of the Aesthetic movement, in their descriptions, tended to emulate the painter's art: "The influence of painting upon English literature which began with the poetry of Keats had now reached its climax, because all educated England was overshadowed by Whistler, by Burne-Jones, by Rossetti; and Wilde—a provincial like myself—found in that influence something of the mystery, something of the excitement, of a religious cult that promised an impossible distinction. It was precisely because he was not of it by birth and by early association that he caught up phrases and adjectives for their own sake, and not because they were a natural part of his design, and spoke them to others as though it were his duty to pass on some pass-word, sign or countersign."

Wilde himself observed, moreover, in *Pen, Pencil, and Poison*, that the arts borrow, in a very ugly and sensible age, not from life but from each other. Nor were the Pre-Raphaelite poets and the Aesthetes the only ones, in their age, to imitate in their writings the devices of painting. Tennyson, so often considered typical of Victorian conformism in the arts, clearly suggests, in *The Lady of Shalott*, the Victorian conception of the medieval illuminator's art; and the very title of his later *Idylls* indicates his desire to convey, in these poems, visual impressions of the scenes that they describe. Gerard Manley Hopkins, painter as well as poet, likewise expresses, in his poetry, many of the preoccupations with those dappled, mottled or stippled qualities of color which had first puzzled him as a painter; and famous painters are the protagonists of several of Browning's poems.

In Wilde's writings, beyond the confusion of literary genres which allowed him to view *Salome*, a play written in elaborately ornate prose, as a poem, a drama in lyrical prose, there thus looms a further confusion, that of the arts and senses. Ever since the Eighteenth Century, when it had inspired scientific and mechanical experiments such as the Abbé Castel's color-organ or Diderot's investigations of blindness, the theory of synesthesia, according to which one sense is able to perceive what appeals to another sense, had haunted the whole tradition of European Romanticism. Hoffmann, in his tales, had frequently suggested confusions of the arts and senses; Leopardi discussed them in his prose-works; they appear often, as a theme, in the fiction of Balzac; they are illustrated in the art of Rossetti, who created *The Blessed Damozel* as a poem when he might have depicted her as perfectly in a painting; they inform much of Baudelaire's imagery, become a doctrine in his sonnet *Correspondences*, and are taken literally by Rimbaud in his puzzling *Sonnet des Voyelles*; finally, the confusion of the senses was proposed by Huysmans, in *A Rebours*, as a veritable way of life which Wilde then preached, for a while, with the fervor of a neophyte. Wilde thus called his critical essay on Thomas Griffiths Wainewright a "study in green," described some of Dvořák's music as "curiously colored" or a "mad scarlet thing," and wrote *The Birthday of the Infanta*, one of his fairy-tales, after the manner of Velásquez, though he never stated it, much as Hoffmann had once written *Princess Brambilla* "after the manner of Jacques Callot" or as the French poet Aloysius Bertrand had composed the prose poems of *Gaspard de la Nuit* after the manner of the same fantastic draftsman.

An analysis of Wilde's various pictorial manners, from the pure Pre-Raphaelitism and the ornately neo-antique of his early poems to the sensuous and elaborately *fin-de-siècle* arabesques of *The Harlot's House*, would reveal the full extent of the poet's progress as his tastes matured, in less than two decades, and as the whole iconography of his imagery changed. In the vase-painting art of *Charmides*, with its nymphs and fauns so closely related to those of Josiah Wedgwood or of Flaxman, we discover an idealized vision of antiquity which Wilde shared with much of nineteenth-century art, with that of mad King Ludwig's Munich, of the mythological world of the German painter Boecklin and the German poets of Platen's school, with that of Walter Pater, of Swinburne and of the somewhat pedantically archaeological paintings of Alma-Tadema and Lord Leighton. And in such other earlier poems as Wilde's sonnet *At Verona*, a Pre-Raphaelitic vignette of Dante's exile, we discover the poet's admiration for the art of the Middle Ages and of the Renaissance, and for much that they had inspired in his own century, to all of which he had been initiated by the work of Rossetti and of Ruskin. Had not Rossetti himself handled the same theme, from Dante's life, in his own far more diffuse and perhaps less immediately moving *Dante at Verona*?

Later, in the piled-up oriental imagery of *The Fisherman and his Soul* and *The Star Child*, born of eighteenth-century translations and imitations of *The Arabian Nights*, improved in the Regency schools of Beckford's *Vathek*, Morier's *Hajji Baba*, Moore's *Lalla Rookh* or the architectural fantasies of the Brighton Pavillion, then perfected by French Romantic art in the odalisques of Ingres and Delacroix till the Orient almost ceased to be exotic in Fitzgerald's *Omar Khayyam*, in the art of Fromentin and in the poetry of Leconte de Lille, we discover Wilde's attempt, through the use of vivid and surprising detail, to maintain the barbaric and exotic values of Orientalism, much as St.-J. Perse has done in twentieth-century poetry: "From the roof of a house a company of women watched us. One of them wore a mask of gilded leather." At the same time, Wilde discovered also a decadently Asiatic Hellenism, more Ptolemaic or Seleucid than the antiquity of *Charmides*, which he displayed in *The Sphinx*, in *Poems in Prose*, his *Prose Poems* and in *Salome*, with their Hermits and Tetrarchs and gilded barges and swarthy Ethiops and hawk-faced gods, all borrowed from the paintings of Gustave Moreau or from the art and literature of other

French decadents. Finally, wearying of so many somewhat theatrical props, it seems, Wilde discovered the nostalgically sensitive line-drawing style of *The Harlot's House* and *The Ballad of Reading Gaol*, an art whose ambiguous arabesques are more closely allied to those of Félicien Rops or of Aubrey Beardsley than the descriptive imagery of *Salome* which Beardsley actually illustrated.

The evolution of Wilde's descriptive style in his poetry, from the museum-piece ornateness of his earlier works to the simpler and more delicate art of his more mature poems, was accompanied, moreover, by an analogous evolution of his poetry's intellectual content, from the discussion of general problems of politics, ethics or esthetics to a greater attention to personal impressions or to the elucidation of particular problems of the poet's life, such as his temptations and moral conflicts. In *The Sphinx, The Harlot's House, Flowers of Love* or *The New Remorse*, for instance, Wilde proved his ability to compose, had he but dared, a body of poems, on themes of sin, suffering and remorse, which might have been the *Fleurs du Mal* of English literature, with much of Baudelaire's concise quality as opposed to Swinburne's vagueness. But on the threshold of discovery, foreseeing the "shameful secret guests" of his own love-life, Wilde turned to the crucifix, in his poetry if not in life, and tried to escape from the bestial phantom which he had at first summoned, in *The Sphinx*, with such longing. He had understood the "monstrous oracles" that the "curious cat" whispered into his ears as it had once into those of Ammon, the "horned" god with "Titan thews" who had been but one of its varied paramours, all doomed, it seemed, to death in its cruel embrace. Forewarned, Wilde rejected the monster from his poetry:

> You wake in me each bestial sense, you make me what
> I would not be.
> You make my creed a barren sham, you wake foul dreams
> of sensual life,
> And Atys with his blood-stained knife were better than
> the thing I am.

But Wilde seems, by this very act of rejection, to have "unmanned himself beneath a pine-tree," as *The Golden Bough* tells of Atys, and to have deprived himself, as a poet, of the source of what might have been his best poetry.

A significant example of Wilde's earlier philosophic poetry is to be found in *Humanitad*. The poem's title and vaguely Socialist deification of man were suggested to Wilde, with a surprising ignorance of Spanish, by Whitman's *Libertad*; but its poetic method, that of pinning one of the poet's moods on some aspect of natural landscape and then drawing general philosophical conclusions from these premises, all this hails straight from Shelley. In *Humanitad*, Wilde progresses, from a conventionally bucolic opening which describes winter scenery, to an invocation of Spring, which will soon revive all nature but the poet's sad emotions: the poet has lost his peace of mind, his innocent and Romantic sense of communion with Wordsworth's or Schelling's Nature, his faith in love, science, learning and the simple verities. The "great unselfish simple life" is no more: its last apostles, Wordsworth and Mazzini, are now dead. In very general terms, Wilde reviles the corruption of his age, its anarchy that betrays freedom, its ignorance, its greed. The arts that once flourished under tyranny have fled; "gentle brotherhood" and "the God that is within us" would be more valuable than art, had we not crucified that God. And the poem's long and curiously confused argument is brought to its conclusion when Wilde expresses the hope that crucified humanity, "that is Godlike, that is God," will soon descend from its cross so that we cease to be "Lords of the natural world" and, at the same time, "our own dread enemy."

To the treatment of such very general arguments, where the poet's individual emotions clothe no concrete plot or myth, a less Romantically subjective manner is perhaps better suited: a more didactic exposition would allow the poet's ideas to emerge more clearly as a poetry of statement whose rational content is as convincing as its emotions and tone seek to be. Wisely, Wilde abandoned, in his later poetry, *Humanitad's* passionately subjective debating, a task for which, as a poet, he seemed so ill-suited. Only in *The Ballad of Reading Gaol* does he again handle as vast a theme, that of love and guilt and retribution; but here it is more deeply rooted in a plot or myth of concrete individual experience, so that the ballad, however diffuse its form, never wanders off, as *Humanitad* so often does, into confused or tangential invocations and descriptions. But it took the most shattering experiences of man's life, such as the deadening proof of a loved one's utter selfishness or the complete degradation of imprisonment, to shake Wilde from his resolve, after *The Sphinx*, never to handle anything but decoratively impressionistic description and moods in his later poetry. The dainty water-color ingenuity of *Lotus Leaves, Impressions, Le Jardin des Tuileries* or *Fantaisies Décoratives*, among the later poems, has the same relationship to the major art of what might have been Wilde's *Flowers of Evil* as an elegantly hand-painted fan has to the art of El Greco. When Wilde's reticence was at last fully forced, in *The Ballad of Reading Gaol*, the pent-up anguish and indignation of his ethical inspiration carried him away, through the floodlike repetitions of his last poem, to total silence.

Between the self-crucifying theme of *Humanitad*, too argumentatively and confusedly general to be the stuff of true poetic experience, and the self-annihilating experience which produced *The Ballad of Reading Gaol*, beyond which no further poetic expression seemed possible, Wilde had thus been compelled to compare himself, in *The Sphinx*, to the victim of a self-inflicted wound. Though symbolic and imaginary, the wound was real enough in its inhibiting consequences from which the poet could henceforth be roused to poetic expression only by a deeper hurt, as in the swan-song expression of his prison experience. Yet Wilde had reached, at that time, a maturity and polish, in the form and diction of his poetry, that promised much and are well illustrated in the very words of his renunciation:

> You wake in me each bestial sense, you make me what
> I would not be.

This simplicity, in a diction purged of much of the florid descriptiveness and rich vocabulary of the earlier poems, allows each word of common conversation, clear and vivid again, loaded with thought or emotion, to transcend, in the strict economy of rhythm and syntax, its usually blurred or vague meaning. As a quality, it informs the best of Wilde's later poetry, the art of which had at last emerged from lush Pre-Raphaelitism to a luminous directness which it now shared with the poetry of A. E. Housman, who began where Wilde left off, at the frontier of what we now call modern poetry, which eschews Victorian poetry's diffuseness and descriptiveness. The whole poem of *The Harlot's House*, for instance, progresses, in a carefully worded arabesque of generally simple but moving diction, toward the climax of its last line, whose dramatic finality is enhanced by its being two syllables shorter than any of the preceding lines:

> Then suddenly the tune went false,
> The dancers wearied of the waltz,
> The shadows ceased to wheel and whirl,
>
> And down the long and silent street,
> The dawn, with silver-sandalled feet,
> Crept like a frightened girl.

The perfection of this poem is marred only when Wilde succumbs, toward the middle, to his own verbal virtuosity and weakens his meanings by expanding them too descriptively, defining the dance first as a waltz, then as a quadrille, then as a saraband, finally again as a waltz; both the dance and the music lose much of their vividness in this cloud of definition whose vagueness, though it might match the manner of one of Swinburne's poems, contrasts here too discordantly with the exact diction of the rest of the poem, like a patch of impressionistic brush-work in the midst of a Poussin landscape. One might also object that the rhyming of "grotesques" and "arabesques," in the third stanza, is a decadent tag which appears again in *The Sphinx* and in *The Ballad of Reading Gaol*; but it fits into the scheme of *The Harlot's House*, and it is only unfortunate that, for extraneous reasons, the reader should be tempted to look upon it as a fault.

In *The Ballad of Reading Gaol*, hastily composed when the sick and weary poet had lost much of his ability to concentrate, the imperfections are numerous. The prison warders, for instance, are described as wearing both "spick and span" uniforms and "Sunday suits." This misuse of the conjunction is but one of many minor defects which all combine to make the poem much more vague, diffuse, shabbily colloquial or repetitious than it might have been. "And his grave has *got* no name" is thus a typically weak verse: the alliteration is achieved at the price of an inexact colloquialism. But some of the *Ballad's* lines also reveal Wilde, as a poet, at his very best; and many of its thoughts and sentiments are typical of a new poetry that is no longer Victorian and to whose flowering Wilde had at that time contributed as much as Housman. A *Shropshire Lad* was published in 1896:

> There sleeps in Shrewsbury jail tonight,
> Or wakes, as may betide,
> A better lad, if things were right,
> Than most that sleep outside.

Two years later, after his release, Wilde read Housman's poem and wrote his own ballad:

> Yet each man kills the thing he loves,
> By each let this be heard . . .
> Yet each man does not die . . .
>
> He does not die a death of shame
> On a day of dark disgrace . . .

The pessimism of Wilde and Housman had little in common with the indignation of such earlier reformers and progressives as Dickens or Thomas Hood, and less with the pathetic fallacies and evasions of Tennyson who, in *Rizpah*, describes the whole tragedy of capital punishment from the point of view of a widowed mother gone insane after her son's hanging, in the eighteenth century, as if the hanging of an orphan or the hangings in the poet's own century were another kettle of fish. In the new pessimism, there are the seeds of a new awareness: A century of belief in progress, of industrialization, of the imperialism of "The White Man's Burden," and of hopeful social and political reforms had but culminated in the pangs that heralded the birth of a new century which promised the most bloody revolutions and destructive wars of all times.

It was Wilde's peculiar destiny, as a poet whose art was one of statement and of experiment in ideas rather than in poetic devices or new forms, to perfect this art and finally achieve a manner of his own, in poetry, only by almost abandoning poetry. During his middle period, he thus refined his ideas, perceptions, tastes, diction and imagery in other disciplines of literature, in poetic prose and in the prose of fiction, comedy or criticism. Perfect as some of Wilde's early poems may be, the perfection which he sought and achieved there, except in rare lines that give a foretaste of his later and more personal manner, all remained strangely impersonal. It was too often the perfection of a gifted student's copy of a passionately admired and brilliantly understood master, whether this master were Milton, Keats, Rossetti or Swinburne. Nor did Wilde imitate only the poets whom he named specifically as his masters, in the invocations of his early poetry or in his critical work. *Ravenna* contains, for instance, distinct echoes of Tennyson, in the repeated use of the epithet "weary," which recalls *Mariana* or *The Lotus Eaters*; the "enchanted stem" of the latter has become, moreover, a "fatal weed" in Wilde's poem and, instead of making it "sweet" for a man "to dream of Fatherland," it now "makes a man forget his fatherland." And *The Sphinx* is written, as if ironically, in the same unusual verse-form as *In Memoriam*.

Until his return from America, Wilde indeed gave to his writing little more than his talent. He wrote his early poetry with a virtuosity of which he was himself, at times, sadly aware, as in *Humanitad*, where he expresses, though in more traditional forms and ornate words, a sentiment that seems to echo Laforgue's complaint that he had read all books:

> But we are Learning's changelings, know by rote
>   The clarion watchword of each Grecian school
> And follow none, the flawless sword which smote
>   The pagan Hydra is an effete tool
> Which we ourselves have blunted, what man now
> Shall scale the august ancient heights and to old
>   Reverence bow? . . . .
>
> Somehow the grace, the bloom of things has flown,
>   And of all men we are most wretched who
> Must live each other's lives and not our own
>   For very pity's sake and then undo
> All that we lived for—it was otherwise
> When soul and body seemed to blend in mystic
>   symphonies.

In the Golden Ages of Hellenism or of Humanism which Wilde proposed more convincingly as ideals in such prose as that of *The*

Soul of Man under Socialism, the poet's task had indeed been easier. Invention and imitation had then been better blended. But learning had now become so meticulously vast and exact that it no longer allowed much scope for the fruitful misconceptions which had once been the source of new art-forms, as when Racine's courtly neo-classical tragedy or Tasso's chivalrous epic were born of imitation of Euripides or Virgil. Wilde had been schooled, as I was still some fifty years later, in the classics as they were taught by the Eminent Victorians of the great English Public Schools and Universities. Young scholars learned, in weekly compositions of Latin and Greek verse, to imitate the poets of antiquity more slavishly, and with a more Germanic philological exactitude *à la* Wilamowitz-Moellendorff, than Milton or Pope ever did. Bulwer Lytton even complains, in *Pelham*, that students were at one time forced to write Latin or Greek almost more fluently and learnedly than English. Even when, under the influence of Matthew Arnold's father, this curriculum of the great Public Schools was reformed, students of the classics were not allowed to develop ideas, forms or a style of their own, as Milton had once done in his fine baroque Latin verse, but had to think and express themselves only in terms of known Golden Age models. Hence the graduation of so many of Learning's changelings, the flight of the grace and bloom of the imitation of the ancients which, but a hundred years earlier, had still blossomed so gracefully. Hence, too, the repetitiousness and constraint of some of Wilde's pastiches of the works of antiquity, the frequent recurrence of the same bucolic topics and imagery derived from Theocritus. In Oxford, Wilde had been taught to avoid, in his Greek and Latin verse, all imagery, topics and diction for which no great classical authority could be quoted as they are for each word by the lexicographers, Liddell and Scott or Lewis. And as the field of profitable classical research became more complex, scholars began, as Housman did, to devote ever more attention to the study of later or lesser poets, such as Manilius or Lucan. Besides, some of the more spirited students, following Pater's discovery of the decadent beauties of the *Pervigilium Veneris*, began to express their "modernistic" dissatisfactions with the rigid scheme of their studies by sometimes employing in their compositions almost Romanesque or Byzantine words for the use of which only an Ammianus Marcellinus or a Tzetzes could be quoted as authorities.

In the poetry of his Oxford years and immediately after, Wilde could not help but unconsciously apply, at times, the same principles as in his Greek and Latin themes. He thus used, in English, the same classical tags, and relapsed into the same purple passages or displayed the same preoccupations with Silver Age models. Though his early poems contain many examples of the Homeric epithet, Wilde's English adaptations of its composite forms are colored by a knowledge, perhaps indirect, of Anglo-Saxon poetry and of the William Morris translations of Homer rather than of Pope's less philological or consciously archaic renderings. In *Ravenna*, the galleys are thus "pine-forest like," the ships "brass-beaked," the islands "wave-circled" and, in *Vita Nuova*, the sea is "unvintageable." It was from this too consciously learned poetry that Wilde eagerly turned to other disciplines, on his return from America, first to poetic prose and the prose poem, then to the prose of fiction or of criticism, till he at last achieved a less traditionally poetic manner, with much of the lost grace and bloom of poetry regained.

In this, Wilde's progress was rapid. The poems published in 1882, however promising, still smacked somewhat of the efforts of the good student who painfully puts together his Latin verses with his *gradus ad Parnassum,* the Latinist's indispensable equivalent of the rhyming dictionary, always well within reach. By 1890, Wilde had already written, if not yet published, most of his mature poetry. And his progress had been esthetic initiation in the very broadest sense. After William Morris, Wilde was indeed one of the first in a now well-established tradition of modern poets who have earned fame and a livelihood as initiators or sponsors of styles in art or interior decorating, as lecturers to women's clubs and editors of women's magazines. In France, even Mallarmé thus edited, at one time, a fashion magazine. And Wilde's interests in some of the more commercial spheres of good taste necessarily led him, already an heir to the dandyism of Byron, Baudelaire, Barbey d'Aurevilly, Bulwer Lytton or Disraeli, to stress, even in his more serious writings, what one might call the sartorial aspects of taste. Hence, his esthetic costumes, his interest in the clothes that his wife wore, the care with which his Tite Street house was decorated and furnished, the detailed descriptions, in *An Ideal Husband,* of the clothes that the characters of the comedy must wear. Hence, too, the elaborate and somewhat chintzy floral pieces in so many of his early poems, where the lilies of a neo-antique Arcady's fields are imported from the same William Morris world as the sun-flowers of Wilde's American lectures on interior decoration. And it was against a similar Second Empire floral extravagance, in Théodore de Banville's poetry or Fantin-Latour's paintings, that Rimbaud had revolted when he had dedicated to Banville his bitterly critical *Ce qu'on dit au poète à propos de fleurs.* Wilde must likewise have wearied of this interior decorator's descriptiveness. The clustered flowers soon began to fade from his writings as his tastes in clothes, wines, draperies or art in general improved with experience; and all his sartorial refinements thus revealed themselves even in his least commercial writings.

Nor were such changes mere flutterings from fad to fad, as in a gushing fashion-columnist's blurbs from season to season. They indicate, on the contrary, a constant improvement in Wilde's experience, knowledge, and sensibility. Until he discovered San Francisco's Chinatown, Ultima Thule of his 1882 American tour, Wilde had, for instance, been rather contemptuous of Chinese art, but enthusiastic about all those *japonaiseries,* painted paper parasols or lacquer knick-knacks, with which the Empire of the Rising Sun had begun to flood the Western world and which, in the decades that followed Perry's expedition, had fascinated even such Parisian connoisseurs of the *bibelot* as the Goncourt brothers. In San Francisco, Wilde changed his mind and developed a taste for Chinese *objets de vertu* too. Unfortunately, he never attained any real knowledge or appreciation of the finer productions of Far Eastern art. His antiquarian discrimination, in this field, barely developed beyond some talk of blue china or of Japanese prints by Hokusai or Hokkei, so that when he wrote *Le Panneau,* an elegant *chinoiserie* which he published, in 1887, in *The Lady's Pictorial,* he still depicts very much the same cute Oriental world as the willow-pattern plates of refined Victorian homes, a world copied from cheap and junky lacquers or porcelains which we now associate with the bazaar rather than with the sophisticated collector's tastes:

> Under the rose-tree's dancing shade
>   There stands a little ivory girl,
> Pulling the leaves of pink and pearl
>   With pale green nails of polished jade.

Had Wilde's last years been less tragically or fruitlessly distract-ing, he might have learned, as indeed the whole Western art-world did toward the turn of the century, to distinguish and appreciate the art of the great periods of Chinese history. He might then have discovered the paintings and sculptures of the Sung and Ming dynasties, the funerary potteries of the Han period, the exquisitely simple bronzes, now green as jade with age, and frail jades, bronze-colored from close contact with human flesh, of the Cheou dynasty. And during his last years in Paris, had he not been so desperately intent on drowning his bitter memories in drink, he might have detected the first glimmerings of modern painting, and been the first to sponsor them in England as he had already been one of the first to sponsor Impressionism and also to recognize its limitations.

Wilde had indeed gone far towards achieving the awareness of all cultural history and the appreciation of all art which was one of the philosophic aims of Benedetto Croce and of Henry Adams. It has now become one of the chief artistic merits of much of the best modern poetry, that of Pound, of Eliot or of Wallace Stevens. In Wilde's generation, the technique of expressing simultaneously an awareness of several ages of history or types of art, as in *The Waste Land*, had not yet been formulated; and Wilde still displayed his awareness of each age or art separately, much as Robert Browning had done, though with a more suggestive subtlety and less crudely journalistic "local color," less positivistic or scientific documenta-tion. Wilde's wisdom was no longer the brash historical knowledge that had also inspired the builders of the great nineteenth-century museums, the great restorers such as Viollet-le-Duc and, at a lower level, Karl Baedeker or the artisans who carefully faked antiques.

In his unending apprenticeship, from a bookish start in his early poems, in the stilted rhetoric and creaking plots of *Vera* and *The Duchess of Padua*, Wilde had learned, at the time of his American tour, to be less derivative and to observe the outside world and his own thoughts and emotions more closely. His sojourns in Paris and his acquaintance with French art and literature had then refined his tastes, taught him the subtleties of his craft and allowed him to view in a somewhat stricter perspective the tradition of the Eminent Victorians into which he had tried to integrate his earlier poems. And from his sufferings, Wilde finally learned to distinguish and express clearly his more intimate emotions. There is thus no reason to agree entirely with Edgar Saltus: "Lord of language he was, but perhaps not always prince of prose. With added years and a fairer fate, that title also would have been accorded." In his poetry, Wilde rarely rose to princely heights, though he did in a few of the poems of the middle period, and in some parts of *The Ballad of Reading Gaol*; but as a result of his poetic experiments, Wilde developed an art of prose that proved him, at least in some of his prose poetry and in his critical dialogues, a veritable prince.

Prose and the Sublime
I — The Lyrical Drama

Few plays by writers reputed great can be as disappointing as Oscar Wilde's two early prose dramas, *Vera or The Nihilists* and *The Duchess of Padua*. *Titus Andronicus* has been ridiculed for its excessively bloodthirsty horrors, the chamber-dramas of Shelley, Coleridge, Byron or Tennyson have been pronounced perhaps fine as poetry but surely unfit for performance, the plays of Edmond Rostand are notoriously bombastic. But all these dramas somehow clothed the bare bones of their plots in some lyrical, philosophical or psychological flesh; and the plots of Wilde's two first plays, though he wrote them in prose, rattle and creak noisily in a resounding void with a kind of bookish rhetoric, falsely poetic at best, which we generally expect from crudely Romantic verse-drama.

The setting of *Vera*, written before Wilde's 1882 trip to America, is Russia in 1800, a Russia borrowed from seemingly superficial readings of novelists such as Turgenev, who were then beginning to be the vogue in England's esthetic circles. But this choice of a setting indicates no special interest in Russia, such as Wilde's interests in the ancient world or in the Italy of the Renaissance: Russian Nihilists were "in the news," and the young esthete hoped that his plot and setting might appeal to a popular audience. Among other absurdities, *Vera* contains anachronistic references to Communists, one of its characters is reported to have "sent two telegrams to Paris," and others are advised to "catch the first train for Paris"; and every character talks, even in asides, as Wilde later, in *The Decay of Lying*, accused Hall Caine of writing, "at the top of his voice." Besides, whenever Wilde felt that any more subtle writing was required, he made his Nihilists speak in the artificially Shakespearean diction which had invaded English drama in the "gothic" era of Romanticism and which Sheridan had already ridiculed in *The Critic.* Whole lines of blank verse, less polished than that of Wilde's unfinished verse-play, A *Florentine Tragedy*, thus protrude awkwardly from *Vera's* prose, like concealed weapons from the costumes of comic-opera conspirators: "Yet would that thou hadst heard the nightingale. Methinks that bird will never sing again."

As for *The Duchess of Padua*, even Wilde admitted, in 1898, in a letter to Robert Ross, that it was "unfit for publication—the only one of my works that comes under that category." With its sixteenth-century Italian plot of political and amorous intrigue such as Vittorio Alfieri might have chosen and animated with some clash of ruling passions, *The Duchess* remains as stiffly melodramatic as *Vera*, though free of the latter's absurd anachronisms and its more obviously store-bought local color. Wilde wrote to Ross, however, that he still found "good lines in it."

The scheming Prime Minister of Russia, in *Vera*, and the tyrannical Duke of Padua both express themselves often in brilliantly cynical epigram and paradox. But this wit tends to freeze momentarily the flow of action and dialogue, being limited almost exclusively, in each play, to the utterances of one character. The Russian Prime Minister's boast, "Experience, the name men give to their mistakes. I never commit any," is echoed by the Duke of Padua: "Failure is the one fault I never know," and "Popularity is the one insult I have never had to abide." Both characters remain, at best, mere pegs for the kind of resounding statement in which ham actors delight because they can then strike an attitude and "steal the show," breaking its kinetic unity in a series of "stills." Wilde, who knew actors and audiences well, later exhumed many of these remarks from his early plays; like borrowed stage-jewelry, they reappear in the comedies, though better integrated in their dialogue so that they no longer freeze the flow of the play.

Neither of Wilde's two early plays illustrates any philosophical theme, neither portrays any deep psychological conflict. They are constructed of sheer plot and somewhat bookish rhetoric, which Wilde borrowed from all the dramas he had ever read; and their characters seem to be pitted against each other like ornamental figures on a mantel-piece, changing their mind or abandoning their set poses with the almost grotesque abruptness of automata obeying a puppet-master's decisions. Vera, when she sees that the soldiers can be bribed, offers her necklace without hesitation, as if this were a daily sacrifice: "It is all I have, it was my mother's." And the Duchess of Padua falls in love with Guido at his mere suggestion, as soon as the plot demands it, without any conflict of conscience, and with no gradations of passion. Even in a much later play, A *Florentine Tragedy*, Bianca pivots similarly from love to love, whichever way the plot blows, with the ease and lack of emotion of a weathercock.

There would be little point in discussing these very mediocre products of Wilde's genius, where it not that they illustrate the larval stage of his poetic prose out of which came, in turn, his later lyrical dramas, *Salome* and *La Sainte Courtisane*. Besides, various elements of plot, from the two early plays, survive in the later ones, and in A *Florentine Tragedy* too, so that the phylogeny of the new literary genre which Wilde created can be clearly followed. All five plays have heroines who are frustrated in their love or who believe themselves frustrated. Both Vera and the Duchess of Padua are ready to revenge themselves on their lovers by plotting their death, just as thwarted Salome later demands Iokanaan's head. Vera accepts to fulfill her duties as a Nihilist in murdering the beloved Czarevitch, then kills herself to save him when she discovers that her love was not unrequited; and the Duchess lets innocent Guido, when he rejects her love, be condemned to death for the murder of her husband, which she herself had committed. In A *Florentine Tragedy*, Bianca falls in love with her suitor, out of love with him, and then in love with her husband, all within the space of one long act; the husband discovers that Bianca is beautiful only when her suitor makes love to her, and she discovers that her husband is "so strong" and attractive only when, before her eyes and indirectly at her instigation, he murders the suitor to whom she had just declared: "Until I see you all my life is vain. . . . Your image will be with me always." Only in *La Sainte Courtisane* does the rejected woman, who has fallen in love, like Vera, the Duchess and Salome, with a veritable saint, not plot any revenge: instead, she becomes a saint while the hermit leaves his cave to live, in Alexandria, the life of sin which she had given up for him and to which she has unintentionally converted him, thus "killing" the qualities that she loved in him. And another element of plot, Herod's fear of corpses and his neurotic rantings, in *Salome*, likewise reflect, from *Vera's* plot, the ambivalent guilt-feelings of the mad Czar.

Frustrated love, revenge, and guilt-feelings are thus the recurrent themes of Wilde's lyrical dramas, which all seem to illustrate the moral of *The Ballad of Reading Gaol*, "For each man kills the thing he loves." Two of these lyrical dramas were written in the manner of Wilde's earlier period; *Salome* illustrates the manner of his middle period, of which *La Sainte Courtisane* is but another fragmentary example, though more integrated and complete than *For Love of the King, a Burmese Masque*, a scenario which indicates only the plot, costumes, and scenery of a sort of pageant or ballet. And *A Florentine Tragedy*, which Wilde never finished, represents a kind of hybrid manner; its verse and setting seem to be derived from the prose and manner of *The Duchess of Padua*, though considerably refined by greater dramatic and literary experience, and its one-act unity indicates that it belongs to the same class of later drama as *Salome*. *A Florentine Tragedy* thus illustrates in some respects, one might say, what the lyrical drama of Wilde's third period might have been, had he written any during his last years in Paris. Originally written before the trials, it was rewritten after Wilde's release, but never finished; and Wilde seems, after *Salome*, to have been striving here toward a more traditional form, much as his later poetry renounced the prose-poem modernism of his middle period.

Nor is it an innovation to define all these plays as lyrical dramas rather than as tragedies: they suffer from many of the limitations of another type of lyrical drama, that of Seneca and the Renaissance Senecans, while at the same time illustrating many of its peculiarities. The *catharsis* of ancient Greek tragedy, the purging of the spectator's passions through pity and fear, had somehow vanished from the more didactic Roman tragedian's works, with their exemplary stress on admiration and horror; and Wilde failed for very much the same reasons to achieve the Greek dramatic ideal whose formula other tragedians, less lyrical or more directly dramatic, had rediscovered since the Renaissance.

In his listing of the elements of tragedy, Aristotle places, immediately after plot and character, a problematic element, *dianoia*, which is generally translated as *thought* or *sentiments*. *Dianoia* represents, however, something more complex than the mere thought, argument or moral of a tragedy's plot, than the sentiments of author or characters; *dianoia* moves the passions of the characters or the spectators and, by constantly mediating between plot, character and diction, integrates all these elements, together with those of choric music and spectacle too, so as to guide the tragedy's action, as drama rather than as narrative, toward the *catharsis* which is the tragedian's ultimate aim. *Dianoia* is thus the element of a tragedy which keeps, for instance, the diction from lapsing into excessive lyricism or rhetoric, where each speech, failing to differentiate between audience and antagonist, would become a lyrical poem or an unequivocally persuasive argument in itself; and it integrates all the speeches and arguments of the tragedy's various characters in a single artistic unit no part of which can be complete in itself. *Dianoia* can therefore be defined as the discussion or argument, the dialectical interplay or conflict of the various characters in action or of the various elements in one character; in fact, as the element of a tragedy which makes all its parts tend outwards, beyond their limits as parts, toward a common whole. In this respect, *dianoia* breathes life into the tragedy's plot and characters and allows the latter to mould and convince each other, to change and suffer before our eyes, to overcome, in monologue and self-analysis, their own passion, doubts or fears.

In a tragedy by Corneille or Racine, for instance, the *dianoia* is, to a great extent, the conflict within single characters, between passion and duty or reason, as in *Le Cid*, between will and fate, as in *Phèdre*; hence the great development of monologue in French tragedy, where so much of the conflict occurs within the individual. In the *Oedipus Tyrannus*, the *dianoia* springs to a great extent from the tragic flaw in the character of Oedipus, from his refusal to believe in the warnings of fate and from his absurd faith in himself, his *hubris*; and Sophocles, with his usual tragic irony, makes it all the more effectively culminate in the *catharsis*, because the audience has been constantly kept aware of the implications of fate's fearful warnings and has at the same time constantly pitied Oedipus for his all too human blindness. Hence, in Greek tragedy, the structural function of the chorus, which adds another dimension to the *dianoia*, extending it toward the audience in more lyrical or rhetorical pieces which determine, to some extent, the audience's attitudes toward the action, voicing its opinions and emotions, but without affecting the attitudes of the tragedy's characters.

In a society where tragedy no longer serves a social purpose as it had once done in Athens, the dramatist is forced to satisfy only the tastes and demands of an antiquarian or literary élite. Seneca found himself in this position, in Imperial Rome; and some centuries later, the Senecans of the Italian Renaissance, writing their tragedies, at first, only for Humanistic courts, followed in his path. T. S. Eliot has pointed out that Seneca's tragedies were probably never performed publicly in Rome, but were read aloud in learned circles. The individual speech, in these works, thus became more of a lyrical or rhetorical exercise, a declamatory *tour de force*; and it assumed some of the esthetic functions of the chorus, aimed more immediately at the listeners and less at the drama's other characters. The extreme of this development is well illustrated in the dramatic monologues of the Alexandrine poet Lycophron or of such Victorian poets as Tennyson and Browning; here, only one character subsists, and the scope of all action and *dianoia* is reduced to this one character's addressing himself immediately to the audience.

Such a development necessarily affects also the very nature of the characters of tragedy. As their utterances become increasingly lyrical or rhetorical, and as the element of *dianoia* grows ever less important, characters become less complex, ever more admirably typical and less pitifully individual as they tower above the problems of increasingly horrible plots. In such lyrical drama, a character's actions are no longer guided, and his passions no longer roused, by the speeches of other characters; instead of illustrating some unique complex of passions that are more or less dominated by a tragic flaw or by a ruling passion, each character illustrates a single passion, an interest or even an *idée fixe.* In most of the Senecan tragedies based on the story of Sofonisba, for instance, the African queen is motivated by her interests, her anxiety to avoid slavery, rather than by any true passion; and her failure, in the end, is due to miscalculation or arbitrary misfortune rather than to any tragic flaw in her character. The *dianoia,* which had once guided the play of passions and facilitated the *catharsis,* is now replaced, in lyrical drama, by more and more elements of plot, such as conflicts of interests, recognition-scenes, arbitrary reversals, and surprising incidents of one sort or another; and the purging of the audience's passions through pity and fear becomes barely possible. Instead, the drama relies, to a great extent, on its diction to generate a lyrical atmosphere which will raise the plot above the level of the mere problem-play; and the passions of the audience, instead of being purged, may actually be stirred, if the diction attains the sublime.

Salome offers a striking example of this development. Iokanaan, for instance, when he meets Salome as he is brought forth from the cistern, addresses the audience, at first, instead of speaking to her: "Where is he whose cup of abominations is now full? . . . Where is she who saw the images of men painted on the walls . . . who gave herself unto the Captains of Assyria? . . . Who is this woman who is looking at me?" As the scene develops, Iokanaan remains rigidly apocalyptic while Salome is more and more dominated by her *idée fixe,* her desire for the prophet's body. Nor is this desire a passion that is stirred within her by any *dianoia* of the drama: it comes upon her arbitrarily, like a fit. At first, she speaks of the beauty of Iokanaan's body, but he rejects her advances. Then, she declares that his body is hideous: "It is of thy hair that I am enamoured." Again rejected, she finds his hair hideous: "It is thy mouth that I desire. . . ." Indeed, she does kiss his mouth later, when Iokanaan's head is brought to her on a silver shield. But throughout the love-scene of their meeting, each one of Salome's speeches comes as another stanza in a lyrical poem, in a sort of ballad-like development whose stages are not determined by any argument of Iokanaan's refusals, but by his mere rejection as an element of plot. The final stanza or "envoi" of this dramatic ballad, whose progression is one of plot and lyrical atmosphere but not of shifting passions, comes at the very end of the play, in the extraordinary monologue that Salome utters as she kisses the dead man's lips: "Ah! thou wouldst not suffer me to kiss thy mouth, Iokanaan. . . ."

In all this, little *dianoia*, no psychological progression, no *catharsis* of the passions through pity and fear, but a curiously emphatic and repetitive lyricism, a sado-masochistic intensity which, by using many of the devices of lyrical poetry, inspires admiration and horror. In *La Sainte Courtisane*, the lack of *dianoia* is even more striking: Myrrhina's first speech to Honorius is a prose poem about the splendors of a great courtesan's life, and Honorius replies in a poem praising "the Son of God." Suddenly, "the scales have fallen from my eyes," he declares; and from hers too, as each has concerted the other. No hesitations, no conflicts of characters and passions, no *ad hominem* appeals from one character to the other: the play consists of plot, typical characters, lyrical or rhetorical appeals to the audience, single units in which a protagonist states his position to the world at large rather than to an antagonist.

In such lyrical drama, where a character cannot illustrate conflicting passions and where conflicts of wills are reduced to elements of plot, all the drama's characters tend to use, in their lyrical or rhetorical statements of points of view, very much the same type of rhetoric or of lyricism; to avoid this monotony and vary the drama's diction, the author may provide each character with typical epigrams or imagery, as Shakespeare provided the cobbler of *Julius Caesar* or as Melville did, in *Moby Dick*, in the dramatic episode of Ahab and the ship's carpenter, where the conceits of the one are determined, in a manner very reminiscent of *Sartor Resartus*, by his trade, and those of the other by his ruling passion. In *Vera* and *The Duchess of Padua*, the epigrams of Wilde's sinister premier and evil Duke likewise distinguish their diction from that of other characters. But these devices leave room for little psychological progression. Each character's epigrams and imagery tend to express, with more or less force or frequency, always the same passion or point of view; and each type constructed in this manner seems rigid and unchanging, at best an illustration of a ruling passion such as Theophrastus or La Bruyère might have drawn. Both Seneca's tragedies and the literary genre of the *Character*, as illustrated in the works of Theophrastus, are moreover creations of the same stoical literature of later antiquity, of the age which also produced the new Comedy of Types in the works of Menander and of Terence; and Congreve's *Letter on Comedy* indicates that a character with a ruling passion is better suited to comedy, as in the works of Terence or Molière, than to tragedy. In a comedy, the very rigidity of the miser, of the hypochondriac or of the boastful man, each of whom reacts to all situations in terms of a single unabated ruling passion, suggests a comic element of excess and of predictability. In a tragedy, only the self-analysis of monologue, as in the dramas of Corneille or Alfieri, can strip the ruling passion of its rigidity and reveal, beneath the type, the other passions of the individual that it dominates; Cinna or Le Cid, for instance, reveal to the audience the full conflict, within themselves, between their ruling passion and their other elements of individual character, such as reason or a sense of duty or of the demands of society. And in Molière's *Le Misanthrope,* the hero's self-analysis raises him above the level of a comic character until, at times, the audience pities him for his folly and fears its effects, so that *dianoia* and *catharsis* almost transmute the comedy into a tragedy.

Critics of the short story have often noted that the masters of the American macabre or fantastic story, such as Poe or Bierce, generally rely, in their tales, almost exclusively on plot and atmosphere, and thus neglect the kind of dynamic verisimilitude that can be achieved through the use of discussion or argument or through the development of character. It is significant, in this respect, that one of the Humanist critics who contributed most to the revival of Senecan lyrical drama in sixteenth-century Italy, Giraldi Cintio, was also a master, in *Gli Ecatommiti*, of the *novella,* the genre from which the fantastic or macabre story is now descended; and that Elizabethan drama, which always tended, whether as comedy, as history or as tragedy, towards a form of drama more lyrical and less "regular" than that of Italy, often borrowed its plots from the novelistic literatures of late antiquity, of the Middle Ages or of Renaissance Italy. Both *Othello* and *Measure for Measure,* for instance, are based on tales from Giraldi Cintio, who also used the plot of *Measure for Measure,* which Shakespeare turned into a lyrical comedy, for one of his own lyrical tragedies; and other plays of the age of Shakespeare are based on plots borrowed from Bandello and other masters of the *novella.*

Whether tragic or comic, lyrical drama makes, it seems, less specific demands, as far as plot is concerned, than ancient tragedy. Though Aristotle's remarks on plot are still valid, on the whole, for lyrical drama, the same plot can apparently be used for both lyrical tragedy and lyrical comedy, except that comedy demands a happy ending and tragedy an unhappy one. But in other details, the plot of lyrical drama, whether fantastic or gruesome, need not be very complex nor conform to any very definite model. With experience, Wilde thus found that a plot as simple as that of *Salome* suited his purposes better than one as complex and full of incidents as that of *Vera*; and the lyrical dramatists of the Renaissance, from Italy to England and Spain, borrowed and adapted plots from each other and from every available type of literature with a remarkable catholicity of taste and esthetic principles, much as the masters of the short story later garnered plot and incident from almost any field of art or of life. Both structurally and historically, the lyrical drama and the short story, especially the macabre or fantastic tale, are thus closely related; and both genres seem to require, of an author, the same kind of talents. Wilde's lyrical dramas, as if further evidence of the affinity of the two genres were necessary, were all written in the first or last years of his middle period, in the course of which he somewhat neglected the kind of poetry that he had previously written, and devoted his talents to poetic prose, to the fantastic in his prose poems and fairy tales, to the macabre in his stories and novel, and to criticism in *Intentions*.

In a review of Walter Pater's *Appreciations*, Wilde told, in 1890, the story of his first meeting with the Master of *Marius the Epicurean*: "Why do you always write poetry? Why do you not write prose? Prose is much more difficult." These had been Pater's words to Wilde, still an Oxford undergraduate but already a poet. And Wilde confessed that he "did not quite comprehend what Mr. Pater really meant."

Of how little he understood Pater, we have evidence, not only in the crude poetic prose of *Vera* or *The Duchess of Padua*, but also in the involved and cumbersome periods of an early essay, *The Rise of Historical Criticism*. "I do not think I knew then," wrote Wilde, "that even prophets correct their proofs. . . . Carlyle's stormy rhetoric, Ruskin's winged and passionate eloquence, had seemed to me to spring from enthusiasm rather than from art." And it was not until he had "carefully studied" Pater's prose that young Wilde began to distinguish the reader's enthusiasm from the writer's calculated purpose, and "fully realized what a wonderfully self-conscious art" English prose-writing could be. This study of prose style must have occurred, in Wilde's life, in his last year at Oxford and in the years that followed. The first evidence of its value can be seen in the preface to Rennell Rodd's volume of poems, written in 1882. But even the prose of *Vera*, self-consciously strained as it is, already shows an improvement on the prose of *The Rise of Historical Criticism*, which had quite neglected esthetic form in its cumbersome handling of rational content. And it was only a few years later, after writing the fairy tales of *The Happy Prince* and the book-reviews of *The Woman's World*, that Wilde finally attained, in *The House of Pomegranates*, in some of his prose poems, in *Intentions* and in *Salome*, a prose style that was masterfully self-conscious, fully aware of all its own powers, its aims and its ease.

Arthur Symons has complained that passion, for Wilde, was a thing to be talked about with elaborate and colored words. Salome, he suggests, is a doll, soulless, set in motion by some pitiless destiny; and Herod is a nodding mandarin in a Chinese grotesque. But Wilde's evolution as a prose artist can be judged when one compares the lyrical prose of *Vera*, with its whirring infernal machine of a plot barely concealed by the unconvincing program music of its Elizabethanisms, and the infinitely more subtle atmosphere of *Salome's* verbal music, where the skilfully contrived monotony of repetition and of well-matched imagery, in the elaborate and colored words, achieves the spell-binding effect of an incantation. Bianca, in *A Florentine Tragedy*, is just as soulless as Salome, a doll set in motion by a more ingenious destiny that Wilde's less skilful blank verse fails to conceal as well as the mature art of *Salome's* prose. And the action of *Vera* is determined by an even more cumbersome machinery of plot, with its two pivotal recognition scenes, when the convict to whom the heroine shows compassion turns out to be her brother and when the Nihilist student whom she loves is revealed to be the politically hated Czarevitch, to say nothing of the final twist of destiny which forces Vera to draw the lot that dooms her to murder the Czarevitch. Though it relies far less than *Vera* on such surprising conjuring-tricks of plot, *The*

Duchess of Padua requires a whole act to establish, in a sort of prologue, how Guido, a child of unknown parents brought up by humble country-folk, discovers his aristocratic lineage and is persuaded to avenge his murdered father by killing the usurping Duke. But the style and tone of a pastiche of Elizabethan drama are better suited to this tale of sixteenth-century Italy than they had been to one of nineteenth-century Russia; and the atmosphere of *The Duchess of Padua* is more convincing while the machinery of plot that it conceals is also less unconvincingly ingenious.

The pitiless destiny of *Salome's* plot is much simpler. It is a mere "take it or leave it affair," like that of a ballad or a parable, and does not need any ingenious devices to establish its probability or necessity; the whole play relies instead on lyrical quality, on the atmosphere generated by its style and diction which, as expressions of Wilde's mature temperament or genius, are both more original and more effective than those of his earlier lyrical dramas. In the development of this drama, the emphasis on complexity of plot had thus decreased while that on atmosphere increased. Stripped of surprising tricks of destiny, plot had finally been reduced, in *Salome*, almost to a legend or a parable, so that it relied even more on diction than the lyrical drama generally does. But the quality of Wilde's prose-style was at last adequate to the task; and the nature of this quality can better be defined in an analysis of Wilde's other works in poetical prose, where the lyrical element was slowly refined until some of the fairy tales, of the prose poems, and of the myths of the critical dialogues at last attained the prose sublime which was their author's aim.

Deprived of the melodic element of the ancient chorus and of most of tragedy's *dianoia*, and reduced to a minimum of plot and character, *Salome* relied heavily on this quality of diction. Pageantry of staging and a diction where the sublime would offer a substitute for the *catharsis* were now the only elements capable, in such simplified lyrical drama, of animating the plot and stirring, though perhaps without purging them, an audience's passions. And it is not surprising that *Salome* should lend itself so easily to operatic adaptation, where music and splendid staging reinforce the spectacular element and add a new element of atmosphere that tends toward an analogous sublime; nor that one of Wilde's followers along the same path, Hugo von Hoffmansthal, should have conceived his dramas so often as operas, and worked so closely with Richard Strauss that the libretto and the score of their works, as in few operas save those of Wagner, can now be analyzed as a single and almost indivisible work of art.

Prose and the Sublime
II — The Poems in Prose

For their form and type of content, Wilde's prose poems are much indebted to Baudelaire and to Pierre Louÿs, one of Wilde's Paris friends who probably helped him write the original French text of *Salome* and to whom the play was dedicated. Other French influences that determined the nature of Wilde's prose poetry were those of Flaubert, Théophile Gautier, Marcel Schwob, and Rémy de Gourmont. From Flaubert was derived the plot of *Salome*, which is based on his *Hérodias*; and his descriptive style, in this work as well as in *Salammbo* or *La Tentation de Saint Antoine*, was a valuable element in Wilde's elaboration of a mythopoeia or "art of lying." To Gautier, Wilde owed other aspects of his art of describing the imagined or the unreal in concrete terms that appeal to the senses of perception; and to Marcel Schwob and Gourmont, theorists and masters of the more learned circles among the French decadents, he owed much of his interest, as to Flaubert too, in all the Asiatic or Alexandrine elements of antiquity to which he had not been initiated by Walter Pater. Of this manner, *La Sainte Courtisane*, on a theme which Anatole France, another friend of Louÿs, developed more fully in *Thais*, is a typical example. The transition from *Charmides* to this antiquity of which *The Sphinx* is also part is as striking, in Wilde's work, as it is, in the history of taste, from the neoclassical antiquity of Addison's *Cato* to that of *Marius the Epicurean*, of *Quo Vadis* or of *The Last Days of Pompeii*; in painting, a similar transition is illustrated in the shift from the antiquity of Lord Leighton to that of Gustave Moreau. An interest in magic, in religious mysteries, and in Gnostic or Early Christian beliefs was prominent in the antiquarian scholarship of Oscar Wilde and the French decadents. It was primarily an interest in aspects of antiquity that Renaissance Humanism had neglected, in all that was obscurely irrational or barbaric or Christian, popularly superstitious or Asiatic rather than luminously classical and rational, in all that was Carthaginian, Persian, Egyptian or Etruscan and that official Athenian or Roman culture had submerged, in the archaic elements that classical culture had concealed. In discovering the beauty of such poetry as the early Latin chorus of the Arval Brotherhood or the popular songs of the ancient world and its magical formulae and incantations, the scholars and esthetes of the last decades of the Nineteenth Century had to reject many of the critical principles of Classicism. In their stead, they relied on the sublime and concluded that it resided to a great extent, in such poetry, in the hallucinatory power of vivid description of objective detail or in the obsessive intensity of repetition and of strict patterns of syntax. It is significant, in this respect, that the earliest known discussion of the sublime should be that of Longinus, an Asiatic Greek of the post-classical era when cultured Greeks had begun to understand and appreciate the thought and art of such "barbarians" as the Egyptians and the Hebrews, and that Longinus should even quote the *Book of Genesis* as an example of the sublime, which no critic in Periclean Athens would have deigned to do.

Baudelaire had similarly stressed the mysterious beauty of medieval Latin poetry, and even imitated, in *Franciscae meae Laudes* and elsewhere, its puns and verbal patterns; and Rimbaud, in *A Season in Hell,* confessed his love for Church Latin. All these tastes of the later Romantics, Decadents, and Symbolists for post-classical Greek and Latin poetry had finally been fused, together with other beliefs, in a new poetics whose aims partook both of thaumaturgy and of psychopathology. On the one hand, those who tended toward Rimbaud's verbal alchemy sought, by vividly descriptive writing, to create the illusion of the thing that the word symbolizes; the poet thus became a magician, emulating God, as some poets and estheticians had suggested from Tasso to Novalis, in his creation of a world that was born of his poem. On the other hand, by obsessive rhythms and alliterations or imagery, the poet sought to hypnotize his reader, to project upon him, as Poe intended, specific moods or emotions; and he thus became, in a way, a psychopathologist or at least a dabbler in theories of madness and of suggestion. The communion of poet and reader, in magic or madness, was achieved through some element that transcends reason, through the sublime; and the chief devices of the sublime, it seems, were vividly descriptive and hallucinatory or obsessively repetitive and rhythmical, the *diatyposis* and the *anaphora* of Longinus.

The declamatory prose poetry of *Salome* illustrates Oscar Wilde's contribution to this new art of poetry. Even in the English translation, which no longer communicates the carefully chosen rhythm and imagery of the original French, the obsessive pattern of the repetitions and the hallucinatory quality of the descriptions are clearly apparent: "The moon has a strange look tonight. Has she not a strange look? She is like a mad woman, a mad woman who is seeking everywhere for lovers. She is naked too. She is quite naked. The clouds are seeking to clothe her nakedness, but she will not let them. She shows herself naked in the sky. She reels through the clouds like a drunken woman. . . . I am sure she is looking for lovers. Does she not reel like a drunken woman? She is like a mad woman, is she not?" Here, the repetitions communicate Herod's own obsessive melancholia, whose nature is strikingly symbolized in the imagery: and when Salome later dances before him, she embodies his obsession even more vividly than the moon.

The forms of such prose poetry illustrate clearly how Neo-Platonist and Romantic esthetics, by stressing the quality of the sublime in poetry and by neglecting all the more formal principles and elements of Aristotelian and Horatian criticism, had inevitably reached the conclusion that the sublime could exist in prose as well as in poetry. Longinus had already discussed the orator's sublime in the same arguments as the poet's sublime, never clearly distinguishing the one from the other. Prose was thus as legitimate a form of poetry as any verse-form; and the more formal artists of the second generation of French Romantics therefore began to experiment consciously with prose poetry and to develop, for the prose poem, forms that were more strict than the rhapsodic prose of

Chateaubriand or Volnay, and more closely allied, by curious analogies, to the verse-forms with which these poets were most familiar. By stripping poetry of its structure of rhythm and rhyme, Baudelaire soon reduced it, in his prose poems, to its elements of factual content, plot, and atmosphere; and his poetics of the prose poem have much in common with those of the fantastic tales of Poe, or of the prose translation of a poem. Rimbaud, a few decades later, neglected the element of fact or of plot which had sometimes made Baudelaire's prose poems almost journalistic, too much like sketches or short stories; instead, Rimbaud developed the lyrical element of atmosphere, till his prose *Illuminations*, by using all the same devices of diction, syntax, and imagery as the verse *Illuminations*, achieved the same elliptical and mysterious perfection.

Oscar Wilde does not seem to have known Arthur Rimbaud's prose poetry, but to have borrowed the esthetics of prose poetry from Baudelaire and a few of his less experimental followers, especially from Pierre Louÿs, whose *Chansons de Bilitis* imitate the manner and forms of translations of late Greek lyrical poems. Before Baudelaire, Aloysius Bertrand, the earliest master of the French prose poem, seems likewise to have imitated, in *Gaspard de la Nuit*, the forms of prose translations of German ballads or of medieval lyrics. In a curious fragment generally printed erroneously as a preface to *A Season in Hell*, Rimbaud had indeed parodied the *New Testament*, much as Wilde did in some of his *Poems in Prose*; and traces of imitation of Biblical style can be found elsewhere in Rimbaud's work. But Rimbaud and Wilde had a common source, in Baudelaire and in the vast Biblical and Satanic literature of Romanticism; both the style and the irony were thus common property, no valid proof that Wilde knew Rimbaud's work.

In English literature, the prose poem has never obtained the same recognition, as a legitimate form of poetry, as in France. No English or American poets of the importance of Baudelaire or Rimbaud have sponsored it in the past, and no school as fruitful as that of Apollinaire or of the Surrealists has made an issue of it in our age. Wilde's *Poems in Prose* thus have something freakish or awkward about them; they follow no known English patterns and must create, as they go, a form that has not been generally imitated, except by such crude or popular writers as Kahlil Gibran, much as Poe's poetic and narrative forms were imitated by jingle-bell rhymesters and pulp-magazine hacks. The *Poems in Prose* now suggest too clearly the forms of non-poetic or pseudo-poetic prose. The more Biblical ones, with their studied archaisms, sound like translations; and *The Artist* or *The Disciple* are like expanded epigrams. Finding no other bronze available, the artist fashions his new image, "The Pleasure that abideth for a moment," out of his earlier image, "The Sorrow that endureth for ever"; and the pool mourns Narcissus, not because he gazed so faithfully into its depths, but because it had always contemplated its own beauty reflected in the youth's eyes. In all this, there seems to be too much wit; the devices of diction and of plot or structure are too apparent, and there is not enough of the lyrical atmosphere of true poetry.

But the very nature of the wit in the Biblical *Poems in Prose* illustrates Wilde's constant preoccupation with themes of guilt and sin. In the artist's development, this preoccupation reveals itself esthetically as a haunting sense of inadequacy, a striving toward an even greater purity of form or content. Wilde was never, as some artists seem to be, satisfied with any of his art. His refusal to rewrite *Vera*, for instance, because it was "a work of genius," in fact all his boasting and exhibitionism can thus be interpreted as manifestations of an ambivalent defense-mechanism, the purpose of which was to silence any critics who might be tempted to affirm what his own artistic conscience never ceased suggesting; or else, to force them to state it openly and thus free him from the anguish of doubt. And Wilde constantly refined his art by banishing, from each genre that he attempted, all elements that proved to be better suited to other genres. From his poetry, he banished all the essayistic thought, the politics, the ethics and the esthetics of such earlier works as *Eleutheria, Humanitad* or *The Garden of Eros,* and most of the decorative and descriptive art of his Pre-Raphaelitic manner, its archaeological or historical reconstruction, till he achieved the almost pure poetry of *The Harlot's House.* He likewise stripped his lyrical drama of much that had marred *Vera,* the unnecessary devices and incidents of plot and the pseudo-realistic detail, for instance, till the genre was reduced to its basic elements in *Salome.* As Wilde sorted his varied gifts, he was able to discover, in his study of each genre, the aspects of his personality which could be cultivated there most fruitfully and which, by their very number and conflicting natures, destroyed the unity of his less experienced work. The element of wit and paradox which still rings so false in some of the *Poems in Prose* was thus something that Wilde later rejected, when he refined his prose poetry enough to permit the writing of *Salome.*

In his earlier poems, Wilde had already expressed his sense of guilt in ethical terms and with less self-knowledge, as in *Humanitad*:

> By our own hands our heads are desecrate . . .
>
> .   .   .   .
>
> And we were vain and ignorant nor knew
> That when we stabbed this heart it was our own
>   real hearts we slew.

Elsewhere, in the early poems, Wilde had proclaimed, as in *Ravenna*, that "The woods are filled with gods we fancied slain," or that "all thoughts of black Gethsemane" were drowned; and he had even spoken contemptuously, in *The Burden of Itys*, of "One I some time worshiped." But the "fond Hellenic dream" of his youthful paganism had apparently proved false; and Wilde slowly returned to Christianity, though to a curiously Alexandrine or Hellenistic heterodoxy which, in *Salome*, the *Poems in Prose* or the fairy tales, adopted Biblical diction and forms, such as the parable, to illustrate a paradoxical ethics of good and evil whose Manichaean identity of contraries is typical of many heresies that once flourished among the more Oriental sects of Gnosticism and Early Christianity.

Nor is this development, from decadent paganism and hedonism to mystical Christianity, at all unusual. It is illustrated in the very history of the ancient world's decline and fall, and in the many legends of pagan sinners who converted and became saints; and several other nineteenth-century decadents who had tried to revive the hedonism and paganism of late antiquity found that these led them almost inevitably back to the Christianity which they had first rejected, though to a more mystical form of it. The most outstanding disciple of the neo-pagan painter Gustave Moreau has thus been the Catholic mystic Georges Rouault; and Wilde's own art, which borrowed so many pagan elements, in *The Sphinx* or *Salome*, from the paintings of Gustave Moreau, also rejected these symbols guiltily, in the last lines of *The Sphinx* and especially in the paradoxical cult of sin which distinguishes much of his later work, from the *Poems in Prose* and *The Harlot's House* to *The Ballad of Reading Gaol* and *De Profundis*. In Baudelaire, in Wilde, and in Rouault, the same Manichaean Christianity leads indeed to the same apotheosis, through sins redeemed, of the prostitute, the spiritual counterpart, in knowledge and rejections of evil, of the saint whom evil has never touched. And the paradox thus becomes an illustration of the Crucifix, its cross-purposes torturing the artist or the mystic with both doubt and certitude.

Paradox and antithesis can suggest, in an *a priori* synthesis analogous to much dialectical reasoning, what cannot be stated logically; and this ineffable of the mystic's intuition of the identity of contraries is analogous, in a different area of experience, to the mathematician's intuition of the infinite or the esthetician's of the sublime. The weakness of Wilde's *Poems in Prose*, as poetry, thus lies in their paradoxical content, which is of an ethical or theological nature rather than of an esthetic nature, so that they express an ineffable rather than a sublime. And a painter such as Rouault has thus solved the esthetic problem of Manichaeanism, with its dualism of good and evil, far more adequately than Wilde: he achieves the sublime in ugliness, beauty in the grotesque, art's equivalent of the body's experiencing the Heraclitean or Taoist identity of contraries in the pleasure of pain.

In *The Master*, among the Biblical *Poems in Prose*, Joseph of Arimathea meets, on the day of the Crucifixion, a young man who is weeping, his body wounded with thorns and his head strewn with ashes. The young man declares: "It is not for him that I am weeping, but for myself"; he has performed the same miracles as Christ and bitterly resents not having been similarly crucified. His plight is indeed that of the many other Messiahs of the age of the Gospels, when some heretical or Essenian sects even believed that Christ was but the supreme Messiah amongst many, and that one of these other Messiahs was to be found living in each age; and Cabbalist Jewish doctrine still distinguishes an ever-present Messiah, Son of Joseph, whose avatars are continuous as those of the Dalai Lama, from the Messiah, Son of David, who is to be the real and last Messiah. In another prose poem, *The Doer of Good*, Wilde portrays a Messiah who discovers that all those whom he has miraculously healed have not morally benefited thereby: the former leper has become a voluptuary, the blind man a lecher, the woman whose sins had been forgiven has started a new life of sin, and the man raised from the dead now spends his days mourning. In a world of the flesh, there is no escape from the sin and sorrow of the flesh.

These *Poems in Prose* expound indeed too much doctrine; they almost fall into what Wilde, in his review of the English translation of Chuang Tzu's Taoist classic, calls "the vulgar habit of arguing." It is elsewhere that Wilde's real prose poetry is to be found, in some of his fairy tales, in *Salome,* and in the myths that glitter like jewels in the dialectical setting of his dialogues. The dialogue on *The Decay of Lying* thus contains a brilliant illustration of the use and purpose of the myth and, at the same time, of the sort of unconditional surrender that Wilde's *Magister* expects, in the dialogues, of his *Discipulus* and of the reader, or that one character, in his lyrical dramas, expects of the other characters and of the audience. When tragedy or dialogue no longer distinguish structurally, in their rhetorical devices, the participants from the public, they can no longer purge the passions of the heart or the errors of the intellect; and they must then depend on the magic spell and total acquiescence which the sublime engenders rather than on the *catharsis* which the more persuasive or argumentative arts of *dianoia* and dialectical elucidation facilitate by moving the passions or exercising the understanding.

In *The Decay of Lying,* Vivian is arguing that the aim of art and of lying is to charm, and that the Truth in art is a matter of style, not of mere fact. But Cyril, the *Discipulus,* is not prepared to believe his *Magister.* Vivian then abandons all argument and illustrates his theory in a vividly descriptive allegory; "Art finds her own perfection within, and not outside of, herself. She is not to be judged by any external standards of resemblance. . . . She has flowers that no forests know of. . . . The dryads peer through the thicket as she passes by. . . . She has hawk-faced gods that worship her, and the centaurs gallop at her side." At this point, Cyril interrupts Vivian, more charmed than persuaded by the descriptive imagery: "I like that. I can see it. . . ."

In the same manner, Wilde convinces his readers more completely, as a poet in prose, only when his imagery and his descriptions of the unreal are most objectively vivid, in some passages of *Salome*, for instance, in the best of his fairy tales and in the myths of his dialogues. Here Wilde's prose poetry follows esthetic principles that are better suited to his temperament than those of Baudelaire's prose poetry, which Wilde imitated almost too schematically, making it seem bare and impoverished rather than adorned and enriched as Rimbaud did. But these new principles established no forms for the prose poem; instead, they developed a poetical manner, an aura of the sublime which was intended to emanate from the whole poem, whatever its form. Of the prose sublime, Wilde already knew magnificent examples in English, in the prose of Ruskin, "whose rhythm and color and fine rhetoric and marvellous music of words are entirely unattainable," and of Walter Pater, "who through the subtle perfection of his form, is inimitable absolutely," or in the prose of Landor and De Quincey and in the Oriental fantasies of Beckford's *Vathek*; and declamatory invocations or descriptions, such as that of Chateau Désir in *Vivian Grey* or those that embellish *Melmoth*, had been, ever since *The Castle of Otranto*, one of the main features of the gothic novel. In French too, there was an older tradition of such rhapsodic prose, in the works of Volnay or Chateaubriand, and especially in Maurice de Guérin's evocation of mythical antiquity, *Le Centaure*, to which Wilde's own visions of Arcady were so closely allied. In one of his book-reviews, Wilde had even written: "It is not that I like poetical prose, but I love the prose of poets."

In his fairy tales, Wilde perfected, to a great extent, his poet's prose, and in much the same manner as he perfected his art in other genres too. The earlier tales, those of the volume that contains *The Happy Prince*, still aim at too many artistic objectives; their pathos is of a more conventional sort than their descriptive art, and their humor too self-conscious for their fantasy. Animals, plants, and inanimate objects here reason and talk and behave like human beings; and human beings, such as the student in *The Nightingale and the Rose*, are oddly obtuse and insensitive, no more human than the water-rat of *The Devoted Friend* or the inanimate hero of *The Remarkable Rocket*. In all this satire, human beings, animals, and inanimate objects think and talk the same selfish language, except the swallow and the statue in *The Happy Prince* or the nightingale in *The Nightingale and the Rose*; but there is something arbitrary and strained in the almost foolish virtue of the few hero-victims, something too contrived in the pathos and the moral of each tale, too much of the schematic in the many shifts from one level of art to another, from the simplicity of tales written for children to the witty artifices of adult irony and satire, and in the shifts from one artistic objective or special audience to another.

In an introduction to Wilde's collected fairy tales, W. B. Yeats once wrote: "The further Wilde goes in his writings from the method of speech, from improvisation, from sympathy with some especial audience, the less original he is, the less accomplished. . . . *The Happy Prince and Other Tales* is charming and amusing because he told its stories. . . . A *House of Pomegranates* is overdecorated and seldom amusing because he wrote its stories." To the Papas and Mamas of the upper-class nurseries of the late Victorian era, such moral tales as *The Happy Prince, The Selfish Giant, The Devoted Friend, The Nightingale and the Rose* or *The Remarkable Rocket,* with their elaborate pathos, sly satire and coy humor, were charming and amusing; and Yeats, who shared some of their rather patronizing views concerning the tastes and reasoning of children as mere miniature adults, assumed that Wilde's earlier fairy tales were perfectly adapted to a children's audience, though they have always been more popular with adult readers than with children. But children are lovers of straight narrative, and generally resent the suspense and delays of a more sophisticated arabesque of ironies; and it is a symptom of a peculiar perversion of taste, in our age that feels such a great nostalgia for the irresponsibilities of childhood, that so many adults should delight in a literature which only pretends to be written for children and still uses many of the devices of adult thinking.

In Wilde's writings, this adult imitation of children's thinking illustrates an attempt to overcome, by making a virtue of it, some deeply-rooted awkwardness or sense of guilt as an artist; and Wilde tried to overcome the same inhibitions, in other works, by imitating the styles of translation or the Biblical manner. What Yeats admired, in the earlier fairy tales, was thus no genuine simplicity, no close rendering of the patterns of Wilde's conversational style, which was always elaborately paradoxical and richly descriptive, but an affectation of simplicity; Yeats quite properly resented, however, some of the descriptive imagery, the "fair pillars of marble," the "loud music of many lutes," the "hall of chalcedony and the hall of jasper," and all the other decorative props which recur so frequently when, in his attempt to emulate the painter's art and thus stimulate the reader's visual imagination, Wilde lapses into careless repetition or hasty description of the same floral pieces, the same imitation antique or semi-precious stones. The fabulous conversations of animals and flowers, in the garden of *The Nightingale and the Rose*, are thus repeated, in a way, in *The Birthday of the Infanta*, when the dwarf wanders into the garden; and *Salome* repeats much of the description of the Biblical *Poems in Prose*.

At his best, in the later tales of *A House of Pomegranates*, Wilde really achieved, in some descriptions, the magic effects which were his real objective; there, his art of lying creates and describes mythically what does not exist, and charms and convinces as utterly as if it did exist. In the Oriental scenes of *The Fisherman and his Soul*, some details of description are perhaps unnecessary to the story. But these arbitrarily introduced details, the woman "who wore a mask of gilded leather," the mountains where "we held our breath lest the snow might fall on us, and each man tied a veil of gauze before his eyes," the strange places and things and people, "the Aurantes who bury their dead on the tops of trees," all these, because each in turn is so exotic and new and surprising, introduce into the story an element of the fantastic or the sublime which Wilde had found in Herodotus, in Mandeville or in Marco Polo and which, while we now read him, we can still see much as Cyril, in *The Decay of Lying*, saw the "hawk-faced gods" of Vivian's allegory.

This is the great art of Wilde's poetic prose, achieved only, among the fairy tales, in the best of *A House of Pomegranates*, in parts of *The Birthday of the Infanta*, *The Young King* or *The Star Child*, and in the whole of *The Fisherman and his Soul*; here, the richness of style and description is not affected, as was the Elizabethan pastiche of *Vera*, nor wearisome, as are some of the floral descriptions in Wilde's earlier poems or the catalogues of rare objects in *The Picture of Dorian Gray*. Even *Salome* is marred by much unnecessary richness, as in Herod's speech: "I have jewels hidden in this place . . . a collar of pearls set in four rows. They are like unto moons chained with rays of silver. They are even as half a hundred moons caught in a golden net . . . I have amethysts of two kinds. . . . I have topazes yellow as are the eyes of tigers, and topazes that are pink . . . and green topazes. . . . I have opals. . . . I have onyxes like the eyeballs of a dead woman. I have moon stones . . . sapphires . . . chrysolites and beryls, and chrysoprases and rubies; I have sardonyx and hyacinth stones, and stones of chalcedony. . . ." Such richness of the jeweler's display is indeed as wearisome as that of a pedantic medieval *Lapidary*; and it now reminds one too much of Huysmans, whom Wilde was imitating, and of *Peter Whiffle*, that clearance-sale of all the curios that Carl Van Vechten had inherited from the "estates" of Wilde, Edgar Saltus, and Ronald Firbank.

All that glitters in nature and life is not necessarily gold in art or poetry. We are not always dazzled by it as we read of it, we do not always see it as Cyril saw the hawk-faced gods. And Wilde's most poetic lies were often those that came most surprisingly, his most vivid and rich descriptions those of objects which had no insurance-value, his most poetic prose that which relied least on the prestige of Elizabethan poetry, of Biblical utterance or of the book-illustrator's art. In *The Young King*, Wilde himself reveals both the esthetic and the moral limitations of mere preciousness, and of the superficial beauty of jewels or brocades and riches which moth and rust corrupt. Brought up in Arcadian simplicity among shepherds, the child of a morganatic royal marriage suddenly inherits the crown and discovers the splendors of a fabulous court; he becomes, at first, passionately addicted to the pursuit of all that glitters, till a series of dreams reveals to him the poverty and agony of the pearl-divers and weavers and other workers who toil to produce his lovely baubles. The young king then abandons these earthly splendors to pursue the absolute beauties of charity and saintliness. In *The Happy Prince*, Wilde had similarly hinted that the gold and jewels of the statue were less lovely than the charity and self-denial of the prince and the swallow; and in *The Nightingale and the Rose*, that the bird's self-sacrifice was at least as lovely as its song or as the rose that its blood had made red. But Wilde discovered in *The Young King* a new source of beauty, and his descriptions of the dismal attic where the weavers toil, a curious resurgence of an ancient Celtic myth of the other-world which had been handed down to Tennyson and the

Pre-Raphaelites from such Arthurian romances as Chrétien de Troyes' *Ivain*, is at least as hallucinatingly vivid as Wilde's descriptions of more glittering beauties. In *The Birthday of the Infanta* too, the pathos of the hideous dwarf's love for the lovely royal child, and of his discovery of his own ugliness in the mirror, then of his broken-hearted death contrasted with the infanta's petulant annoyance at the loss of this human toy, all these are marred by no self-conscious humor or affectation of beauty; and the little monster's physical ugliness is as vividly depicted as that of a Velasquez dwarf, and indeed as poetic as the beautiful infanta's ugly insensitivity. With unerring strokes, Wilde here depicts rapidly, without stopping to moralize, to over-decorate or to entertain with unnecessary wit or humor.

In his later fables, Wilde thus rejected mere physical beauty in favor of a more transcendent beauty of art whose light shines forth from appearances often less glittering and sometimes even ugly. And he achieved his aim of dazzling not so much by the richness of what he described as by his way of describing it, by a kind of sublime that emanates, to a great extent, from the vivid description of contrasts, from a more firmly guided dialectic than that of the earlier tales, and from a greater unity of plot or singleness of purpose in the narrative's atmosphere. As a narrator, Wilde was less frequently tempted to err from his course through stagnant pools of description or wayward humor; and his atmosphere was at last perfectly suited to his plot, in an esthetic similar to that of the German *Maerchen*, of the macabre story or of the lyrical drama, where character development, by rooting the narrative too deep in the reality of verisimilitude, might mar the mythical reality of the unreal.

We cannot easily evaluate Wilde's techniques for attaining the sublime, or the theory that would justify them, without situating them first in a quest or controversy that has now lasted some two thousand years. But our task allows little scope for a detailed historical survey of the topic; and brevity soon suggests misleading generalizations, unless one is careful to think in terms of the contexts of particular theories rather than in terms of the theories themselves. Each theory of the sublime must thus be viewed here as an attempt to organize and clarify the data and opinions of its age and of a controversy the general problems of which determine much of the theory's particular nature.

Most of the critics of antiquity, when they first examined poetry or poetics, analyzed them dialectically, as Plato did, in terms of the known values of another science, such as ethics or politics. But Aristotle's formulation of analytical logic, the terms of which are applicable to all sciences and belong to none, soon made it possible to determine rationally the elements of poetry; and those of tragedy thus came to be defined in Aristotle's *Poetics*. It was then found, however, that an unknown element which escaped logical analysis yet remained to be defined. This element was the sublime, whose existence and nature such critics as Longinus determined intuitionally or psychologically, by observing in themselves or in others the emotions that it aroused and by attempting to correlate these with the passages of a poem that produced them. The element of the sublime thus became the primary aim of many poets; but an emphasis on the poem's educational effect on its audience led to a confusion between oratory and poetry, which broadened the scope of a discussion that was more and more devoted to morals or to rhetoric. Longinus, for instance, identified the sublime, on the one hand, with the communication of the poet's own moral virtues or those of his topic and, on the other hand, with the rhetorical devices which allow art to imitate fitly the beauties of nature, in fact to reproduce, for instance, in abrupt or disordered syntax, the abruptness or disorder of the passions or the scene described. And when Sir Joshua Reynolds, many centuries later, returned to a similar discussion of the sublime in the art of painting, for which no rhetoric had yet been formulated, he still reduced it so clearly to the depiction of moral virtues that he preached little more than an art of illustrating noble rather than merely elegant deportment.

By reducing to a limited number of theological mysteries all that defied rational analysis, medieval scholasticism absorbed the sublime within the miracles and confused the rest of poetics with rhetoric. Virgil thus came to be variously revered, throughout the Middle Ages, as a prophet or magician among rhetoricians or a pre-Christian saint; and apocalyptic allegory became the aim of poets who, like Dante, hoped to transcend the *trivia* of grammar, logic, and rhetoric and attain the anagogical sublime.

The Humanists of the Renaissance again distinguished esthetics from theology, the esthetically miraculous from the theologically miraculous, the poet as creator of the beautiful from God as Creator of the Universe. They tended, however, especially Giangiorgio Trissino and Sperone Speroni, to think that a tragedy's audience could be moved to pity or fear only when its characters illustrated pity or fear; and this type of literal thinking led them also to identify the sublime with a poem's miraculous or marvelous content. Pagan myths and marvelous legends of chivalry, with their monsters and magicians, thus became favorite topics among such poets as Ariosto or Tasso; and the sublime, in the poetics of Tasso or Minturno, and later in the critical writings of Corneille, was variously identified with a magic which made the poet analogous to God, with the marvelous of profane legends or, if an ethical content were required, with the "merveilleux chrétien" of Tasso's epic, of Corneille's *Polyeucte* or of Milton's *Paradise Lost* as distinguished from the profane marvelous of Ariosto's epic, of *Le Cid* or of Spenser's *The Faerie Queene*.

But the sublime still seemed to elude all rational analysis; and gradually such critics as Gravina and Dubos returned to discussing it as an unknown quantity, a "je ne sais quoi," till the middle of the Eighteenth Century, while poets almost gave up all hope of attaining it, except by some chance felicity of sentiment or of wording. A new interest in epistemology, however, then revived discussions of the sublime, first in England and then in Germany, but with a new emphasis on taste and on the dimension from the work of art to its audience rather than from artist or subject-matter to work of art. Initiating this fruitful and more empiric or pragmatic type of investigation of the sublime, Edmund Burke made esthetics a study of the sensual and intellective rather than of the moral pleasures of art. And Hogarth suggested that the unknown quantity might reside in devices that do not follow known or rational canons of art, in the irregular rather than the regular, in the "clear serpentine line" and in sinuously indirect curves, in the winding streams of nature, for instance, rather than in the formally architectonic structure of the Palladian temples of art. If the analogy between geometry and logic were valid, this would mean that the poetic sublime resides in sinuously indirect statement rather than in direct proposition. In

Germany, discussion of the beauties of non-classical masterpieces slowly led also to the formulation of various intuitional theories of judgment and of the sublime; and Romantic poets tended toward these views, at first, and developed a poetics of periphrasis and self-expression which allowed more scope for emotional or impassioned inspiration and, while stressing a renewed interest in the irrational and in the marvelous, generally preached what one might call a non-Euclidean conception of form.

The later Romantics, however, were not satisfied with these views. In an age of scientific experiment, of inventions and discoveries, they returned to a more exact and mechanistic conception of form and devised an inductive method which, positing the sublime as an actual infinite, worked toward it with the aid of techniques and devices which seemed likely to attain it. Such were, for instance, the experimental poetics of Poe, Baudelaire or Rimbaud; as magicians or hypnotists, in a curious mixture of scientific method and of the showmanship of the charlatan, these poets experimented on their readers with techniques of hallucination or obsession, with vividly objective description of hauntingly rhythmical repetition, the *diatyposis* and the *anaphora* which Longinus had recommended. And it was Oscar Wilde's distinction to be one of the first to apply these theories in English; but it was also his misfortune to achieve his ends less frequently than Poe.

With his brashly American sense of expediency and showman-ship, Poe had understood that his task demanded a total effort in which he could afford to despise no device, however trite or crude. Wilde was more fastidious and under-estimated the value of whole classes of devices which dazzle or deceive less sophisticated readers. In *The Canterville Ghost*, he could bring himself to use the conventionally melodramatic props of the macabre story only apologetically, with self-conscious humor; but Poe had used them without betraying any emotion that might weaken their effect. And in *The Picture of Dorian Gray*, Wilde avoided many of these props and substituted descriptions of rare and precious objects which demand of the reader more taste or learning and contribute little to the narrative's total atmosphere. In *The Sphinx*, whose apparition is so closely patterned on that of *The Raven*, Wilde likewise avoided the doggerel devices of obsessive rhythms and jingling rhymes which

Poe had used so successfully. Wilde's failure to achieve his objective as often as Poe can thus be attributed, to a great extent, to his intellectual or esthetic prestige-needs and to inhibitions which prevented him from using some of the more crude or trite devices of his art. In his empirical quest of the sublime's actual infinite, Wilde had ignored whole categories of evidence, so that his inductive method was less reliable and his success less probable.

Criticism as Art

An artist who is as concerned as Oscar Wilde was with the purposes and devices of his art, with its ends and means, must demonstrate his esthetic beliefs very frequently and not always directly. The very form or structure of some of his works may illustrate them, while the characters of other works may expound them as other characters expound beliefs that their author rejects. Critical theory can thus be distilled from almost any example of his creative art as well as from the contents of his more directly critical works.

Most of Wilde's creative works can be analyzed, to some extent, as critical works. Lord Henry, in *The Picture of Dorian Gray*, expounds very much the same doctrines of art and of life as Ernest in the critical dialogue on *The Critic as Artist*; and in *An Ideal Husband*, Lord Goring illustrates, though satirically, similar opinions and tastes, those of the ideal dandy. Wilde found illustrations of his own tastes and beliefs even in real life; in *Pen, Pencil, and Poison*, an essay on Thomas Griffiths Wainewright, we discover curious analogies between Wainewright, the essayist, painter, and poisoner who was a friend of Charles Lamb, and Wilde's Dorian Gray. The historical character and the fictional hero both exercised a "strange fascination" on all who met them, each young dandy "sought to be somebody, rather than to do something," both "recognised that Life itself is an art, and has its modes of style no less than the arts that seek to express it," both collected more or less the same precious coins, antique gems, cameos and other knick-knacks, and both came to grief, by way of crime, when they abandoned their dispassionate dandyism and allowed themselves to be dominated by their passions, greed or self-love.

But many of the appreciations and critical views that are scattered throughout Wilde's poetry, drama, and fiction have been restated in a more organized form in his critical dialogues, *The Decay of Lying* and *The Critic as Artist*; and the preliminary observations for these more formal discussions of artistic problems are to a great extent available in Wilde's more important essays, in *The Truth of Masks, The Soul of Man under Socialism, On the Rise of Historical Criticism* or *Pen, Pencil, and Poison*, as well as in his many book-reviews and other occasional writings where, though often discussing works that are of little interest or importance to us today, he constantly uses his ephemeral topics as illustrations of the philosophy of art and of life that was his permanent concern.

As editor of a fashionable women's magazine, Wilde was indeed limited, in much of his book-reviewing, to the works of women-writers or to other topics which were of special interest to women readers. We thus find him reviewing such charming period-pieces as The Princess Emily Ruete of Oman and Zanzibar's *Memoirs of an Arabian Princess*, discussing such forgotten novels as Lady Augusta Noel's *Hithersea Mere* or Harriet Waters Preston's *A Year in Eden*, devoting much attention to the works of very minor poetesses, such as Miss Chapman's *The New Purgatory and Other Poems* or Graham R. Tomson's *The Bird-Bride*. Wilde even pursued these acquired interests in book-reviews that he published in periodicals, such as *The Pall Mall Gazette*, whose readers were of both sexes; there Wilde discussed books on embroidery, cooking or on *How to be Happy though Married*, "the Murray of matrimony and the Baedeker of bliss."

In all this reviewing that might have been so frivolous or insipid, Wilde lost no opportunity to pursue his mission as a serious and original critic. Reviewing the ballads of *The Bird-Bride*, for instance, he expressed the same objections to the Mid-Victorian revival of dialect-poetry as in his review of Swinburne's *Poems and Ballads.* He points out that dialect is "dramatic" and a "vivid method of recreating a past that never existed," but "so artificial that it is really *naive*," and that it tends to express "simply the pathos of provincial-

ism," though "to say 'mither' instead of 'mother' seems to many the
acme of romance." In discussing *Hithersea Mere*, Wilde finds occasion to discuss the development of the nineteenth-century novel
and to object to the art of Henry James in much the same terms as
in his far more important *The Decay of Lying*. He states that "an
industrious Bostonian would have made half a dozen novels" out of
the good lady's roaring plot, and still "have had enough left for a
serial"; and, while outlining the history of the English novel and
deploring the lack of any real schools of fiction, Wilde points out
that there are at last "some signs of a school springing up amongst
us." This school, he observes, "is not native, nor does it seek to
reproduce any English master," but "may be described as the result
of the realism of Paris filtered through the refining influence of
Boston. . . . Analysis, not action, is its aim; it has more psychology
than passion, and it plays very cleverly upon one string, and this is
the commonplace."

Wilde's book reviews likewise express the same admirations, for
Balzac or Meredith, for instance, as his dialogues, and decry the
same propagandistic aspects of the realist novel whose object "is not
to give pleasure to the artistic instinct, but rather to vividly portray
life for us, to draw attention to social anomalies and social forms of
injustice." And much that Wilde wrote hastily in his reviews of
forgotten poets of the 'Eighties is still so true that it applies to a
Benèt or a MacLeish in our own day: "It is always a pleasure to
come across an American poet who is not national, and who tries to
give expression to the literature that he loves rather than to the land
in which he lives. The muses care so little for geography!"

In his mature critical writings, Wilde seems to have aimed very
carefully at a consistent doctrine of art, and to have contradicted
himself, except in paradoxes, only inadvertently, and in rare moments of carelessness. In *Shakespeare on Scenery*, a relatively unimportant article published in *The Dramatic Review*, Wilde states, for
instance, that it is impossible to read Shakespeare "without seeing
that he is constantly protesting against the two special limitations of
the Elizabethan stage—the lack of suitable scenery and the fashion
of men playing women's parts." Though the latter contradicts the
theory expounded with such relish in *The Portrait of Mr. W. H.*,
where Wilde ambiguously suggests that love for a boy actor inspired
many of the beauties of Shakespeare's plays, the article's main

argument, an analysis of Shakespeare's verbal description of settings as a substitute for the visual appeal of scenery, corroborates Wilde's other analysis, in *The Truth of Masks*, of Shakespeare's descriptive joy in details of costume.

Such inconsistencies are indeed very minor, of an accidental rather than of a substantial nature, in the appreciation of objects of value rather than in the elucidation of values according to which they are to be appreciated. In Wilde's discussion of these values or standards, on the contrary, one observes a constant and consistent development. In his politics, for instance, he was at first an ardent Ruskinian Socialist, with all the naiveté of Romantic idealism, from his Oxford years until he chanced to review, in 1890, a translation of the works of a Chinese Taoist anarchist: *Chuang Tzu, Mystic, Moralist, and Social Reformer*. Wilde's socialism was then refined and enriched, as a philosophy, until the politics of *The Soul of Man under Socialism*, already more sophisticated than his earlier beliefs, finally became, in the second part of *The Critic as Artist*, a consciously Taoist anarchism of inaction.

Though Wilde's opinion and tastes constantly changed as he learned to appreciate more varied or subtle types or styles of thought and art, and though his skill and elegance as a critical writer improved with practice, his fundamental principles remained substantially the same, from his earliest writings, such as *On the Rise of Historical Criticism*, to his mature dialogues. Wilde believed, for instance, that the purpose of art was to delight rather than to inform or to propagandize: "The aim of most of our modern novelists seems to be, not to write good novels, but to write novels that will do good. They wish to reform the morals, rather than to portray the manners of their age. They have made the novel the mode of propaganda." He believed indeed that "the supreme advantage that fiction possesses over fact" was that "it can make things artistically probable; can call for imaginative and realistic credence; can, by force of mere style, compel us to believe." And because most nineteenth-century novelists neglected this force of sheer style and imagination, Wilde deplored the decay of lying, of the ability to create what Plato called myths.

As Wilde himself learned to use with greater skill the devices of this art of mythopoeia, he developed more complex and convincing forms for his critical writings, until they became as fictional, in some respects, as his stories and plays, deriving much of their persuasiveness from the immediately dramatic qualities of their plot or dialogue form. In his early essay *On the Rise of Historical Criticism*, Wilde did not hesitate, for instance, to stress the stages of his argument by resorting to cumbersome outlining devices: "Having now traced the progress of historical criticism in the special treatment of myth and legend, I shall proceed to investigate the form in which the same spirit manifested itself as regards what one may term secular history." In *The Truth of Masks* too, he points out the dialectically ambiguous nature of his argument in an oddly appended conclusion which has little to do with the essay's topic but treats the essay itself as its topic. In the dialogue entitled *The Decay of Lying*, however, Vivian reads to Cyril his article on the decay of lying, and discusses it with him in dramatic form; Cyril is then convinced by the mythopoeic quality of the essay and by the gist of the discussion in which he participates, and the reader shares the conviction of this unreal character who, thanks to a trick of artistic perspective similar to that of the play within the play in *Hamlet*, communicates some of his reality and of the reader's own reality to the essay itself, to the argument within the argument of the dialogue. Within the fictional frame-work of *The Portrait of Mr. W. H.*, the ambiguity of Wilde's theory concerning Shakespeare's sonnets likewise pervades the whole story and is brought out much more immediately, by devices of plot, than the ambiguity of *The Truth of Masks*. These two examples of the loftily creative art of the critic are as illustratively convincing as any argument in Wilde's other dialogue, *The Critic as Artist*, though the latter's dramatic form and argument and one character, Gilbert, mediate constantly between the reader and the other character, Ernest, as Gilbert's objections to Wilde's argument, expounded by Ernest, are voiced one after the other and disposed of by Ernest until Gilbert and the reader are simultaneously convinced by Ernest and by Wilde.

In *The Critic as Artist*, however, the argument is perhaps too long and complex to be successfully expounded and discussed in a dialogue which has but two participants. A more experienced dialectician and craftsman in this dramatic art of exposition would have presented his material with a greater number of participants; and this would have enhanced the mythopoeic quality of the fictional form and strengthened its devices by varying the points of view of the objections raised and refuted, so that the argument's verisimilitude would have been greater in the eyes of readers whose points of view vary and whose objections may not all be voiced by Wilde's one character and disposed of by the other.

Wilde believed that the aim of the artist or "liar" is "simply to charm, to delight, to give pleasure," and frequently dismissed as merely "tedious" or "a bore" all art that failed to delight him. It would therefore seem legitimate to suggest that *On the Rise of Historical Criticism*, in spite of its brilliant and exact distinctions between the philosophy of history of Herodotus and that of Thucydides, and in spite of its many excellent insights into historiography, is rather "a bore," for lack of sheer elegance or artistic form and of persuasive mythopoeia in its cumbersomely and compulsively argumentative periods: "Besides, Herodotus, I may remark, had he reflected on the meaning of that Athenian law, which, while prohibiting marriage with a uterine sister, permitted it with a sister-germane, or, on the common tradition in Athens that before the time of Cecrops children always bore their mothers' names, or, on some of the Spartan regulations, he could hardly have failed to see the universality of kinsmanship through women in early days, and the late appearance of monandry." According to the same hedonistic standards, one might likewise find *The Truth of Masks*, brilliant and delightful as it is, more "tedious" than *The Portrait of Mr. W. H.*; and *The Critic as Artist* might, for the same reasons, seem "tedious" to more readers than *The Decay of Lying*. The proof of art, according to Wilde's theory, would indeed lie, as in Salvador Dali's theory of "comestible" art, in the "eating"; and more readers will be delighted by *The Portrait of Mr. W. H.* than by *The Truth of Masks* or by *The Decay of Lying* than by *The Critic as Artist*.

Not that the topics of *The Truth of Masks* or of *The Critic as Artist* are in themselves at all "tedious." *The Truth of Masks* is as entertaining, and as well documented and ingeniously organized, as many an essay by a critic generally considered great, such as Hazlitt or T. S. Eliot. But Wilde had found, for *The Portrait of Mr. W. H.*, a new form which allowed him to discuss such material with additional delight for readers of essays, and which might even delight many readers of fiction who do not derive, in general, much pleasure from essays. The story's formal perfection, though no greater, is thus of a creatively higher order than that of the essay. As for *The Critic as Artist*, which presents Wilde's philosophy of art and of life as a whole, its contents should be far more interesting than those of *The Decay of Lying* or of any of Wilde's other critical works; but the form of this dialogue is not as ingeniously adjusted to these contents as that of *The Decay of Lying*, so that the discussion lacks, at times, dramatic verisimilitude and tension. The whole dialogue indeed tends to lapse, for lack of more participants or more varied points of view, into long monologues whose form is that of separate lectures or essays and whose various parts, as one reads, seem more closely integrated into each monologue than into the dialogue as a whole.

"Socrates questioned, but did not answer; for he pretended not to know," wrote Aristotle, analyzing the Socratic method as it is illustrated in the Platonic dialogues. And throughout Plato's many dialogues, Socrates rarely expresses any opinion of his own but generally forces the other participants to formulate and then, in discussion, to correct their own latent beliefs. With but two participants, Wilde finds himself involved, in his two dialogues, in expounding his own philosophy in the words of one participant, who acts as "magister," which is what Plato generally avoided, while the other participant listens most of the time as a mere "discipulus." Wilde's philosopher thus tends to lecture, as the master does in the dialogues of the *Upanishads* or as the Gautama Buddha does in the ancient Indian dialogues, more often than he forces his listener, by dialectical questioning, to formulate and modify his opinions. And besides presenting but one disciple to mediate between the master and the reader, Wilde does not make this master, as Socrates does in those Platonic dialogues which have but two participants, reveal "many faces" so as to vary his point of view. The dialectical structure of Wilde's dialogues thus tends to follow the pattern of the Neo-Platonic dialogues of late antiquity or of the early Renaissance, those of Saint Augustine or of Leone Ebreo, rather than the more complex patterns of the Platonic dialogues. And Wilde is unable to correct more than one wrong attitude of his disciple toward his topic, whereas Plato, even in a dialogue such as the *Cratylus*, whose dramatic structure is relatively simple, could modify two opposed and equally exaggerated views, and in other dialogues could correct even more than two such views.

Nor is there any greater similarity, in their structure, between Wilde's dialogues and those of *Il Cortegiano* which is, in the literature of Humanism, to the dialogues of Plato what the neo-classical tragedy of Racine is to ancient tragedy. The participants in Baldassare Castiglione's discussions are drawn from real life, as were those of Plato, so that the dialectic of *Il Cortegiano* is rendered more complex by the contrasts and conflicts between its various characters, whereas Wilde's characters, if at all delineated, are all very much alike, save in their opinions. Whether as fiction or as drama, Wilde's dialogues indeed reveal their author's ideal world, as opposed to the merely idealized world of his stories or his novel, and to the caricature of his ideals which is revealed in the world of the comedies. There is no plot or action, in these dialogues, save those of philosophical discussion, though *The Critic as Artist* is divided into two parts by a purely conventional device of plot when Ernest and Gilbert interrupt their discussion to partake of a supper of "delightful" ortolans and "perfect" Chambertin, and though evening falls at the end of one dialogue and dawn rises at the end of the other. Significantly, two of the four citizens of Wilde's ideal world, Cyril and Vivian in *The Decay of Lying*, bear the names of the author's own children, as if to express some pious hope of a more perfect future; and, though the masters of both dialogues expound more or less the same doctrines as Lord Henry in *The Picture of Dorian Gray*, their disciples, unlike Dorian, are not led thereby to discover any narcissistic and evil elements in their nature, nor inspired, through knowing themselves, to be themselves in self-indulgence, crime and all the other corrupting realms of action. In *The Picture of Dorian Gray*, Lord Henry practices his own doctrine of inaction and does not approve of Dorian's falling in love; but, had not Dorian been one of those whom Vivian, Lord Henry's counterpart in *The Decay of Lying*, calls "the tedious people who carry out their principles to the bitter end of action," there would have been no action and no plot to Wilde's parable of the fallen dandy who is not enough of a "tired hedonist" and is still "too fond" of his pleasures.

Wilde's stories, his novel, and his plays illustrate moreover the need for plot and action in a world which, however idealized, still imitated the world as the author knew it rather than as he would like it to be; and here the author was forced to let his philosophical dandies become infected, as their clay feet trod the soil of action, with the corruption of this real world. But the dialogues imitate Wilde's ideal world of pure speculation where no action is necessary, his heaven where neither moth nor rust doth corrupt, where a Lord Henry may instruct a Dorian without the latter's debasing the dandy's saintly philosophy of art and of life in self-indulgence, where there are no women to tempt the hero into the selfishness that is his punishment for abandoning in action the arduous task of self-perfecting contemplation.

In Wilde's "New Hellenism," which he defined in *The Soul of Man under Socialism* as "the new Individualism," action stands where knowledge stood in the ancient "Hellenism" that Wilde imitated. Our civilization, with its ethical pragmatism and its stress on progress and production, estimates action as the ancients once valued knowledge; and Wilde set himself the task, as a new Socratic, to point out that all action can be the cause whence evil effects spring, as in his prose poem *The Doer of Good*, and that the only absolutely good action is thus inaction, much as Socrates once taught that no knowledge is identical with wisdom or Truth, and that a knowledge of the limitations of our knowledge is paradoxically the only wisdom that man can attain. The pursuit of wisdom is thus more important than any one of the knowledges that we may acquire in this pursuit, and the infinite task of self-perfection more valuable than any good actions that we may perform in the momentary belief that we have attained this perfection.

Though Socratic in the negative and even aporetic character of its dialectic as it contradicts so many of the popular beliefs and prejudices of its age, Wilde's thought is not Socratic in the structure of the dialogues themselves. The Magister, in both dialogues, relies more on lyrical or rhetorical devices of persuasion than on intellectual or dialectical devices, and the various parts or lectures, where he expounds his philosophy between the disciple's brief interruptions, are Augustinian in form and related to the whole dialogue too loosely; the long lyrical or rhetorical passages of Senecan tragedy are similarly related more loosely to the whole drama than are the parts of a Sophoclean tragedy, whose more closely-knit structure is analogous to that of a Platonic dialogue. And as Wilde failed to keep the dialogue's characteristic aim constantly in view but allowed himself to be carried away, in each part of it, by the pyrotechnic brilliance of set speeches, so too he was sometimes led into unnecessary contradictions and was not always conscious of their full implications. In the beginning of *The Decay of Lying*, for instance, Vivian declares that "people tell us that Art makes us love Nature more than we loved her before"; his own experience, however, is that "the more we study Art, the less we care for Nature," and that "what Art reveals to us is Nature's lack of design." But he also declares later that Nature "quickens to life" only "in our brain," that "things are because we see them, and what we see, and how we see it, depends on the Arts that have influenced us"; and Vivian then goes on to point out that "at present, people see fogs, not because there are fogs, but because poets and painters have taught them the mysterious loveliness of such effects," though "there may have been fogs for centuries in London." But is not all this a proof of the doctrine that Vivian first set out to disprove, according to which, "after a careful study of Corot and Constable," we see things in Nature "that had escaped our observation"? Vivian had indeed protested that only "the dullard and the doctrinaire" want to be consistent; but in a dialectical discussion, inconsistencies of this sort tend to obscure or pervert the aim of the argument, unless they are resolved into conscious paradox. And it was, among other reasons, to avoid this apparent aimlessness of the rhetorical sophist who is carried away by his own brilliance, that the Platonic Socrates, in general, refrained from expounding his own views and more often forced his listeners first to formulate and then to correct their views.

Oscar Wilde's critical writings illustrate a rare devotion to art, that of the saint to his religion, as Baudelaire described it, or of the soldier to his cause. Not content with expressing his philosophy of art and life, Wilde sought to present it in a worthy and beautiful form. And if he failed to achieve perfection in the dialogue, the most perfect form for philosophical discussion, he at least, by imitating the more perfect models of antiquity, revived this form from the decadence into which it had fallen. In the *Imaginary Conversations* of Lucian, Fontenelle or Landor, purple passages of wit or of archaeological learning had taken the place of the philosophical lectures into which, in Neo-Platonic writings, the Platonic dialectic had already degenerated. Regressing toward lost perfection, Wilde went but half the way, which was already further than most of those who, at various times, have sought to revive the glory that was Greece. And he seems, moreover, to have been obscurely aware of the weaknesses of his own dialectic; for he felt that it was necessary to recapitulate the master's doctrine toward the end of each dialogue, lest the disciple or the reader, confused by the complexity of a discussion whose tactics had more often been those of rhetorical debating than of dialectical elucidation, forget the points on which agreement had been reached. In a truly Socratic or a perfect Freudian analysis, no such confusion can subsist, and no recapitulation is ever necessary.

Oscar Wilde's failure to achieve his high aim, in his dialogues as in other writings where he emulated classical models, can in general be attributed to the vague nature of the concept of form in his philosophy of art. In the somewhat Neo-Platonic theories of art which were propounded, throughout the latter half of the Nineteenth Century, by the hierophants of "Art for Art's sake," the sublime occupied very much the same position as the concept of grace in the scholastic systems of an earlier age. The artist, being one of "the elect," was relieved of much of the responsibility of "works," of the toil of laborious construction. Mere expression, in the esthetics of Benedetto Croce, who later tried to organize this whole philosophy in a *Summa*, created the basic form of a work of art; the rest was polish, superficial ornament, style. In his critical writings, Wilde repeatedly states that form is "the beginning of things" and "everything"; but he identifies form with style rather than with structure, and affirms that "nothing but style" can make us believe a thing, and that style is also "everything." In discussing the novels of Turgenev, Wilde identifies style as a "spirit of exquisite selection" and a "delicate choice of detail"; in discussing the form of Pater's prose, he speaks of its "subtle perfection." Evanescent and almost indefiniable, form has thus ceased, hypostatized by the sublime, to be anything as definable as structure, which may not be immediately apparent and often demands detailed analysis; instead, it has become an immediately expressed and immediately perceptible beauty, a mystic communion through expression and impression.

But the most complex forms of Western literature and thought, tragedy which purges the passions and the philosophical dialogue which purges the intellect, must rely, for their perfection, on a form that is more carefully and curiously devised, on a structure that is neither immediately expressed nor immediately apparent, a beauty more substantial than polish, ornament or style.

Fiction as Allegory

When Wilde began to write straight fiction, after poetry, lyrical drama, poetic and critical prose, he had prepared himself for his new task by carefully studying the novels and stories of most of his more distinguished contemporaries. He had already expressed, for instance, very definite views concerning their particular qualities or faults and the art of fiction in general. In *The Decay of Lying*, Wilde had accused the modern novelist of presenting "dull facts in the guise of fiction . . . He has his tedious *document humain*, his miserable little *coin de la création*, into which he peers with his microscope . . . shamelessly reading up his subject. . . . If something cannot be done to check, or at least to modify, our monstrous worship of facts, Art will become sterile."

It was left for a later age to discover, in the novels of newspaper correspondents, how sterile the art of fiction can become when it borrows all the factual devices of the reporter's craft but still fails to achieve the immediate urgency of his reality. Wilde already found even R. L. Stevenson guilty of "robbing a story of its reality by trying to make it too true," and Rider Haggard, who had once had "the makings of a perfectly magnificent liar," of lapsing into seeking "cowardly corroboration" for his inventions. Turning to Henry James, whose worship of facts was more scientific than journalistic, Wilde observed that he "writes fiction as if it were a painful duty, and wastes upon mean motives and imperceptible 'points of view' his neat literary style." Nor was Wilde any less critical of French novelists. It was in France that the new pseudo-scientific or positivistic doctrines of literary Realism had been elaborated and applied most consciously. Wilde dismissed Maupassant rapidly as an artist who wastes "a keen mordant irony . . . and hard vivid style" on petty themes; he found that Zola's characters "have their dreary vices, and their drearier virtues," and he observed that Bourget forgets "what is most interesting about people in good society," that is to say, "because we are all of us made of the same stuff . . . the mask that each one of them wears, not the reality that lies behind."

In Balzac, Wilde found, however, "a most remarkable combination of the artistic temperament with the scientific spirit." Balzac "created life, he did not copy it"; his characters have "a kind of fiery-coloured existence" and "defy scepticism." But he also "set too high a value on modernity of form . . . a huge price to pay for a very poor result," so that no book of his, "as an artistic masterpiece can rank with *Salammbo* or *Esmond*, or *The Cloister and the Hearth*, or the *Vicomte de Bragelonne*." Nor did Wilde mean, by modernity of form, any modernistic structural or stylistic innovations such as those later proposed by Proust, Gide or Joyce; he seems rather to have been thinking of a sort of journalistically documentary or scientific quality which he found "always somewhat vulgarizing" in that it tends to make art serve the purposes of some propaganda: "The public imagines that, because they are interested in their immediate surroundings, art should be interested in them also, and should take them as her subject-matter. But the mere fact that they are interested in these things makes them unsuitable subjects for art," which should never, as it has so often in our own generation, compete with the newspapers. And Wilde concludes: "To art's subject-matter we should be more or less indifferent." In a conversation with his friend Coulson Kernahan, Wilde expanded this doctrine to insist that the novelist should "never have any intention other than to tell a story," and especially never, as Dickens "who means so well" so often did, "snap the thread of the story to explain what he means."

It is in the light of these poetics of fiction, classical in formal constraints but romantic in plot and atmosphere, that Wilde's only novel and his few short stories must be examined. A novelist, Wilde believed, must avoid preaching, "drawing attention," for instance, "to the state of our convict-prisons," as Charles Read had done, wasting too much of his artistic career, than which the poor unprophetic future inmate of Reading Gaol knew nothing more sad "in the whole history of literature." And Wilde's ideals, it seems, were the elegance of Thackeray and the scrupulous art of Flaubert, the sheer narrative virtuosity of the elder Dumas, the visionary power of Balzac and the "true sense of beauty" of Charles Read. To these one must add Wilde's paradoxical admiration for Meredith: "As a writer, he has mastered everything except language; as a novelist, he can do everything except tell a story; as an artist, he is everything except articulate."

But there was a blind spot in Wilde's vision of the novelist's art. He does not seem to have understood that the preaching of a doctrine of esthetics can be as foreign to true fiction as that of any social or political doctrine, and that detailed descriptions of rare jewels and brocades or gorgeous interiors can require the same realistic technique, and the same shameless reading up of a subject, as do Zola's descriptions of factories and slums. Coulson Kernahan points out, besides, that the novelist, in Chapter XI of *The Picture of Dorian Gray*, intrudes to the point of exclaiming: "Is insincerity such a terrible thing? I think not." But without saying "I" each time, Wilde preaches his own doctrines of the dandy's philosophy of life, of art and of interior decoration throughout his novel, either in the words of Lord Henry or in the actions of the hero, or again in those tedious descriptions, repeated from his prose poetry, of jewels and antiques and knick-knacks and *objets de vertu* which make some parts of the novel read like a decadent "on and off the Avenue" shopping column to guide the perfect dandy in the selection of all the details of his wardrobe, his interior, and his hobbies. In *The Spoils of Poynton*, Henry James barely describes the magnificence of Poynton's art-collections; he suggests it, however, most powerfully by describing its importance in the lives of his several characters. Yet the works of art themselves, from what little he describes, must have been very much of the same types and quality as those that decorated Dorian Gray's home.

Two of the French novelists whom Wilde admired or imitated most faithfully, Flaubert and Huysmans, were masters, significantly enough, both of imaginatively exotic or decadent description and of painstakingly realistic reportage. The magnificent backgrounds of *Salammbo* are just as carefully documented, and described with as realistically detailed a technique, as are the scenes of contemporary bourgeois life in *Madame Bovary* or *L'Education Sentimentale*; and a more classically minded novelist, such as Stendhal, would have objected to the same exuberance of descriptive detail in both, protesting that the true novelist is no painter or interior decorator but must rely, for verisimilitude, as Henry James did, on the psychological motivations of his characters and their actions rather than on the stereopticon-like deceptions of meticulously contrived surroundings.

But Wilde, in his fiction as in his lyrical drama, generally neglected the *dianoia* and the development of character which typify tragedy and the novel at their loftiest level, and relied almost exclusively, as did the Senecans in drama or the masters of the macabre in fiction, on plot and atmosphere. Besides, Wilde wrote most of his fiction, with the exception of *The Portrait of Mr. W. H.*, much as he later wrote his comedies, hastily and almost as commercial literature. In several of his earlier stories, he thus neglected atmosphere too, so that the plot of *The Canterville Ghost* or *The Model Millionaire* develops cancerously on its own, no longer adjusted to dove-tail harmoniously with any of the other elements of fiction. In *The Canterville Ghost*, the Americans who have bought the old English haunted house are peculiarly well prepared for every one of the poor ghost's very irregular and varied appearances; and the reader begins to wonder what gift of prophecy or what detective-service warns them when and where to expect the spook, at what time and behind which door, and always armed with the objects that will disconcert him most. Instead of clothing his plot in an appropriate atmosphere, Wilde relies, in this story, on stock witticisms and heavy satire on the bad tastes and manners and the prejudices of Americans; as in his English lecture-tours, Wilde thus avenged himself for the many humiliations he had suffered in America, though he admitted, at the same time, his admiration for American efficiency in practical matters.

This venting of the author's opinions concerning the manners and modes of society, and his illustrations, in other stories, of the esthetic doctrines which he preached indirectly in his fiction as much as he did more directly in his American lectures, all this weight of padding and plastering not only snaps the thread of the story repeatedly but also, in several cases, throws the whole structure of the plot out of balance. How gravely this distortion can cripple a story is best demonstrated by comparing Wilde's handling of an unusual theme, the relationship of artist to model and of model, as actor or interpreter, to "the real thing," with another writer's handling of it—Wilde's *The Model Millionaire* with Henry James' *The Real Thing.*

James confesses in his note-books that an anecdote told him by his friend Du Maurier was the source of *The Real Thing,* which "should be a little gem of bright quick vivid form." It seems indeed almost as if James, stung by Wilde's criticism of his work, had decided, some ten years after the publication of *The Model Millionaire,* to show the world how much better he could handle the same theme. In the James story, Major Monarch and his wife, who are "the real thing" socially, have become destitute and now approach a young artist in the hope of earning a living as models for his illustrations to society novels. The painter's regular model is a Cockney girl with a great histrionic gift for assuming the airs of any character for whose portrait she is posing, whereas the Monarchs fail utterly to be anything but themselves, never even transcending their individual personalities to become types. Out of pity, the artist tries to use them as models, but his art deteriorates and he is forced to revert to his Cockney model for the ladies, and to his Italian man-servant for the gentlemen, while he cannot employ the needy lady and gentleman even as servants. F. O. Matthiesen has pointed out that this story involves "James' whole-hearted repudiation of realism as mere literal reporting"; and James himself concludes that "in the deceptive atmosphere of art even the highest respectability may fail of being plastic."

In the James story, Mr. and Mrs. Monarch are central characters around whom the whole plot and action revolve. Each one of the other characters, the artist, the Cockney model, the Italian man-servant or the artist's friend who points out to him the deterioration of his art, illustrates one of the several dimensions of the theme: the relationship of art to reality, that of model to reality, of artist to model, of artist to work of art or of "appreciator" to work of art. In the Wilde story, however, this fascinating theme is almost lost in a load of unimportant and rather conventional wrappings. A young man "with a perfect profile," like so many of the young dandies who drift through Wilde's satirical pictures of London society, is in love with a girl whom he cannot marry because neither of them has enough money. He chances to call on an artist friend whom he finds busy painting the portrait of a truly pitiful old beggar. While the artist is out of the room, the poor young man is moved to give a sovereign, his whole week's cab-money, to the poor old man. But the model turns out to be an eccentric millionaire who wanted to be painted as a beggar and who, delighted with the success of his disguise and with the young man's generosity, gives him the ten thousand pounds which make his marriage possible.

The central figure of Wilde's story is neither the artist nor the model, but the outsider, the one whom James put to work, in his story, as the "appreciator." The girl is quite unnecessary to the development of the theme of the beggar model who paradoxically turns out to be a model millionaire; and the love-element throws the whole plot out of focus. Wilde thus neglects to investigate any of the complex relationships of artist to model, of model to "real thing" or of model or "real thing" to work of art, or any of the weird implications of guilt-feelings or superstition which would prompt a millionaire to pose as a beggar, as if to ward off, by acting it out ritualistically, a deserved or feared fate. Wilde seems to have appreciated none of these opportunities to develop, out of the story, a philosophy of art; instead, he wastes his theme and his talents on a superficial estheticism of paradoxes, in title, plot and dialogue, all preaching to the reader an attitude toward life which is illustrated not so much in the life of the story as in the story-teller's own life as dandy and editor of a women's magazine similar to those where most of his tales were first published. And the weaknesses of *The Model Millionaire* serve only to illustrate the great superiority of a multi-dimensional art of "imperceptible points of view," such as that of Henry James, over Wilde's narrower art where only the artist's point of view is ever illustrated or expounded.

In *The Portrait of Mr. W. H.*, Wilde seems, however, to have at last overcome these defects of his fictional art by adapting to the development of plot much of the brilliance which he revealed as an essayist and critic in *Pen, Pencil, and Poison* or in *The Truth of Masks*. And here too it is interesting to compare Wilde's methods and those of Henry James, as the latter illustrated them in *The Figure in the Carpet*; for the theme of both stories is very much the same, the problem of analyzing a complex work of art in order to discover its essentially secret and ambiguous meaning.

In Wilde's story, the work of art is Shakespeare's sequence of love-sonnets. The author of the story tells how, while he is dining with his friend Erskine, they chance to discuss artistic forgeries. The author insists that we have "no right to quarrel with an artist for the conditions under which he chooses to present his work . . . to censure an artist for a forgery was to confuse an ethical with an esthetical problem." But Erskine then quotes the case of a forgery committed in order to prove an unusual theory about a work of art; this, the author agrees, is "quite a different matter." Erskine shows him an example of what he means: a portrait of a young man in Elizabethan costume, presumably the Mr. W. H. to whom Shakespeare's sonnets were dedicated as their "onlie begetter." And Erskine explains that he inherited this portrait from Cyril Graham. Convinced by some intuition as well as by ambiguous internal evidence contained in the obscure sonnets, that Mr. W. H. had been a boy-actor who had inspired both the sonnets and many of the dramas whose heroines he had impersonated, Cyril Graham had failed to find any conclusive historical proof of the existence of a boy-actor named Will Hughes and had finally had this portrait painted as an authentic proof of his theory. Erskine had, however, then stumbled upon proof of its being a forgery, and bitterly reproached Graham with his dishonesty; and Graham had then shot himself, bequeathing to Erskine the portrait with a letter explaining that it had been produced "simply as a concession" to allay Erskine's doubts, but that this did not invalidate the truth of the theory concerning the sonnets.

The author of the story becomes convinced of the truth of Graham's theory, in which Erskine no longer believes, and devotes many months to a meticulous analysis of the sonnets, all of which appears in Wilde's story. At last, "not merely restoring Cyril Graham to his proper place in literary history, but rescuing the honour of Shakespeare himself from the tedious memory of a commonplace intrigue," the author expresses in a letter to Erskine all his enthusiasm and faith. No sooner is the letter mailed, however, than a curious reaction sets in: "It seemed that I had given away my capacity for belief in the Will Hughes theory of the Sonnets, that something had gone out of me, as it were, and that I was perfectly indifferent to the whole subject." The author then calls on Erskine to apologize for his letter; but convinced by the letter, Erskine goes abroad to seek further historical evidence in the archives of German courts where Elizabethan troupes of actors had performed. Two years later, the author receives a letter from Erskine, who has failed to find any new proof for the theory and is determined to take his own life as Cyril Graham had once done: "The truth was once revealed to you, and you rejected it. It comes to you now, stained with the blood of two lives,—do not turn away from it." Horrified, the author hastens abroad to prevent his friend's death, but arrives too late. He discovers, however, that Erskine did not kill himself: he died of consumption, bequeathing to him the forged portrait and this forged account of his own death, both of which now, at times, revive the author's old faith in Graham's theory of the sonnets.

In the last paragraph of *The Truth of Masks,* in just such a mood of equivocation, Wilde had concluded: "Not that I agree with everything that I have said in this essay. The essay represents simply an artistic standpoint, and in esthetic criticism attitude is everything. For in art there is no such thing as a universal truth. A Truth in art is that whose contradictory is also true." The plot of *The Portrait of Mr. W. H.* illustrates this point perfectly: Graham's theory of the sonnets is both true and untrue, and the discovery of the portrait's being a forgery no more disproves the theory than the non-existence of an authentic portrait leaves it unproven. It is significant that Wilde actually had this portrait painted by one of his friends, and that it was one of the most prized works of art in his Tite Street home.

In the Henry James story on the same theme, the author is asked, by his friend Corvick who has no time to do it himself, to review a new book by a favorite author, Hugh Vereker. Corvick insists that the review must "try to get *at*" Vereker who gives him "a pleasure so rare; the sense of . . . something or other." Of what? "My dear man, that's just what I want *you* to say." The review is then written and published, and its author chances to meet Vereker who disappoints him bitterly by declaring that he has failed to perceive "the particular thing I've written my books most *for*," an intention expressed "with every stroke of my pen." The young critic, puzzled and incensed, devotes many months to an analysis of Vereker's work, fails to find what he is seeking and abandons the search. Corvick then takes up the quest of this "figure in the carpet," with his fiancée. After a while, Corvick dies, but not before having found what he sought and revealed it to her; but she refuses to reveal it to the young critic, marries another man and, some years later, after Vereker's death too, dies in turn. The baffled critic then tries to discover the secret from her widower, but the latter has never heard her express any interest in Vereker's work or discuss any theory concerning it.

With all the subtlety of its imperceptible points of view and the economy of its plot where each character serves to illustrate a different degree of interest in the problem, and with all its analysis of these attitudes toward a work of art and of the latter's complex and ambiguous nature, *The Figure in the Carpet* yet fails, in one element of sheer plot, where *The Portrait of Mr. W. H.* succeeds brilliantly. With the reticence which was so successful in *The Spoils of Poynton*, James never describes, for his readers, any of Vereker's works, never quotes anything, never gives us any hint of the critical and analytical methods which his characters follow in their quest of the hidden meaning of Vereker's work. The reader thus never develops any real interest in a problem which remains so vague that he never shares the enthusiasms and despairs of the characters nor follows them in their quest. Wilde, however, by stating his problem more concretely, by quoting the sonnets and revealing to his readers all their ambiguities, allows us to step into the very life of his far less complex story till its more conventional and more arbitrarily constructed characters become convincing because we share all their perplexities. The problem, in *The Spoils of Poynton*, did not concern the nature of the works of art, so that no detailed description was necessary; but the problem of *The Figure in the Carpet* was of a different order, and required some description of the problematic work of art.

Nor could one find a better illustration of how well sheer atmosphere or a display of Wilde's own tastes, beliefs, and curious erudition could be made to become an integral part of a plot. In Wilde's *The Fisherman and his Soul*, the descriptions of strange Oriental worlds whereby the soul sought to tempt the fisherman had all, in the same way, been necessary elements of the story, like the descriptive extravaganzas of Flaubert's *La Tentation de Saint Antoine*, rather than superfluous and awkwardly adjusted ornaments such as the long descriptions of jewels, for instance, and the other displays of erudition or of paradoxical wit which, from time to time, snap the thread of Wilde's narrative in *The Picture of Dorian Gray*.

All Wilde's short stories except *The Portrait of Mr. W. H.* can be dismissed as mere sketches where the author tested his techniques and played with various types of plot before attempting what turned out to be his only novel and his major fictional achievement. *The Sphinx without a Secret*, Wilde himself calls an "etching"; it is a fictional elaboration, in terms of fashionable magazine art almost reminiscent of the Parisian drawings of Steinlen or Evenpoël, of an epigram concerning women that reappears in Wilde's comedies. In *Lord Arthur Savile's Crime*, Wilde approaches for the first time the Satanic theme of the dandy turned criminal, while at the same time testing the possibilities of introducing the supernatural into the world of contemporary society manners; and he does all this playfully, superficially, with a skill that is admirably adapted to the tastes of the readers of fashionable magazines, but with none of the macabre atmosphere of his later novel and none of its loftier artistic or philosophical intentions. In *The Canterville Ghost*, Wilde again tries his hand at the supernatural in modern high society, but with heavier humor and more atmosphere than before, though a consciously false atmosphere which, unsure of his skill and ridiculing his own art, he describes to a great extent in terms of borrowed theatrical props and of "Wardour Street" imagery. In *The Model Millionaire*, Wilde first tests, though without much skill, the effectiveness of a portrait, a work of art, as an element of plot. In the plot of *The Portrait of Mr. W. H.*, Wilde places the portrait much more centrally and effectively, though he still fails to make it an essential plot-element; a forged letter might have served just as well as proof of Graham's theory. In the plot of *The Picture of Dorian Gray*, the portrait comes at last to life as an indispensable element of the story's action.

In two of his more effective stories, *Lord Arthur Savile's Crime* and *The Canterville Ghost*, Wilde had self-consciously burlesqued the manner of the macabre, introducing a note of satire to conceal his own awkwardness in creating atmosphere. In *The Portrait of Mr. W. H.*, Wilde inserted, within a macabre plot of forgery and suicide, another element of mystery or of the puzzle which had much in common with Poe's cryptographic interests; but the plot of his last fictional work, *The Picture of Dorian Gray*, placed it in the lineage of the greatest of the "gothic" novels of at least fifty years earlier.

From the eighteenth-century vogue of Ann Radcliffe and Horace Walpole to the success, in the early decades of the nineteenth century, of the novels of "Monk" Lewis, a whole literary genre had culminated, in 1820, in the publication of *Melmoth the Wanderer*. Its author, Charles Robert Maturin, was, by marriage, an uncle of Wilde's mother, the poetess Speranza. Wilde knew *Melmoth* well, and was proud of this relationship. When the old novel was reprinted in 1892 with a long biographical introduction, the editors expressed their thanks, in a preface, "to Mr. Oscar Wilde and Lady Wilde (Speranza) for details with regard to Maturin's life." And when Wilde retired to France after his release from Reading Gaol, he lived there under the name of Sebastian Melmoth which he used as a pseudonym until his death. From Reading Gaol, in a letter to Robert Ross dated April 6th, 1897, Wilde wrote, of Rossetti's letters which he had just read and considered forgeries, that he had been interested, "to see how my grand-uncle's *Melmoth* and my mother's *Sidonia* have been two books that fascinated his youth." Though certainly ignorant of Lautréamont's passion for the Satanic wanderer, Wilde surely knew that Baudelaire had praised *Melmoth* in *De l'Essence du Rire*; and he was proud of the high esteem in which two of his favorite authors, Byron and Balzac, had held his mother's uncle.

Of Maturin's influence on Wilde we have ample proof. Maturin's biographers state that "he always showed an extravagant taste for dressing up" and that "throughout his life a love of masquerade and theatrical display never deserted him." His eccentricities of dress were noted, besides, by many contemporaries: Byron described him, in a letter, as "a bit of a coxcomb." Speranza likewise attracted much attention, in Dublin society and later in London, by her none too tasteful splendors, recorded by several contemporaries. Wilde's own sartorial extravagances thus seem to have been inspired to some extent by a family weakness, though a well-established tradition of dandyism, from the age of Byron and Maturin, through that of Bulwer Lytton and Disraeli, still encouraged the affectations of a Brummel among artists of Wilde's generation.

Much as Wilde may have been influenced, in his art and his life, by the more dandified Romanticism of such novels as Bulwer Lytton's *Pelham* or Disraeli's *Vivian Grey* and *Lothair*, with their epigrammatic brilliance and foppish haughtiness inherited from the Regency bucks, there is also, in *The Picture of Dorian Gray*, distinct evidence of direct borrowings from *Melmoth*. In the opening chapter of Maturin's novel, when Melmoth, the young student, comes to his miserly uncle's death-bed, he is sent to fetch some wine from a closet "which no foot but that of old Melmoth had entered for nearly sixty years." There, amidst "a great deal of decayed and useless lumber" such as that which later furnished the locked and abandoned school-room where Dorian Gray concealed his compromising portrait, young Melmoth's eyes were "in a moment, and as if by magic, rivetted on a portrait" whose eyes "were such as one feels they wish they had never seen, and feels they can never forget." This portrait represents an evil ancestor, a third Melmoth who, by a pact with the devil, has been permitted to live one hundred and fifty years without showing any signs of aging, much as Dorian Gray was mysteriously permitted to retain the appearance of his youth in spite of his crimes and debauchery. And this ancestor, Melmoth the Wanderer, is still alive: fear of him has even caused the old miser's death.

Maturin's whole romance then unfolds as a tangled series of episodes from the Wanderer's legendary life. And when, in the last pages, the evil ancestor returns to the place of his birth because "the clock of eternity is about to strike," in his last moments of life he suddenly ages: "the lines of extreme age were visible in every feature. His hairs were as white as snow, his mouth had fallen in, the muscles of his face were relaxed and withered—he was the very image of hoary decrepit debility."

The magic formula of Dorian Gray's sinister youth was thus an heirloom in Wilde's family, handed down like some choice recipe from old Maturin, from one of the sources of the Dracula myth to novels and movies to the author of *The Picture of Dorian Gray* which, when it was finally filmed, was acclaimed by the poet Parker Tyler as "the last of the movie Draculas." And Dorian Gray himself, whose mere presence, as his lasting youth became more and more sinister, would "make a man like the Duke of Berwick leave the room," whose friendship "was so fatal to young men," is a half-brother of Lautréamont's Maldoror. The arch-fiend of Surrealist satanism is indeed but another scion of the same Melmoth who boasts: "It has been reported to me, that I obtained from the enemy of souls a range of existence beyond the period allotted to mortality—a power to pass over space without disturbance or delay, and visit remote regions with the swiftness of thought—to encounter tempests without the *hope* of their blasting me, and penetrate dungeons whose bolts were as flax and tow at my touch."

From Melmoth, Dorian Gray thus inherited his lasting youth, and Maldoror his gift of ubiquity, of travel without disturbance or delay, and "that singular expression of the features, (the eyes particularly), which no human glance could meet unappalled." But both of these Draculas outdid, in one respect, their ghoulish sire. The Reverend Maturin, a worthy Anglican minister with what even a snob in a Somerset Maugham novel calls "a good old Irish name," was apparently unwilling to permit his monster to lead any victims to damnation. And as he is about to die, the Wanderer exclaims: "No one has ever exchanged destinies with Melmoth the Wanderer. *I have traversed the world in the search, and no one, to gain that world, would lose his own soul.*" Maldoror and Dorian Gray, however, were both more successful as tempters, and each of them left a trail of blasted lives behind him.

The portrait concealed in Melmoth's closet is bound to the ghoulish wanderer by no such ties of sympathetic magic as those which bind Dorian Gray to his portrait; it occupies no such central position in Maturin's story and remains a mere accessory which is destroyed, without dire consequences, shortly after it is discovered, so that one barely remembers it as one reads the rest of the romance. Between its literary avatars in *Melmoth* and in *Dorian Gray*, this portrait had indeed undergone a strange metamorphosis, under the influence of the magical portrait, as Richard Aldington has pointed out, of Max Rodenstein in Benjamin Disraeli's *Vivian Grey*, published in 1826, and also of the magical skin in *La Peau de Chagrin*, written by Balzac in the period in which he was most deeply affected by his readings of Maturin, only a couple of years before he wrote his sequel to the Wanderer's tale, *Melmoth Reconcilié à l'Eglise*. Dorian Gray's portrait is thus born of the Wanderer's, but by Disraeli's miraculous portrait of an incidental character in *Vivian Grey*; and it inherited its central position in Wilde's novel from Balzac's magical skin, together with analogous qualities which reveal themselves just as accidentally and prove just as dire a source of temptation.

As a macabre novel, in spite of this noble ancestry, *The Picture of Dorian Gray* is not entirely successful. The thread of its narrative is too frequently interrupted by Wilde's esthetic preaching, by useless displays of esthetic erudition, by unnecessary descriptions of works of art and by paradoxical table-talk which have little bearing on the plot, except where Lord Henry dazzles and convinces Dorian. The conversation, at times, even distorts the plot. It allows a vague number of duchesses and other characters, doomed to vanish almost immediately after their first appearance, to wander into Wilde's novel, straight from the pages of *Vivian Grey* or of *Pelham*, in a frenzy of brilliant repartee and shrill laughter like the extras who suddenly give life to a court-scene in an old-fashioned light-opera. Between these pauses, where the atmosphere has been slapped on so thick that it clogs the machinery of plot, Wilde's plot itself reveals several curious weaknesses; had not the book been so hastily written that it is almost unjust to analyze it as if it were a carefully devised work of art, these weaknesses would suggest an unexpected mixture, in the author, of amateurishness and prudish guilt-feelings.

Wilde's naively romantic descriptions of low life, for instance, are full of pathetic echoes of the melodrama of earlier decades, of De Quincey's years of misery in the London slums where he met Ann, of the drug-addict poet James Thomson's *The City of Dreadful Night*, and even of Charles Dickens; and they contrast oddly with Wilde's infinitely more sophisticated and knowing descriptions of high society. When Wilde's young men with perfect profiles stop flinging themselves petulantly upon the divans of their extravagantly furnished bachelor quarters or dining out with duchesses in a haze of epigrams, they stalk forth, as Vivian Grey or Lothair had done some decades earlier in their moments of tension or despair, into the vast wilderness of London. And there, in the night, Wilde's dandies discover another world, whence they return, at dawn, with "a dim memory of wandering through a labyrinth of sordid houses, of being lost in a giant web of sombre streets" or of "narrow shameful alleys."

Victor Hugo's *Les Misérables* and Eugène Sue's *Les Mystères de Paris* had contributed much to Wilde's romantic vision of London's nocturnal underworld, with its grisly prostitutes, its drunken brawls before the doors of degraded dock-land taverns, its foul opium-dens, and its sinister Jewish theater-owner like De Quincey's money-lenders or the hideous Jews of Rowlandson's cartoons. All the props, save the sewers, of Victor Hugo's Paris had been imported to England in such popular melodramas of the Seventies as *The Streets of London* or *London by Gaslight*; and it is from this naive pan-orama of the sinful city that Wilde's young men at last emerge in Covent Garden, among the vegetables glistening in the dawn light and the rustics who, "rude as they were, with their heavy, hobnailed shoes, and their awkward gait . . . brought a little of Arcady with them."

Between these two worlds, no decent or comfortable middle class, no quiet family life, no dormitory sections in Wilde's vision of the big city. From the brilliantly lit society with which the author seems so well acquainted, we step straight into a dim slum-land of which he seems ignorant, scared or ashamed, whose denizens are all stock characters from almost "gothic" melodrama, like Sybil Vane's mother in *Dorian Gray*, living in poverty almost too proverbial to be convincing. And it is perhaps significant that Marcel Proust, who translated Ruskin into French and was influenced by his thought even more than Wilde, likewise neglected, in general, to describe, except his own family, a mean of people who live and work decently, between the maximum of the idle Guermantes world, with its dependent servants and its less brilliant gate-crashers such as the Verdurin set and Madame Cottard, and the minimum of Jupien's den of prostitution.

In his handling of crime too, Wilde seems just as ill at ease and inhibited as in his descriptions of the surroundings of crime and poverty. The Reverend Maturin, in *Melmoth the Wanderer*, had never been able to bring himself to write the exact terms of the pact that his Satanic character offered to his prospective victims: "Every night he besets me, and few like me could have resisted his seductions. He has offered, and proved to me, that it is in his power to bestow all that human cupidity could thirst for, on the condition that—I cannot utter! It is one so full of horror and impiety that, even to listen to it, is scarce less a crime than to comply with it!" In *Dorian Gray*, Wilde likewise refrains from ever revealing the exact nature of Dorian's evil influence on the many friends, such as Adrian Singleton or Alan Campbell, whose lives his friendship has irremediably seared; and even when Dorian blackmails Alan into helping him dispose of the murdered painter's corpse, he writes "something" on a paper and hands it to Alan, "something" that makes Alan shudder and comply, but that is never revealed to the reader. Such a curious blockage, in both Maturin and Wilde, can suggest, to the psychoanalytically inclined reader, only a crime which is terribly repressed by the prejudices of the age, perhaps what Lord Alfred Douglas called "the Love that dare not speak its name." And Wilde's unwillingness to name this sin in *Dorian Gray* makes one all the more sceptical of his authorship of *The Priest and the Acolyte*, a strangely sacrilegious and outspoken story which is sometimes attributed to Wilde and, though it handles Wilde's favorite theme of "each man kills the thing he loves," contains none of his ubiquitous paradoxes and epigrams. At the time of Wilde's trial, it was moreover proved conclusively that he had not written *The Priest and the Acolyte*, nor ever met its author, an obscure Oxford undergraduate.

Wilde's unwillingness to handle the details of vice, crime, and the underworld as firmly and realistically as he does those of the world of fashion is indeed more than a mere concession to Victorian prudery. He shrinks from it, in his art if not in his life, with the neurotic's resistance, as if from a confession or from the discovery of a maëlstrom of experience into which, as in the tempting visions of *The Sphinx*, he fears being irretrievably drawn. And this squeamishness imposes, on the plot of his novel, some odd distortions which the more objective author of an ordinary mystery-novel would easily have avoided. When Dorian Gray, for instance, seeks "to cure the soul by means of the sense, and the senses by means of the soul," he presses a spring in a cabinet in his home and thus releases a secret drawer where he keeps a box of an unnamed "green paste waxy in lustre, the odour curiously heavy and persistent." This paste is opium; but Dorian Gray, unlike all addicts who always have their pipes at home even if they occasionally run out of "junk," has the opium, it seems, but no pipes. Putting his good opium back in the secret drawer, he therefore rushes out into the night, takes a cab and goes far into London's dock-land, in a low den frequented by sailors and derelicts where the "junk" is surely inferior to what he left at home.

Why this unlikely twist in the novel's plot? The habits of opium-addicts were probably little known to Wilde, and Dorian Gray had to be brought somehow to dock-land in order to be recognized there by dead Sybil Vane's avenging sailor-brother. But James Vane is then so clumsy in shadowing Dorian that he follows him onto a moor, in the midst of a shooting-party, and gets killed accidentally, as he hides behind a bush, by a shot aimed at a hare! This whole episode of frustrated revenge is thus introduced by means of one unlikely scene and resolved in another; and the awkward lack of verisimilitude of its beginning and end reveals Wilde's ignorance and fear of a world of crime with which, in real life, he was doomed to become all too familiar.

In spite of its many weaknesses, *The Picture of Dorian Gray* yet remains, in many respects, a great novel. Though hastily written and clumsily constructed, it manages to haunt many readers with vivid memories of its visionary descriptions. As a masterpiece of the macabre, it is infinitely less diffuse or rhetorical, and told with more economy and fewer tangles and snappings of the thread of narrative, than *Melmoth the Wanderer*. Wilde had indeed profited by the art of Balzac and Flaubert; and when he revived the obsolete genre of the "gothic" or sartorial novel, he avoided much of the formlessness of *Melmoth*, *The Monk* or *Vivian Grey*, so that his tale now reads better than most of its literary ancestors and conforms more exactly to our stricter and more sober standards of plot, of atmosphere, and of probability for the improbable.

But the true greatness of *The Picture of Dorian Gray* resides in the philosophical doctrine which the novel is intended, as a myth, to illustrate. The *Erziehungsroman* of dandyism pretended to instruct the nineteenth-century reader much as Lord Chesterfield had once taught his son, but in a more fictional form, better suited to the tastes of an age which had outgrown even the eighteenth-century taste for the epistolary novel. As a genre, it produced, in England, four resounding successes: *Tremaine*, by Robert Plumer Ward in 1825, Disraeli's *Vivian Grey* in 1826, Bulwer Lytton's *Pelham* in 1828 and, half a century later, *The Picture of Dorian Gray* in 1890. For all its success, *Tremaine* has little doctrine beyond a pious conformism or conservatism and is of no interest today; both *Vivian Grey* and *Pelham* refer to it sarcastically as a favorite among fashionable women. The doctrine of Disraeli's youthful work, for all its refined tastes in Romantic art and scenery, was one of brashly unscrupulous ambition. In his Machiavellian intrigues, Vivian was guided by immediately practical considerations; as a more business-like and less foolish Beau Brummel, he failed to achieve his ends, though he accepted all the corrupt standards of his society, only because he found himself pitted against Mrs. Felix Lorraine, an even more unscrupulous enemy. Bulwer Lytton's novel portrays a "man of fashion" who is saved, by his intellect and his more fastidious moral judgment, from being corrupted by the fashionable society in which he is so successful; *Pelham* portrays Brummel, in Russelton, as a man who came to grief not so much because he failed to manage his affairs according to the principles of the world of fashion as because he lacked the sound sense of values which only a more intellectual or prudential attitude toward life can provide.

The ethical message of *The Picture of Dorian Gray*, though rarely understood because rarely sought, is no less clear than that which Bulwer Lytton explained in his preface. Lord Henry, Wilde's perfect dandy, expounds to Dorian a paradoxical philosophy of dandyism which shocks Basil Halward but appeals to the young narcissist. In the passion of his self-love, Dorian Gray distorts this doctrine and becomes a fallen dandy, corrupting all those who accompany him along his path and murdering his conscience, Basil Halward; finally, in self-inflicted death, Dorian meets the punishment of excessive self-love. But Lord Henry's true doctrine, more spiritually and less prudentially intellectual than Pelham's, was a philosophy of inaction: beyond good and evil, for all his evil-sounding paradoxes which only illustrate the Taoist identity of contraries where both conscience and temptation are placed on the same footing but then transcended, Lord Henry never acts and never falls.

Comedy as Self-Degradation

"Wilde in his poetry represents all that is worst in decadent romanticism, and in his comedies all that is vital in the rising comedy of manners," writes Allardyce Nicoll, a historian of drama whose literary appreciations, especially of poetry, are rarely valid. And he thus invests with the authority of his specialized scholarship the general unthinking view that Wilde's comedies, because still popular, must be better than his less popular works and as "good" and "vital" as all the other box-office successes of the last fifty years. But if we now read a representative selection of these other successes, we immediately realize that the "rising comedy of manners," as a new and vital art-form, was as still-born as the movie industry; the few outstanding achievements of the commercial theater and the cinema have generally been flukes, and their average success zooms, like some newly marketed cosmetic, to a zenith of popularity on a wave of sheer publicity, and then sinks into a weirdly meaningless obsolescence that appalls us if we ever dare look at it again a few years after it was first produced.

Like most modern plays that have any lasting value, Wilde's comedies transcend the average of our dreary age of commercial drama only by virtue of qualities that they share with other forms of literature, less popular or commercial, or with the drama of less commercial ages. But in his eagerness to make money, Wilde made too many concessions to the bad dramatic tastes and habits of his own times; and he failed throughout *A Woman of no Importance* and *An Ideal Husband*, and in several aspects of *Lady Windermere's Fan* and *The Importance of Being Earnest*, to achieve the lasting perfection of the true classic rather than the ambiguous survival of works that are treated as classics for lack of any better examples of their genre.

The Nineteenth Century had seen the legitimate theater develop, in London, into a huge entertainment industry that catered to masses of customers whose cultural levels ranged from very low to very high. In eighteenth-century London, only three theaters held licenses to produce legitimate drama. Throughout the early decades of the Nineteenth Century, the demand for dramatic entertainment, in the expanding metropolis, grew so rapidly that a whole crop of unlicensed "speak-easy" theaters arose and finally had to be licensed too. Authorized at first to produce only musical entertainments or what was then called "melodrama," they had, however, before they were allowed to produce legitimate drama, fostered a taste for sensational plays which, the vogue for "gothic" romantic drama aiding, had affected the productions of the licensed theaters too. Scarcely a play that could be enjoyably read or seen today was produced on the London stage from 1800 to 1880. Almost the only dramatic masterpieces of that era were the plays of such poets as Byron, Shelley, Coleridge, Beddoes, Tennyson, Browning, Matthew Arnold or Swinburne, most of them composed as "chamber drama," lyrical plays to be read, as those of Seneca had once been, rather than produced before popular audiences. On its mediocre diet of plays actually produced, the English theater finally sank, toward the middle of the century, into such a decline of stale repetitiousness and stilted conventions that only foreign influences, from France and Norway, were able to infuse new life into it in the last decades of the century.

The most popular dramatist of the middle Victorian era, Thomas William Robertson, imported the problem-play from France and initiated what the London critic Hawk's-eye, in 1871, called "the Robertson era, in which he showed what a man of brilliant genius could do in the present day, and with the present time, and how well refined comedies can be played." Robertson's "refined comedies," *Society* (1865), *Ours* (1866), *Caste* (1867), *Play* (1868), *School* (1869), *M.P.* (1870), *War* (1871), initiated the English public into the relatively simple mysteries of the art of Scribe and of other French wholesale dramatists; presenting each year a new problem under another laconic title, Robertson thus borrowed elements of plot from all the successes of the Parisian Realist theater. W. S. Gilbert, in his early prose comedies, likewise borrowed extensively from the problem-plays of the French Realists and from farces such as those of Labiche. And when Wilde began to write his comedies, in the early Nineties, the English theater was still thriving on the art of Alexandre Dumas *fils*, Emile Augier, Octave Feuillet, and even Georges Ohnet. The plots of three of Wilde's comedies, *Lady Windermere's Fan* (1892), *A Woman of no Importance* (1893) and *An Ideal Husband* (1896), with their problems of the fallen woman trying to regain a respectable position in society or to drag a respectable family down to her own sordid level, remind one immediately of those of *La Dame aux Camélias, Le Demi-monde, Le Mariage d'Olympe* and of countless other plays of Dumas *fils*, Augier and their imitators; and Wilde's fourth comedy, *The Importance of Being Earnest* (1895), has many farcical elements in common with the plays of Eugène Labiche.

In these plots, Wilde contributed nothing new to the English theater or to the theater in general. He wrote his comedies in order to make money, and he carefully selected, as their themes, stories which would appeal to the tastes of his London audiences. Writing in the same years, Henry Arthur Jones, in *The Liars* (1897) and *Mrs. Dane's Defence* (1900), or Sir Arthur Pinero, in *The Second Mrs. Tanqueray* (1893) and *The Notorious Mrs. Ebbsmith* (1895), chose the same type of plot, dealing with much the same problems; and even George Bernard Shaw, in *Mrs. Warren's Profession* (1898), though far more outspoken than most of his contemporaries, remained faithful to their very Second Empire preoccupations with sin.

Queen Victoria's reign, by maintaining for so long the same domestic tone and policy in English life, had helped the isolationist British middle class (in an age of colonial expansion when the manners of Africa or Asia attracted almost more attention than those of France) to cultivate, far longer than other formerly more liberal bourgeoisies, the Holy Alliance's philosophy of conservative respectability. Wielding his umbrella as a sort of middle-class sceptre symbolizing constitutional monarchy, Louis-Philippe had represented this philosophy, for a while, in France. Throughout Europe, the Treaty of Vienna had indeed inspired governments to curb "the excesses of the French Revolution" and also those of the era of dandified immorality which had blossomed from the Conciergerie, in the French Directoire, and then spread rapidly to Regency England, to the yoyo-playing small German courts where French refugees called the new toy "le coblence," or to the decrepit Venetian Republic which was crumbling away splendidly in a last flowering of rococo gambling-dens, guilded blackamoors, pox-ridden dominoes, and fantastic stage-machinery.

But the July Monarchy had not lasted long in France. Soon bored with a monarch who was not even decorative, the French tried variously, after 1848, to revive all the excitements of the revolutionary republic, of the Napoleonic empire and of pre-revolutionary court-life. La Païva then became a new Dubarry; *"Louis XVI Impératrice"* was, for a while, the style for furniture, before its ormolu fantasies were shipped to Chicago and further West, where frontier millionaires and the proprietors of Bonanza Inns mistook them for "genuine Louis XV"; and Victor Hugo went into dignified exile while absinthe and time-bombs became constant preoccupations among the more socially conscious intellectuals, and Baudelaire's esthetics spread slowly among the more contemplative.

In the last decades of Victoria's reign, a similar restlessness was felt in England too. The class which was later to set the tone of the Edwardian era and finally to degenerate into our own Café Society became impatient of tedious Victorian ideals of commerce, Empire, and morality; and English taste began to revert to earlier traditions of Romanticism which, though kept alive by small groups, had generally been frowned upon as immoral in Balmoral and Osborne. As the dandy came back into his own, the art and literature of the French Second Empire began to interest a class of sophisticated Londoners who somehow felt, as in A *Sentimental Journey*, that they order these matters better in France, and that any novel bound in yellow paper, were it even by Georges Ohnet, must be more modern and more naughtily entertaining than an English three-decker. With a more guffawing humor and less subtle music, Gilbert and Sullivan then imitated the *opérettes* of Offenbach and Meilhac and Halévy: a good steak-and-kidney pie trying to pass off as a divine *vol-au-vent*. And the English decadents, from Oscar Wilde to George Moore, tried hastily to catch up, in a mere decade, with almost half a century of French art movements that ranged from Realism and *Le Parnasse* to Symbolism, Impressionism, and the neo-antique of Pierre Louÿs or Jean Moréas.

It is in terms of this general background, with its curious inhibitions and restlessness and its guilty sense of a culture-lag, almost as great as that of the American upper classes of the same era, that Oscar Wilde's comedies must be interpreted. "The aim of social comedy," wrote Wilde, "is to mirror the manners, not to reform the morals, of its day." Wilde had already neglected his own art-for-art's-sake precepts to preach esthetics and ethics in his fiction; and now he began, in an even more general manner, to preach estheticism and to moralize in his comedies too, so that their esthetic nature is that of a photographic double exposure, with the banter and *marivaudage* of the comedy of manners superimposed, in the frothy dialogue, on the more earnest plot of a problem-play which tends to reform morals or at least to correct current moral attitudes. It is almost as if these plays were the work of two authors, of Oscar Wilde writing the dialogue, so similar, in style and tone, to that of his own conversations or of Lord Henry's in *The Picture of Dorian Gray*, and of some hack, the "Spirit of the Age" that supplied Wilde with the plots and all the emotional scenes and tirades where the action progressed.

But the hack was Oscar Wilde himself, harried by his creditors and his expensive habits, desperately anxious to achieve commercial success and to market, in the more profitable form of plays, all the brilliant epigrams that he had, for years, been unprofitably squandering on social conversation or on less popular forms of art. If one were patiently to sift the epigrams and paradoxes of his complete works into a card-index, one would soon discover that many of them flutter dazzlingly through his writings, settling on each work with about as studied a relationship to its structure and tone as a butterfly has to the shape and color of the flower where it momentarily rests. *The Sphinx without a Secret* is thus the title of one of Wilde's earlier fictional sketches; as an epigram applied to all women, it reappears on Lord Henry's lips in *Dorian Gray*, then again on Lord Illingworth's in *A Woman of no Importance*. "Experience, the name that men give to their mistakes," is another of Wilde's more faithful gags, uttered for the first time by the evil Russian prime minister in *Vera*, repeated in a dialogue-scene of *Dorian Gray*, reappearing on the lips of Cecil Graham in *Lady Windermere's Fan*. "I never talk scandal, I only talk gossip" is a maxim of all Wilde's dandies, of Cecil Graham, of Lord Illingworth, and of Lord Goring in *An Ideal Husband*. All these exquisites, together with Algernon Moncrieff in *The Importance of Being Earnest* and Lord Henry in *The Picture of Dorian Gray*, express themselves in the same dandified language of elegant *fin-de-siècle* paradox and epigram, the *obiter dicta* of an attitude toward life which Wilde raises to the level of an organized philosophy in the critical dialogues of *Intentions*, in *The Decay of Lying* and in *The Critic as Artist*. And the feminine counterparts of these dandies are Wilde's very "modern" young women, sophisticated dowagers or cynical adventuresses, Gwendolyn Fairfax, Cecily Cardew or Lady Bracknell in *The Importance of Being Earnest*, Mabel Chiltern, Lady Basildon, Mrs. Marchmont or the evil Mrs. Cheveley in *An Ideal Husband*, Mrs. Erlynn, Lady Carlisle or the Duchess of Berwick in *Lady Windermere's Fan*, Mrs. Allonby in *A Woman of no Importance*, and the various society women who flit across the stage of *Lord Arthur Savile's Crime* or *The Picture of Dorian Gray*.

Contrasting with these, and almost strangers to their world of wit, we find worthy characters of stock Victorian drama, Lord and Lady Windermere, Sir Robert and Lady Chiltern in *An Ideal Husband*, or Mrs. Arbuthnot, the stuffy Mary Magdalen of *A Woman of no Importance*. Their problems, such as the injustice of "one law for women and another for men" or the folly of "a high moral tone" that sees no gradations between black sin and white virtue, determine the plots of three of Wilde's comedies; for the banter of the dandies and their mates, like the poetry or "atmosphere" of lyrical drama, would rarely lead anywhere, in terms of dramatic progression, were it not cut out of the endless cloth of Wilde's wit to fit neatly on some sturdy plot, whether problem or farce, with its beginning, its middle, and its end.

As in the lyrical drama, the macabre story, or the fairy tale, Wilde's real esthetic problem thus lay in fitting his atmosphere neatly to his plot. And in three of his comedies, the seams that join his two materials, that of the comedy of manners and that of the problem-play with a social moral or of the farce, are often none too elegantly concealed. It has been pointed out that Wilde is most sincere, as an artist, when depicting insincere characters; and that there is always some artistic falseness and insincerity in the declarations of his few sincere characters. Lady Windermere, for instance, is delightfully convincing as long as she prattles elegantly; but as soon as her maternal instincts begin to ferment in her, the resulting dialogue is no longer the same light champagne but some flat and cloudy wine that has turned sour. In *A Woman of no Importance*, Mrs. Arbuthnot joins the gay party with the inappropriateness of a grisly dead bat pinned as a corsage on a charmingly frivolous dress. Her black velvets and veils, as absurdly conventional as mad Tilburina's white satin in Sheridan's parody of neo-Shakespearean tragedy, her ancient grievances and her brooding utterances, all these immediately transmute the whole nature of the play. And she soon degrades even Lord Illingworth to her own melodramatic level when he forgets his studied urbanity to snap at her, with all the Satanic arrogance of an evil Regency buck in the plays of an earlier age: "It's been an amusing experience to have met amongst people of one's own rank, and treated quite seriously too, one's mistress and one's—"

"Bastard," he would have uttered, but the stern dramatist, like fate in Sheridan's *The Critic*, made Mrs. Arbuthnot snatch up a glove and strike Illingworth across the face with it, cutting short the sentence and his most unseemly mood at once. In *An Ideal Husband* too, Mrs. Cheveley and Lord Goring relapse into some pretty melodrama over the stolen diamond pin-bracelet, when the "immoral" dandy begins to moralize as if he were Lady Chiltern, and the smooth and lovely adventuress goes to pieces so that "a curse breaks from her . . . her face is distorted. Her mouth awry. A mask has fallen from her. She is, for the moment, dreadful to look at. . . ."

In such scenes, the comedy of manners becomes, as a work of art, just as dreadful as its characters: a mask falls, and the ugly melodrama of the Victorian problem-play is revealed. But Wilde's three first comedies were, as John Drinkwater has pointed out, "frank surrenders to a fashion of the theater which Wilde had too good a brain not to despise." Wilde had learned that the public, like Shylock, demands its pound of fleshly problem, of informative facts or of moral instruction, to allay the guilt of sheer enjoyment, before it will acclaim a new dramatist. Later, once captivated by his magic, it may forget its demands or begin to find, for its pleasure, some justification in his mere art. And Wilde had reached the point, in *The Importance of Being Earnest*, where he could at last, it seems, rely on his earlier success, as an author of problem-plays, to carry him ahead, as an author of light comedies, on the crest of a wave of sheer popularity. In his last comedy, we find no fallen women, whether anxious to regain their lost respectability or to undermine the reputations of more worthy characters, no good women who must learn, through bitter experience, that sin and virtue are not clear-cut absolutes. Instead of the moral problem which the author must solve, Wilde now uses, as plot, a purely farcical intrigue, though perhaps still too much of an infernal machine, too loudly ticking beneath the light dialogue and too well timed, with all its happy couples paired off in the last act, to achieve the less obviously contrived or less self-conscious perfection of one of Sheridan's comedies of manners.

Between *The Importance of Being Earnest*, with all its plot and sub-plots, and Sheridan's *The Critic*, which is all situation and no plot, a happy mean can be found; and Wilde might have found it, had not the catastrophes of his private life smashed his popularity with the public and killed his desire to write any more. The perfect comedy of manners, for all its satirical characterization, should never preach. "It may be questioned," Wilde wrote, "whether the consistent reward of virtue and punishment of vice be really the healthiest ideal for an art that claims to mirror nature." In mirroring the society that surrounded him, Wilde was most faithfully realistic when he abandoned the conventions of a superficially Realist school in favor of a more original satirical fantasy. In his comedies, moreover, where his aim is to create an almost perfect illusion of reality, Wilde rarely had recourse to the device of the "interior monologue," though it was still to be found quite frequently in the plays of French Realists, even in Becque's *Les Corbeaux*. Inherited from the tragedies and comedies of an earlier age, where an outburst of lyrical self-analysis or an aside addressed to the audience in a Punch-and-Judy tone of complicity had some artistic verisimilitude, such monologues as Algernon's, when his man-servant leaves him alone on the stage in the first act of *The Importance of Being Earnest*, are no longer justified in an art which pretends to mirror

life without any stylization. It required the new style of such dramatists as Eugene O'Neill to justify these monologues again, by pro-
posing a new psychological realism where several levels of discourse
correspond to the several levels of consciousness of the play's characters, so that a different "key" of acting or of diction distinguishes
each level. In his more melodramatic problem-plays, Wilde avoided
the monologue less scrupulously. The grisly Mrs. Arbuthnot, a
veritable prose tragedy queen, is almost constantly on the verge of
uttering a tirade on an empty stage; and it is only with difficulty, it
seems, that her frantic feelings can be constrained within a few
monologues, each one of them rationed to a mere couple of lines.

But Wilde seems, in *A Woman of no Importance*, to have emp-
tied his whole bag of melodramatic problem-play tricks, in a final
clearance-sale before removing to the new premises of farce. This is
his usual procedure, in the curious artist's progress that he followed,
from the many errors and impurities of a generally bad start to the
artistic purity which he always preached but generally found it so
difficult to practice. In his poetry, from the cluttered art of *Humanitad* to the simple arabesque of *The Harlot's House*, in his lyrical
drama, from the absurd melodrama of *Vera* to the unity of tone of
Salome, in his poetic prose, from the two humorously self-conscious
tales of *The Happy Prince* to the far purer art of *The Fisherman and
his Soul*, he had achieved perfection and unity of tone only after
using and rejecting, in each art-form in turn, a mass of discordant
elements that belonged more properly in other art-forms. His fiction
and his comedies, it seems, might have undergone to a greater
degree this process of "sorting out," had Wilde's life permitted him
to devote a few more years to these two genres. The doldrums of
witty dialogue, where Wilde's narrative is so often becalmed while
he satirizes himself and offers his cruder readers what they expect of
him, would then have vanished from his fiction. In his comedies, he
had found a better use, artistically and economically far more
profitable, for all this wit that he had wasted in his own conversation
or in that of the birds and flowers of his early fairy tales or of the
unnecessary "extras" who crowd the parties of his fiction.

But in Wilde's first three comedies, the light dialogue of the
satirical comedy of manners was not yet properly fitted to the
heavier plot of the problem-play. In *The Importance of Being*

Earnest, the remarks and the character of Lady Bracknell seem far more appropriate, less affected and less unrealistically stylized, against their background, than those of the Duchess of Berwick in *Lady Windermere's Fan*, where Lady Windermere's unrelieved earnestness contrasts too violently with the frivolity of most of the other characters. We thus seem to be witnessing, in some scenes of Wilde's first three comedies, the improbable commerce of two different species of imagined humanity, *homo moralis* and *homo immoralis*, who could not conceivably live together on such amicable terms in the same small society: one of them would surely expel the other very soon, by some Gresham's Law such as that which drove fallen Adam and Eve out of the angels' Garden of Eden or which later caused the aboriginal Tasmanians to die out as soon as Victorian Englishmen appeared on their shores.

Though the characters of Wilde's farce are all of the same species, its plot is at times too heavily contrived, especially in the last act: the sudden revelation of Miss Prism's past solves too conveniently the problem of the hero's origin, and too many of the embarrassing lies of the play are too neatly resolved into truth. Such reliance on the whimsies of chance weakens the satire of a comedy of manners; its plot should seem to grow more directly out of the follies of its characters, mirroring the irrationality of an absurd society of human beings responsible for their own predicaments rather than the irresponsible tricks of a contemptibly frivolous destiny.

In spite of the polished brilliance of its paradoxical dialogue and the sure pace of its surprising action, *The Importance of Being Earnest* thus never transcends, as a work of art, the incomplete or the trivial. Its tone is that of satire, but of a satire which, for lack of a moral point of view, has lost its sting and degenerated into the almost approving banter of a P. G. Wodehouse. Satire, whether in the comedy of manners or any other genre of satirical literature, must be founded on more than a dandy's mere tastes and opinions; from some sounder moral philosophy, it must derive a necessary bitterness without which the satirist remains ineffectual while the manners of his comedies, not yet structurally integrated, seem superimposed as mere ornament on an arbitrary plot of farce.

With more experience as a writer of comedies, Wilde might have outgrown the contemptible destiny of too farcical plots just as he had already outgrown the too contemptibly vengeful destiny of the problem-play. He might, it is true, have rather outworn it than outgrown it, by writing a farce to end all farces, a sort of *Charley's Aunt*, much as he had, in *A Woman of no Importance*, exhausted all the tricks of melodramatic coincidence when, for instance, Mrs. Arbuthnot enters the scene for the first time just as her future daughter-in-law insists that "all women who have sinned be punished," or when young Gerald Arbuthnot recognizes his unknown father in the benefactor who has just insulted his beloved and whom he is threatening to kill. In over twenty centuries of artistic decline and fall, the great recognition-scenes of ancient tragedy, where angry gods of destiny and retribution vengefully displayed their flouted powers, had degenerated into petty coincidences in the ambiguous lives of fallen women and illegitimate children.

Oscar Wilde was conscious of this cheapening of the artistic standards of drama. In *The Soul of Man under Socialism*, he attributed much of it to "the exercise of popular authority" in the arts and concluded that "a true artist" should take "no notice of the public." Too slavish an awareness of the public's crude tastes and absurd demands had indeed led the English dramatists of his age to produce "more silly, vulgar plays" than those of any other country. And to escape this slavery, Wilde abandoned such "higher forms of the drama" as the problem-play, where "the public dislike novelty," in favor of farce, where "the artist in England is allowed very great freedom." Though the public "like the obvious," Wilde knew that "they do not like the tedious"; and he felt that "burlesque and farcical comedy," the two most popular forms of drama in his day, "are distinct forms of art." But he also declared, in *The Soul of Man under Socialism*, that "art should never try to be popular," and that "the public should try to make itself artistic." As a dramatist, however, Wilde could no longer be content to practice his doctrines before an empty house, so that *The Importance of Being Earnest* illustrates a compromise: he hoped to be able to enjoy more artistic freedom in a lower form of art while still reaping the financial benefits of popularity.

It is the true artist's privilege and duty to transcend the artistic folly of his age, the bad taste and bad habits displayed in its too lazily conventional or superficial imitation of life. Nineteenth-century English drama had sunk to such a nadir of bad taste and bad habits that it was almost impossible for an artist to transcend so much artistic folly and yet see his plays produced before a public accustomed only to the coarsest fare. And it took several decades of various foreign influences and of varied effort, on the part of our more creative or less corrupt dramatists, to free English and American drama from the toils of ranting melodrama or guffawing farce. Wilde was among the first to attempt this Herculean task. He came well prepared, with a broad knowledge of the great drama of the past and a sound understanding of acting and of the technical problems of the modern theater. There was, moreover, a strong histrionic streak in his character as in that of any dandy: as a narcissist poseur, the perfect dandy is an accomplished actor whose posing never bores nor offends any but true bores and the truly offensive. A Wilde manuscript of an unfinished poem, sold a few years ago in an important sale of autographs, is perhaps psychologically significant: it contains, as doodles, what the catalogue describes as "three palpable attempts to forge the signature of Henry Irving."

Of Wilde's understanding of the actor's art, his self-identification with actors and his friendship and sympathy for them, we have less ambiguous proofs at more conscious levels of his thought. His critical writings and *The Portrait of Mr. W. H.* reveal unusual insights into the art of interpreting; his American tour, with his public appearances in knee-breeches and his other showmanlike displays of affectation, gives ample proof of his histrionic exhibitionism; and we know from his letters and biography what close ties of friendship and sympathetic understanding he developed with many of the great actors of his time. When he saw Sarah Bernhardt again after his release from prison, an end came to their momentary estrangement which had been caused by her somewhat cowardly fear of compromising herself by appearing in *Salome*. Wilde then wrote to Robert Ross that "she embraced me and I wept—and the whole evening was wonderful."

With his sense of drama and his clear understanding of its devices and of their limitations, Wilde was able, in his comedies, to reduce to some extent the gaping chasms that separated the theater of his day both from art and from life. Others, in his generation and immediately after, were dedicated to the same task; and their combined influences have helped the commercial theater, in our own day, to avoid, from time to time, many of the pitfalls where Victorian dramatists almost inevitably made fools of themselves. We need but read any collection of the more distinguished box-office successes of this century to recognize at once how inspiring was Wilde's example, and how fruitful has been his revival of the comedy of manners, even in the hybrid form in which he revived it. Wilde's dignified man-servants may indeed, in many English plays or novels, have become very stereotyped in their "inimitability"; but the Noel Cowards who have imitated Wilde have generally failed, for lack of satirical integrity, to raise their art to the level of perfection that it deserves. There are few successful comic dramatists today, in England or America, to whom one might not repeat, if they dared speak lightly of Wilde's contribution to modern comedy, the words of Mrs. Arbuthnot to her son who is about to strike Lord Illingworth: "Stop, Gerald, stop! He is your own father!"

Wilde's importance, in the history of the commercial theater, is moreover significant as an indication of the artist's relationship to a society in which we still live. Wilde believed that there can be "no great drama without a noble national life, and the commercial spirit of England has killed that too." And when he began to write his comedies and to be a successful artist in terms of popular acclaim and royalties, he had already progressed, as thinker and stylist, far beyond the somewhat meretricious glitter of many of the epigrams that constitute the chief merit of these works. Such a dandified art of conversation was a relic of an earlier attitude toward art and life; and Wilde, in his more important works, had already transcended this attitude so that the rational content of his later epigrams often belongs to the politics, ethics, and esthetics of his youth rather than to the thought of his mature years. But society remembered Wilde's flamboyant youth, his Bunthorne days; and Wilde was expected to remain equal to himself, never to change or to progress. It was to this earlier dandyism that he now had to return, when he decided to commercialize his art. Had not the scandal of his trial and imprisonment cut short his career as a writer of successful comedies, Wilde might have experienced, a few years later, the anguish or "crackup" of so many artists of our own age, who have turned back because Broadway or Hollywood demanded it, and then discovered, though too late, that their paralyzed wit has become but a pillar of lifeless salt. Wilde's comedies thus suggest that his life, as a serious or creative artist, had perhaps ended before his trials and tribulations, and that his only future, in 1894, was that of the successful writer. But in *De Profundis*, Wilde seemed to believe that his misfortunes might facilitate a rebirth, in a different form, of the more serious and creative art which he had abandoned. Had he lived, Wilde might indeed, though it now seems psychologically improbable, have profited as an artist by this moral or spiritual regeneration. In any case, what he once wrote unprophetically, in a review of some poems by Wilfred Scawen Blunt, another poet who experienced imprisonment, is now true of *The Ballad of Reading Gaol* and of *De Profundis*: prison converted Wilde back to being "an earnest and deep-thinking poet."

The Politics of the Dandy

"Really, if the lower orders don't set us a good example, what on earth is the use of them? They seem, as a class, to have absolutely no sense of moral responsibility." Of such witticisms, on social and political problems, Oscar Wilde's writings are full; and a reader who misses some of their author's complex intentions will readily conclude, from their supercilious tone, that Wilde was politically immature or snobbishly reactionary. But most of these remarks are made by characters, in the comedies especially, whose very foibles they satirize. Algernon, in *The Importance of Being Earnest*, is clearly of no social use and prides himself on his irresponsibility; and when Lady Bracknell remarks, in the same play, that if education produced any effect in England, which it fortunately does not, it would prove a serious danger to the upper classes, Wilde certainly does not intend to suggest that the proletariat should be kept ignorant, but rather that an educated upper class might develop an uneasy conscience instead of taking, as Lady Bracknell does, so many of its privileges for granted.

Of society's stratifications and conflicting class interests, Wilde was indeed as conscious as any artist of his age. The politically idealistic philosophies of Saint-Simon and Fourrier or Owen and Ruskin had injected some notions of Socialism into the Romanticism and Estheticism of most French or English poets some years before the ideas of Marx or Proudhon began to spread appreciably among artists and writers. The French Revolution and middle-class democracy had failed, after the Napoleonic wars, to satisfy many of the great hopes that they had aroused. Instead of the ideal equality of Republican Rome which intellectuals inspired by two centuries of Humanistic study of Plutarch had been led to expect, the Industrial Revolution had come, an age of crass commercialism which even Queen Victoria's conformist Laureate described in *Maud* as "When the poor are hovelled and hustled together" and "only the ledger lives," and from whose "vile traffic-house" Oscar Wilde, some twenty years later, began to seek refuge "in dreams of Art and loftiest culture."

This frightening new world of the gas-lit city, with its industries and slums, was already beginning to throw out tentacles to enslave science, art, and the intellect. Most of us have now become, through habit, quite insensitive to the full horror of our Inferno and of the many wiles whereby Satan, as Baudelaire wrote, deceives us into believing that he does not exist; but the nineteenth-century intellectual, with his Humanistic eighteenth-century background and education which we have lost, generally resented every political or economic pressure that was intended to commercialize or nationalize the intellect. He felt estranged from this new world and, especially after the disappointments of 1848, either sought escape from the present in the past or the future, or adopted an attitude of solitary disapproval whereby he hoped to signify, as Baudelaire suggested that the dandy should proudly do, that he was "less base than" the average man of his age.

To nineteenth-century escapism we thus owe both the persecuted religion of Art for Art's Sake and the persecuting totalitarian doctrines now derived from Marx or Gobineau and de Maistre; and the orthodoxies of both revolution and reaction, of both those who sought a solution in the future and those who sought it in the past, are now tending, though more directly and brutally than the old bourgeois order once did with its mere offers of money and prestige, to put the escapist intellectual to politically useful tasks. But Baudelaire, who was "Not base enough to be convinced of anything," wrote that "to be a useful person has always seemed to me something particularly horrible"; and Rimbaud added, thinking of all the industrious platitudes about the hand that guides the plough or holds the pen or steers the ship or wields the sword, that he himself would "never have a hand," meaning some useful trade, in his "century of hands." As a conscientious objector to the social order in which he lived, many a nineteenth-century artist thus sought evidence of his own integrity in his utter uselessness.

Today, both the dandy and the conscientious objector are as unpopular with conformists of the right or the left as they once were with the bourgeois majority which believed in the middle way and the established order. Neither fascism nor communism can tolerate citizens who proclaim that politics and material problems are less important than ethics or esthetics. But in Oscar Wilde's age, the political doctrines of the dandy and the esthete, who so often professed sympathy with extreme views of the right or the left, were considered dangerous only by the mildly liberal or conservative majority. Had not Lassalle, the German Socialist, been a notorious dandy? Was not Heinrich Heine, esthete and dandy, a close friend of Karl Marx, and had not Wagner at one time been a friend of Bakunin? Had not Baudelaire, bitter critic of bourgeois democracy, advocated theocracy and communism and even warned all non-communists that "all is common property, even God"? In being a "pariah," rejected by the order which he himself rejected, Baudelaire found evidence of his own "true greatness" and concluded: "When I inspire universal horror and disgust, I shall have conquered solitude."

Few dandies or "literary lions" were doomed, however, to inspire, as Oscar Wilde did in the end, such universal horror and disgust that they no longer emulated Mr. Wormwood who, in Bulwer Lytton's *Pelham*, "was too much disliked not to be sought after." The deaths of nineteenth-century dandies and esthetes, in Brummel's madness or that of Hoelderlin, in the paralysis of Hoffmann, Heine or Baudelaire, the suicide of Novalis or Nerval, in syphilis, alcohol or drugs, were often frighteningly solitary; they seem to have been meticulously planned to appear as macabre as the last moments of the Satanic or damned hero of a gothic novel, or to satisfy all the pent-up guilt-feelings of a life of systematic debauchery. The solitude that Wilde experienced in Reading Gaol, and later as an exile and outcast in Paris, was no less intense in degree, but not of his own choosing in its form; and he failed to transcend it as an artist, overwhelmed by the horror of his fate. The two letters on prison life that he published, after his release, in the London *Daily Chronicle*, are indeed symptomatic: Wilde no longer attempts to conceal his anguish and indignation, no longer seeks to dazzle, as an artist, or to delight, but states his argument in pathetically simple terms, bitterly accusing society of stupid cruelty and irresponsibility in its treatment of delinquent children and prisoners in general. The tone of these two letters is indeed that of all Wilde's writings of the tragic aftermath, when he seemed to be merely waiting for death to release him from the memory of experiences which had been too painful to serve as the materials of art, save in the curiously repetitious *Ballad of Reading Gaol*, where the poet is endlessly haunted by his memories, as if his poem were his pain and there were no end to either.

Not that Wilde, before his trial, had ignored the cruelty and stupidity of the society in which he lived. As early as his Oxford days, when he was more an esthete than a dandy, he had become imbued with Ruskinian Socialism and had talked about the dignity of manual labor, and even gone, with other Ruskinians, on a road-building expedition. In his early poems, he also proclaimed a Byronic admiration for Mazzini, much as Disraeli or Elizabeth Barrett Browning had, and frequently chose political themes in which he revealed, however, great ambiguity and immaturity. Later, while touring America in 1882, Wilde expressed sentimental and optimistic views about a Renaissance of art: industry should permit its workers to enjoy their work and produce, instead of the hideous wares of cheap and careless mass-production, beautiful objects which would satisfy their esthetic sense and their pride of craftsmanship.

But his travels in America seem to have opened his eyes to the naive and unworldly nature of this Romantic Socialism; as a dandy and man of the world, he abandoned, on his return to Europe, the

Pre-Raphaelitic politics of the esthete, though he never lost interest in political or social problems. Of this more sophisticated interest, we have proof in the witticisms and paradoxes of the comedies and fiction, but especially in three important pieces of critical writing: Wilde's review of the English translation of the writings of the Chinese philosopher Chuang Tzu, his essay *The Soul of Man under Socialism*, and a long passage in the second part of his dialogue *The Critic as Artist*. As all three of these pieces were first published in 1890, it may safely be assumed that they were written, though not necessarily in the order of their publication, within a very short time; and as *The Critic as Artist* mentions Chuang Tzu by name and *The Soul of Man under Socialism* contains many of the ideas of the Chinese Sage, there is enough evidence to conclude that the discovery of Taoism made it possible for Wilde to transcend at last the political dilemmas of the dandy in a new creed of his own.*

The politics of the more callow esthete are stated in a number of Wilde's early poems, several of which are predominantly political. Repeatedly, Wilde proclaims the anti-monarchist and republican faith which he had inherited, it seems, partly from his Irish background and Speranza, his Byronic mother, and partly from his own readings. In *Ave Imperatrix*, while still under the spell of the imperial myth which inspired Tennyson, Disraeli, W. E. Henley, Kipling and Buchan, with its fears of "the treacherous Russian" and its new legendary Rolands of the Khyber Pass, Wilde thinks too, in a mood that foreshadows *A Shropshire Lad*, of "Cromwell's England" which must yield "For every inch of ground a son":

> In vain the laughing girl will lean
>   To greet her love with love-lit eyes:
> Down in some treacherous black ravine,
>   Clutching his flag, the dead boy lies.

---

*Oddly enough, George Woodcock had come on his own to the same conclusions as I concerning the influence of the Heraclitean or Taoist theories of the Identity of Contraries on Wilde's wit and especially on his frequent use of paradox as well as on many of his more profound thoughts, such as those expressed in *The Soul of Man under Socialism*. Both Woodcock and I thus traced much of Wilde's more mature and profoundly paradoxical wit back to his review of the English translation of the Chinese philosopher Chuang-Tzu.

But Wilde concludes hopefully that, "when this fiery web" of conquest is at last spun, England's watchmen shall see from far:

> The young Republic like a sun
> Rise from these crimson seas of war.

In his sonnet on the death of Louis Napoleon, the Emperor Napoleon the Third's exiled heir who was killed in Zululand while fighting one of Britain's colonial wars, Wilde rejoices that France is now "free and republican." In his sonnet *To Milton*, he again hails Cromwell; in *Quantum Mutata*, much as the Neronian poet Lucan once mourned Cato's ideals, Wilde mourns Cromwell's "great Republic," when "no man died for freedom anywhere, But England's lion" at once "Laid hands on the oppressor"; and Wilde attributes England's moral decline, as did the Stoic writers of Imperial Rome, to luxury which clutters "with barren merchandise" what, in *Theoretikos*, he calls "this vile traffic-house" where "wisdom and reverence are sold at mart."

But all these republican moods were oddly ambivalent, like those of Speranza who, while professing anti-monarchist views, was yet delighted when the Queen knighted Oscar's father. In his *Sonnet to Liberty*, Wilde thus admits that he does not love Liberty's children "whose dull eyes See nothing save their own unlovely woe, Whose minds know nothing, nothing care to know"; but Liberty's "reigns of terror" and "great anarchies" mirror the poet's "wildest passions" and give his rage a brother for whose sake he is not, as he might else be, unmoved by tyranny; and he concludes that he is, "in some things," with "These Christs that die upon the barricades." In another sonnet, however, in *Libertatis Sacra Fames*, though still "liking best that state republican Where every man is Kinglike," Wilde prefers "the rule of One, whom all obey," to letting "clamorous demagogues betray Our freedom with the kiss of anarchy"; and here, he concludes that he loves not those "whose hands profane Plant the red flag upon the piled-up street For no right cause, beneath whose ignorant reign Arts, Culture, Reverence, all things fade."

In the one sonnet, Wilde is thus with those whose anarchy mirrors his wildest passions and his rage against his age; in the other, he is against them in his desire to preserve a cultural heritage which they destroy together with the order which both they and Wilde hate. Matthew Arnold, in the two sonnets which he dedicated, in 1848, *To a Republican Friend*, had consciously faced the same dilemma, and stated it in very similar terms. On less general issues too, Wilde wavered in his revolutionary faith, much as the poet and dandy Vittorio Alfieri had enthusiastically supported the American Revolution and then the French Revolution, until his personal losses in the latter made him protest against its violences. Though he proclaimed his passionate admiration for Mazzini in *Human-itad*, Wilde thus objected to the unification of Italy, in which Elizabeth Barrett Browning had vested such hopes, on the grounds that it "desecrated" Rome where "In evil bonds a second Peter lay" while on the city's walls, there fluttered "The hated flag of red and white and green." Indeed, the thought of the Pope's "bondage" seems to have marred much of the joy of the young poet's trip to Italy, if one is to believe the sentiments expressed throughout the lyrics of *Rosa Mystica*; but Wilde did rejoice later, as he wrote *Ravenna*, when he looked back upon other achievements of the Italian Revolution: "The Austrian hounds are hunted from the land" and Dante's "dream is now a dream no more," since the cry "Of light and Truth, of Love and Liberty . . . Rings from the Alps to the Sicilian shore."

In Wilde's early lyrical dramas too, in *Vera* and *The Duchess of Padua*, the dilemma of the Romantic-liberal esthete's curiously ambivalent politics is clearly illustrated. In *Vera*, the idealistic Czarevitch seems more liberal than most of the narrow-minded Nihilists with whom, before inheriting the crown, he had secretly associated and plotted, disguised as a poor student; and the play's political tangle becomes all the more complex when its villain, Prince Paul, the Machiavellian Prime Minister, suddenly turns Nihilist, in his disgrace, in order to obtain revenge. From an ethical point of view, the Czarevitch is the play's hero; but he seems to have been created by Wilde with very little sympathy, interest or inspiration and, as a character, lacks energy as he is carried away by the rush of incidents and plot. Prince Paul's evil or cynical motivations, however, interested Wilde much more, so that the play's villain turns out to be esthetically its hero, or at least its most complex and interesting or attractive character. However crudely, Prince Paul illustrates, for the first time in Wilde's writings, an attitude toward life which is symptomatic of the dandyism which Wilde affected on his return from America, when he began to abandon Ruskinian esthetics, with their naive Socialism, in favor of a more sophisticated philosophy of art and life. Many of Prince Paul's paradoxes are repeated in Wilde's later works; and they are typical of the wilful philosophy of the dandy who, reputedly, "would stab his best friend for the sake of writing an epigram on his tombstone, or experiencing a new sensation," who prides himself on his unpopularity and desires but a frivolous immortality, "to invent a new sauce." The politics of Disraeli's *Vivian Grey*, for all their complexity of intrigue, had been no more sociologically or ideologically motivated than those of *Vera*; and purely personal ambitions or resentments seem to have provided much of the energy of a whole class of Romantic heroes, from Julien Sorel or Vivian Grey to Prince Paul.

In *The Duchess of Padua*, the villainous and tyrannical Duke, for all his ostentatious cruelty and haughtiness, seems likewise intended to be esthetically attractive; he has the magnificent pride of the *uomo di virtu* tyrants of Renaissance Senecan tragedy, where the most evil characters were intended to inspire admiration and horror, and also much of the macabre cynicism of the dandy. But the play's hero, however much we may prefer him on ethical grounds, seems characterless and esthetically less interesting, a virtuous pawn in an intricate chess-game of plot. Nor do these ambiguities make the plot or the characters of either play any more complex or convincing; they merely illustrate the indecision of the author, and an ambivalence, in political, ethical or esthetic matters, which was not peculiar to Wilde.

The standards which govern evaluations in the various branches of axiology, in esthetics, ethics and politics or economics, have always tended to be closely connected or confused, so that a thinker's attitudes, in one branch of axiology, frequently affect his evaluations in another branch. The standards of ethics and esthetics, and of ethics and politics, in particular, have now been, for close on two centuries, almost inextricably commingled in most philosophies. The idea of progress, for instance, was first formulated in early eighteenth-century controversies about the relative excellence of the ancients and the moderns in the arts. The Humanists of an earlier age had assumed that all the ancients, as artists, were absolutely superior to the moderns; but a closer study of ancient literature had then revealed that some writers of later antiquity had been more decorous, according to courtly Renaissance standards, than most earlier writers, so that it began to be argued, in the Sixteenth Century, that Seneca or Virgil were more decorous than Euripides or Homer. In the first two decades of the Eighteenth Century, a group of members of the French Académie went one step further and argued that classical French literature had improved on the standards of antiquity, so that there was clear proof of progress in the arts. From this controversy, the idea of progress soon spread to other fields and, with relative standards accepted in esthetics, it began to be argued that ethics too had improved with Christianity, that modern science, since Copernicus, Galileo and Descartes, was more true than that of antiquity, or that modern man was better in all respects than man had been in antiquity.

Progress, it seemed, was still to be expected in every field. And thus was born the notion of the perfectibility of the common man as a citizen rather than as a soul to be saved, so that the whole structure of absolute monarchy, with its aristocratic élites, was undermined when the French *Querelle des Anciens et des Modernes*, an esthetic controversy, spread to other branches of evaluation until, within a few decades, it had affected politics too. In the French Revolution, this idea of progress and of the perfectibility of the citizen was first put to the test.

The intellectual élite of France had, for over half a century, taken part in these various controversies; and most artists or thinkers of any talent had either helped formulate the theory of progress or were ardent believers in it. When the millennium of the common man revealed itself first as a Reign of Terror, then as an age, after the Directoire, of ruthless power-politics and unprincipled economic expansion and exploitation, many of these artists and thinkers became, in their disappointment, what Cyril Connolly has now called, in *The Unquiet Grave*, "liberals without belief in progress, Democrats who despise their fellow-men, Pagans who still live by Christian morals, Intellectuals who cannot find the intellect sufficient,— unsatisfied Materialists."

Chamfort, French moralist and dandy, was one of the first victims of this *mal du siècle*, when the Revolution, in which he believed, began to persecute him as it did its enemies. And Connolly describes his frightening predicament, now far more common, as "that of the revolutionary whose manners and way of life are attached to the old régime, whose ideals and loyalties belong to the new, and who by a kind of courageous exhibitionism is impelled to tell the truth about both, and to expect from the commissars of King Stork the same admiration for his sallies as . . . from the courtiers of King Log."

In the eyes of such disappointed men, the tyrannicide, once so superb in his self-sacrifice, now seemed more intolerant of criticism than the tyrant who had proved weak enough to be overthrown. And in the new democracy of the common man, with all its shoddy expedients and brutal pent-up hate, the vanished tyrant began to appear, in retrospect, superb at least in his absolute contempt for all the cheap values of an order that was too often demagogic disorder or the amateurish tyranny of the self-made leader. The new champions of ethics, from Robespierre on, were proving themselves blind to beauty and unethical too; at least some beauty and elegance and magnanimity could be discerned in the old representatives of evil.

In this dilemma, the dandies of the early Nineteenth Century began to formulate an attitude toward life which would maintain the best of the old aristocratic values of medieval chivalry and of the Humanistic *uomo di virtu*, but without any encouragement from the society in which they lived. In what Baudelaire called "the pleasure of astonishing and the proud satisfaction of never being astonished," the faith of the dandy thus became "the cult of one's self," something "spiritual and stoical, but never vulgar," in fact "a kind of religion" in which an élite, "a new aristocracy founded on the most precious faculties, the most indestructible, and on heavenly gifts that work and money cannot grant," expressed its "opposition and revolt." As an "unemployed Hercules" in an age that had no use for him, while "the rising tide of democracy drowns day by day these last representatives of human pride," the dandy represented, in Baudelaire's eyes, "the last flash of heroism in an age of decadence." In a century whose arts and morals seemed ever more corrupt, the elect of dandyism were the saints of a new religion of art and of living without faith in anything beyond secular salvation or damnation.

Rejecting the vulgarly bourgeois idea of progress and all its political corollaries, most of the dandies of the later Nineteenth Century withdrew completely from politics. Some of them later repented and became involved, together with the more dogmatic Catholics who had never accepted the principles of the Age of Enlightenment or with dispossessed or apprehensive aristocrats who could not forget "the worst excesses of the French Revolution," in a political reaction which was but the negation of liberalism and an inversion of the idea of progress. But Oscar Wilde, in the political writings of his maturity, transcended the dandy's dilemma and resolved its conflicting elements in a new political anarchism where the ideal government, as in Saint Augustine's *City of God*, would be a state where no governing is necessary. In *The Soul of Man under Socialism*, Wilde thus describes his "New Hellenism" as a "new Individualism," an ideal state whose slaves, since all great civilizations require slaves to perform their more unpleasant but still necessary tasks, would be soulless machines. Nor would this mechanization lead to any of the painful unemployment which is now the macabre caricature of leisure. Instead of competing against man, machines would only serve him, and thus allow every citizen to enjoy, at last, all the dandy's privileges of leisure, freedom and culture, much as the citizens of Saint Augustine's *City of God* would all enjoy the virtues of sanctity, or as all would be poets in the ideal culture which haunted the dreams of Rimbaud or Lautréamont.

Biographical accidents, psychological factors or intellectual influences may have made it easier for Wilde to transcend as he did the political dilemma which had frustrated so many of the dandies of his century. Born a few decades later than most of the men whose creed of elegance Baudelaire and Barbey d'Aurevilly had formulated, Wilde may have been more conscious of the increasing social tension and of the need to resolve its conflicts. His homosexuality, in some respects a strangely democratic passion which often flouts class distinctions in a fantastic fraternization of those who are economically most and least privileged, may also have given him a more emotionally sympathetic understanding of the resentments and aspirations of "the white-smocked carters, with their pleasant sunburned faces and coarse curly hair." Liberal beliefs may have been more deeply rooted in him as a result of his Irish upbringing and his mother's life-long devotion to revolutionary causes; and the more strict philosophical and dialectical habits of his thought, as a student of Plato and Aristotle, may have impelled him to examine his opinions with enough care to develop them fully and formally. In any case, Wilde abandoned the political opinions of the typical dandy to the ironical self-portraits contained in his stories and comedies, to Lord Goring in *An Ideal Husband* or Lord Henry in *The Picture of Dorian Gray*; for himself he reserved, in *The Soul of Man under Socialism*, in a few of his book-reviews and in *The Critic as Artist*, the expression of views that seem less irresponsible and, however Utopian, posit an ideal toward which society should strive, though perhaps only with the hope of improving itself without ever attaining its aim.

Of George Sand's philosophy of social regeneration, Wilde once wrote that, "if it is Utopian, then Utopia must be added to our geographies"; and in discussing the possibilities of political reform in England and the Empire, he stated that "England will never be civilized until she has added Utopia to her dominions." In an age whose political theorists are nearly all content with merely practical and attainable ends, the planner of an ideal society is likely to be scorned or ignored; we tend to forget how many practical benefits we now owe to the Humanistic planners of Utopias, to Campanella, Saint Thomas More or Rabelais, whose clearly stated ideals stimulated the political thinking of two centuries until ways of attaining some of their aims were formulated in the Age of Enlightenment. In many respects, Wilde's political thought has thus been sadly neglected by those who could most profit by it; and *The Soul of Man under Socialism* contains many an observation that should be useful to those who now pretend to be planning full employment and "a more vital democracy."

Wilde's ideal Socialism would release all citizens from "the sordid necessity of living for others which . . . presses so hardly upon almost everybody." Our sympathy for the sufferings of others too often prompts us now to waste our energies in seeking remedies which, without curing the disease, merely prolong it. We keep the poor alive, or we seek to amuse them, whereas "the proper aim is to try and reconstruct society on such a basis that poverty will be impossible"; and Lothair, in Disraeli's novel, had similarly wanted to devote his life to "the extinction of pauperism." But charity,

Wilde insists, merely degrades and demoralizes; and it is immoral and unfair "to use private property in order to alleviate the horrible evils that result from the institution of private property," which disposes of the theories of Lothair, who intended to devote his vast private income to his task. Wilde's new Socialism, by leading to Individualism, proposes to change all this. But Wilde is aware, like Proudhon, of the dangers of Statism; and he insists that his Socialism must avoid being Authoritarian because, if governments are "armed with economic power as they are now with political power, if . . . we are to have Industrial Tyrannies, then the last state of man will be worse than the first."

Private property, Wilde concedes as did Proudhon too, allows at least a large privileged class to develop some individualism; from its ranks come our great poets, supreme artists, great men of science and fine critical spirits, men of culture, "real men" who have "realised themselves, and in whom all Humanity gains a partial realisation." It is Wilde's aim, through Socialism, to extend this privileged class until it embraces the whole human community.

Wilde dismisses briefly the merely material advantages of Socialism, under which "each member of the society will share in the general prosperity" and be secure from seasonal unemployment and the other parodies of leisure with which the poor are now afflicted. After all, Wilde knows that he is no economist, and his topic is man's soul rather than his body. He admits that the individualism generated under conditions of private property is not perfect, and that the poor now have many virtues. But both the possession of property, under our present institutions, and the lack of it are "demoralising," so that the abolition of private property would remove the cause of the moral imperfections of both rich and poor. The virtues generally ascribed to the poor are, moreover, none too glorious. The best among the poor are never grateful for charity, but remain ungrateful, discontented, disobedient and rebellious, thus retaining real virtues which indicate, in healthy protest, their true personalities as individuals, and which, throughout history, have been the source of all progress. As for those poor who are generally deemed virtuous because they are thrifty, grateful, content and obedient, they have but come to terms with their enemy and sold their birth-right "for a very bad pottage." And because misery and poverty degrade and paralyze, "no class is ever really conscious of its suffering," so that agitators, presumably from another class, "are absolutely necessary," to arouse men to an understanding of their plights as the Abolitionists of Boston once roused the slaves of the South. The true perfection of man lies indeed, not in what he owns, Wilde insists, but in what he is. Under our present system, most "personalities" are obliged to waste "half their strength as rebels"; but "the true personality of man" should express itself "naturally and simply," without any such discord, without having to argue or dispute or prove. In this "Christ-like life," each man would be "perfectly and absolutely himself," for "all imitation in morals and life is wrong." And because "Art is the most intense mode of individualism," and "the unique result of a unique temperament," Wilde affirms that the citizens of his ideal state must all be artists for whose "unique temperaments" the most suitable form of government would be "no government at all." Opposing Plato, who banished all poets from his Republic, Wilde would have none but poets in his; but he agrees unconsciously with the Taoist philosopher Lia Yu Kou or Lieh-Tzu who tells similarly (Book II, 1) how the legendary Lord of The Yellow Earth, China's earliest recorded ruler in a mythical Golden Age, once worried about the problem of good government and found no rational solution until, in a dream, he discovered the Utopia of Hua Su, where there was no government at all, so that the problem had been solved by the intuition of a dream rather than by any arguing or reasoning.

All known modes of government are indeed failures, and Wilde concludes that the only purpose of the State is to accomplish merely useful tasks, "to organise labour, and be the manufacturer and distributor of necessary commodities," so as to leave the individual citizen free to "make what is beautiful." But the duties which Wilde thus entrusted to the State were precisely those which Her Majesty's Government, with its faith in free enterprise, had never yet considered.

In the course of his argument, Wilde digresses frequently to criticize, much as Bulwer Lytton had done some sixty years earlier in *Pelham*, the British public's stupid attitudes toward art; and in these criticisms lie the flaws of Wilde's argument. Wilde's preoccupation with Art blinds him, it seems, to the existence of the other forms of pure individualism which he had considered at the beginning of his essay: the great man of science, for instance, is forgotten soon after the essay's start and not included among the citizens of the final Utopia. In analyzing the follies of the public which has "an insatiable curiosity to know everything, except what is worth knowing" and should "try to make itself artistic" instead of expecting Art to "try to be popular," Wilde fails moreover to indicate how this erring public is suddenly to be redeemed of its vices, when his Utopia is established. He never explains how, having disposed of the tyranny of the Prince, "who tyrannises over the body" and of that of the Pope, "who tyrannises over the soul," we are to dispose of that of the People, "who tyrannises over soul and body alike" and, in doing this, yet avoid establishing, instead of the New Individualism, but another version of what Plato's philosopher's state has generally been understood to be. Might not Wilde's artist merely be another benevolent despot who would impose on the public what he thinks best rather than what Caliban's "blind, deaf, hideous, grotesque, tragic, amusing, serious, and obscene" authority demands?

In this last flaw resides, however, the very Utopian nature of Wilde's argument: "A practical scheme is either a scheme that is already in existence, or a scheme that could be carried out under existing conditions." And Wilde objects "exactly" to these "existing conditions," so that he is not concerned with any apparently practical steps toward the attainment of his ideal, but assumes that it can be attained if these conditions are first abolished. Then the public, the mass of mankind, would transcend its present follies and attain, in a sort of universal Pentecost, the "New Individualism" which would emanate from all of us as soon as we are released from the conditions which now demoralize and degrade us.

The purely transcendental nature of Wilde's ideal state, which must be considered more as an ideal toward which man should constantly strive than as something attainable within the span of history, is explained even more clearly in his review ("A Chinese Sage") of the English translation, by H. A. Giles, of the political, religious and moral works of the Taoist philosopher Chuang Tzu, and in the political part of the second dialogue of *The Critic as Artist.*

In his Taoist philosophy of self-culture and self-improvement, Chuang Tzu neglects the whole classical conception, common to

Greek thought and to Confucianism, of man as a "political animal," a citizen who has duties toward his family, toward other citizens or toward the state. Instead, Chuang Tzu develops an Evangelistic and almost solipsistic doctrine of the individual's duty to become "a perfect man" who "does nothing beyond gazing at the universe." He believes in "leaving mankind alone" because "there has never been such a thing as governing mankind" and "all modes of government are wrong," all more or less bad rather than good; and Chuang Tzu's politics thus become identical with an ethic of the mere individual. By pointing out "the uselessness of all useful things" and proclaiming a creed of the identity of contraries and of inaction, he indeed denies the validity of the very concept of social living and reduces the Good Society to the proportions of a group of good individuals who all happen to be leading the good life together. The object of Chuang Tzu's good life is not only, as in a Freudian analysis, "to get rid of self-consciousness," but also "to become the unconscious vehicle of a higher illumination." Nor can this ideal ever be attained through any education, any teaching or learning: "it is a spiritual state to which he who lives in harmony with nature attains."

If all men were perfect, there would be no need, in the infinity where the parallels of politics and ethics meet, for any laws, any policing, any government. And no education, no policing, no governing can lead the imperfect citizens of any finite state toward this perfection of moral and intellectual virtues which can be attained only through the efforts of each individual. In the political parts of *The Critic as Artist*, Wilde merely repeats, though in somewhat different terms, the basic principles of his new non-political politics of the citizen who is perfect as a man. "It is to do nothing that the elect exist," Wilde concludes: "Action is limited and relative. Unlimited and absolute is the vision of him who sits at ease and watches, who walks in loneliness and in dreams." But this perfection of the Augustinian elect is not necessarily a privilege of the few: "The development of the race depends on the development of the individual." To educate oneself rather than others, to ignore society whose security "lies in custom and unconscious instinct" so that the basis of its stability, as a healthy organism, "is the complete absence of any intelligence among its members," these should be the aims of one and all, until each individual is perfect and all are of the elect.

The Ethics of the Dandy

In *Pen, Pencil, and Poison*, Wilde reports that Wainewright, when a friend reproached him with the murder of his young sister-in-law, shrugged his shoulders and said: "Yes, it was a dreadful thing to do, but she had very thick ankles." And in *The Picture of Dorian Gray*, when Sibyl Vane kills herself after Dorian has abandoned her, Lord Henry says to the young dandy: "Things like that make a man fashionable in Paris. But in London people are so prejudiced." Cynical remarks of this type appear frequently in the works of Wilde's maturity, in his fiction, critical writings, and comedies; they enliven the dialogue of his characters, and the morally surprising or shocking quality of their wit and paradox contributed very much to the popularity of Wilde's comedies and to their author's success, in society, as the brilliant conversational heir to the tradition of Brummel and Byron, Disraeli and Bulwer Lytton. Unwisely, Wilde published a collection of such apophthegms, *Phrases and Philosophies for the Use of the Young*, in the first issue of *The Chameleon*, a questionable Oxford undergraduate periodical published by a friend of Lord Alfred Douglas. But the standards of Regency society no longer prevailed, and Queen Victoria's ruling middle class was not amused, so that these remarks, though no more immoral than many that could be found in the early novels of Her Majesty's dear Dizzy, were cited in court, at the time of Wilde's trials, as evidence of his immorality.

In Wilde's comedies and conversation, such remarks generally served to illustrate ironically the more shocking attitudes of the perfect dandy who, like Bulwer Lytton's Henry Pelham, should be "impertinent enough to be the rage." Barbey d'Aurevilly, in his essay on Dandyism, had written that the dandy, "while still respecting the conventions, plays with them," and that he seeks "to produce the unexpected . . . which could not logically be anticipated by those accustomed to the yoke of rules," so that, "in a hypocritical society, weary of its hypocrisy," he always "tries to create surprise by remaining impassive." As a "great mystificator," the dandy does not necessarily express his own beliefs, if he entertains any. He seeks rather to produce an effect, often Satanic, sinister or macabre, as that of Brummel or Byron in real life or, in fiction, of Melmoth the Wanderer or of Glanville in *Pelham*; and Barbey d'Aurevilly pointed out that silence is also a way of producing an effect and that, "for dandies, as for women, to *seem* is to *be*."

To deduce a consistent ethics from Wilde's paradoxical remarks on moral problems would thus be a thankless task. Too often, Wilde's wit serves but the negative purpose of a *Pseudodoxia Epidemica* which reveals, sometimes by the device of parody, the follies and ambiguities of popular opinions and prejudices rather than any of the author's own opinions. The development of Wilde's ethical beliefs can be traced, however, through the changing tone of his writings. His moral philosophy developed, closely patterned on his politics, from a naive and unworldly Romantic idealism, first expressed in the poems of the Oxford period, through a somewhat ostentatious display of dandified cynicism and paradox, satirized in the dialogue of the comedies, to a transcendental philosophy where ethics, having already absorbed politics, is absorbed in turn by esthetics, and Wilde's mature ethical beliefs, as his political and his esthetic, are to be found in the critical dialogues and the more important essays that he wrote at the height of his middle period, before he began to commercialize his talents and caricature these beliefs and tastes in his comedies.

But the accidents of Wilde's private life and sexual habits often conflicted with his ethical beliefs. In his anxiety, Wilde would then offer esthetic justifications for his actions; and, from real life, this evasion of the issue was easily reflected in his writings, so that his whole philosophy of values, in its transit through ethics, became at times tainted with the blind folly of a tragic hero. Wilde's politics, on this side of his ethics, remained clear, consistent and philosophically valid, though ultimately dependent on an ethic whose principles were still to be formulated elsewhere in full. When these principles are finally deduced from the body of Wilde's mature writings, they are found to be similarly dependent on those of his esthetics; but the relationship of his ethics to his esthetics fails to be always as clear as that of his politics to his ethics. Between ethics and esthetics, personal problems intervened, passions which perverted Wilde's thought until it often lost its dispassionate clarity or consistency and was blurred by his habit of concealing the unpleasant truth from both the world and himself.

In esthetics, one of Wilde's fundamental principles was his "recognition of the primary importance of the sensuous element in art," his insistence on a "love of art for art's sake." In one of his earlier critical writings, the preface to Rennell Rodd's volume of poems, Wilde calls this insistence "a departure definite and different and decisive . . . from the teaching of Mr. Ruskin." Throughout his life, Wilde continued to maintain that ethical standards are irrelevant in esthetic evaluation. He reaffirmed it in his book-reviews whenever the occasion arose; it is one of the main principles of the discussion of esthetics in *The Soul of Man under Socialism*; it is implied in *The Portrait of Mr. W. H.*, and is one of the chief doctrines of Lord Henry in *The Picture of Dorian Gray*; it is one of the main arguments of the two critical dialogues, and is the theme of many of the satirical paradoxes in the comedies: "The amount of women in London who flirt with their own husbands is perfectly scandalous. It looks so bad."

Ruskin, wrote Wilde, "would judge of a picture by the amount of noble moral ideas it expresses," much as Sir Joshua Reynolds did in his discussions of the Sublime. But, to Wilde and his friends, "the channels by which all noble work in painting can touch, and does touch, the soul are not those of truths of life or metaphysical truths"; to the apostles of the "English Renaissance" which was the topic of Wilde's lectures in America, "the rule of art is not the rule of morals." Even in court, at the time of his trial, Wilde still declared, with the temerity of religious conviction and in the face of an easily antagonized jury, that "there is no such thing as an immoral book"; and he affirmed that *The Priest and the Acolyte*, Bloxham's sexually and religiously Satanic or perverse story which, published in *The Chameleon*, had erroneously been attributed to him, was but "badly written," in fact that it "violated every artistic canon of beauty" rather than any moral principle.

Though he constantly strove to make others accept, at least in their evaluations of art, this clear distinction between art and nature or life, Wilde was more and more often forced, by his inability to justify ethically some of his own actions, whether in his own eyes or in those of others, to have recourse to esthetic arguments in ethical matters. Unwilling to admit that some of his actions were evil, or unable to prove that they were good, he would seek to justify them on grounds of beauty; and he thus helped to spread, especially toward the end of his life, the confusion of ethics and esthetics, in ethical matters, which he so fervently sought to clarify to esthetical matters.

This confusion is not yet apparent in Wilde's early poems, though they are full of the same vague Romanticism, in their ethics, as in their politics. A "fond Hellenic dream," in *Ravenna*, haunts Wilde with memories of a sinless and conscienceless Golden Age, drowning "all thoughts of black Gethsemane," much as in Swinburne's *Laus Veneris*. In the mildly pagan and conventionally pastoral Eden which is the setting of *The Burden of Itys, Athanasia, Endymion, Charmides, Panthea,* and *Humanitad*, it sometimes seems to Wilde as if "The woods are filled with gods we fancied dead"; but the poet is impatient both of the constraining moral limitations of Christianity and of the guilt that he feels in expressing his discontent. "Surely there was a time," he exclaims in *Hélas*, when he might have expressed himself without guilt:

> I did but touch the honey of romance—
> And must I lose a soul's inheritance?

The poems which celebrate Wilde's discovery of Italy express just as inconclusive a longing for the untroubled certitudes of Catholicism. Throughout his life, in moments of great crisis as, for instance, when he was released from prison, Wilde always returned to the notion of converting to the one religion whose pomp, "bright with purple and with gold," would delight him esthetically while its clear-cut moral philosophy would at the same time relieve him of the anguish of indecisions and decisions. Finally, in *De Profundis*, the transfigured artist, in prison, longed for the beauties of nature which, in *The Decay of Lying*, he had once compared so unfavorably to those of art; and, in his despair, he turned to a Franciscan

Catholicism, no longer for the beauty of any liturgy, but because he had come to think of this church, through the years, as the only one. Throughout the early poems, Wilde's moral problems remained comfortably theoretical and vague. In *Taedium Vitae*, the poet could still unhesitatingly renounce all that he knew of worldly pleasures for a life of ascetic contemplation, of the undisturbed *ataraxia* which the Epicurean philosophers of antiquity identified as the only pleasure. In those years, there was indeed much truth in Wilde's answer to a Washington reporter's prying questions, in 1882, about his private life: "I wish I had one." All Wilde's biographers agree on one point: throughout his years of school and university and until after his return from America, he remained a remarkably pure young man, both in deed and in speech, and seemed content with the spectacular Platonicism of such passions as the one that he dotingly advertised for Lily Langtry, the "Lily of love, pure and inviolate," of his rather Pre-Raphaelitic poem *The New Helen*.

Some qualms, concerning the true nature of his desires, must have disturbed Wilde in these more care-free years. He thus began composing *The Sphinx* when hardly had, for him, "Some twenty summers cast their green," that is to say when he was probably still an Oxford student; but it is significant that he did not complete this poem or publish it until 1894. During all those years, as he carefully analyzed and expressed his fantasies while re-writing his poem, Wilde slowly came to realize, like Ishmael in *Moby Dick*, that "those same things that would have repelled most others, were the very magnets that thus drew me." And Wilde banished the Sphinx and its suggestions from his poetry, which was always chastened by the same oral inhibitions as his speech, if not from his life.

Had Wilde been content to explore evil at the intellectual or esthetic level from which he generally banished it, he might have discovered the value of the work of art as a check to action. In the alternative of art, Wilde might have purged the passions or sublimated the forces which drove him to self-degradation and self-destruction. But he shunned the *catharsis* of art, perhaps because he feared the exposure of publication in an age which confused art with life; and he chose the course of life, with its false promise of a privacy maintained in the confused crowds of the modern metropolis.

Though banished from his poetry, the Sphinx that, unlike woman, was not "without a secret" thus continued to haunt Wilde in his life and even in some of his later writings. Half woman and half beast, it was but the more bestial reincarnation, under the spell of conscious guilt, of another hybrid monster, half girl and half boy, that had earlier haunted the poet's more innocent fancies. In *Madonna Mia*, a Pre-Raphaelitic vision of a Florentine Platonism such as that of Marsilio Ficino whom Wilde praised extravagantly in *The Portrait of Mr. W. H.*, he had lovingly described, in his youth, an idealized portrait of Lily Langtry, "A lily-girl not made for this world's pain." But *Wasted Days*, among Wilde's uncollected poems, reveals to us an earlier version of the same poem, a description of a picture, "painted by Miss V. T.," though of "A fair slim boy, not made for this world's pain," most of whose features are the same as those of the lily-girl of *Madonna Mia*. Boy or girl, however, the object of esthetic love, in such ornate pictorial or poetic fantasies, does not necessarily reveal any biographical or psychological facts about the artist. *Wasted Days*, or the description of the young Greek boy's beauty in *Charmides*, though they might prejudice an undiscriminating jury of the artist's political equals, offer us little valid evidence concerning Wilde's love-life. Had not Tennyson published *In Memoriam*, where he avoided the physical descriptions which distinguish the "fleshly" poetry of Swinburne or Wilde, but where he frankly or naively explored his despair at the loss of "The human-hearted man I loved" and even compared himself, in his bereavement, to a girl whose lover has been killed? At the crude level of biographical interpretation, *Charmides* is less compromisng than *In Memoriam*; the emotions of Wilde's poem are more general and less personal, and its descriptiveness is that of an established art-style which the poet shared with Pater, Rossetti, Swinburne, and other writers and artists whose love-life it did not necessarily reflect.

The average juror of today, together with the majority of our unread readers, is no longer aware of the great tradition which, ever since classical antiquity, has inspired artists to describe, with an esthetic passion and sensuality that emulate and simulate those of physical love, objects which they need not love physically in their lives as citizens. From Homer and the poetry of the Greek Anthology or of Catallus, a tradition of such art had been kept alive, by studiously enthusiastic imitators of the ancients, even in dark ages and benighted lands where homosexuality was punished with death, in the writings of such saintly medieval Churchmen as the Latin poet Hilarius or of such doughty knights as Sir Thomas Mallory, who were haunted by the unearthly beauty of a Galahad. Surely, these men would have avoided such topics had they believed them unequivocally sinful or compromising.

Wilde was conscious of this artistic tradition; it is the theme of *The Portrait of Mr. W. H.*, and it is again illustrated in the painter Halward's "curious artistic idolatry" for Dorian Gray. But Wilde knew too that he lived "in an age when men treat art as if it were meant to be a form of autobiography," as it is still believed to be by the majority of critics and biographers. It had thus been left to the late Nineteenth Century, the heyday of all the corrupt politics, phony art and sham ethics of a smug and smutty middle class, and to know-all jurors or amateur psychoanalysts in our own day, to decide that art is but a big Freudian slip, and that the artist is apparently the only type of neurotic who is not compelled to conceal, in his conscious utterances and his art, the nature of his real ailment; yet Edmund Bergler's psychoanalytical studies now indicate that the artist is generally compelled to simulate, in his art, less disturbing ills than those that his strategy conceals. The popular fallacy of the biographical explicitness of art has, however, made many artists so self-conscious, especially since Wilde's trial, that they either prudently avoid all incriminating topics or rashly flaunt them in an orgy of confession.

The general problem of the autobiographical value of art is too complex to be solved here; its solution is often to be found, in particular cases, rather in small details that recur almost accidentally or unconsciously in an artist's work than in the broad lines of what is consciously or misleadingly displayed. Oscar Wilde was thus attracted to an Alfred Douglas or a Dorian Gray, for instance, not so much by the boy's mere sex, it seems, as by his selfishly pleasure-seeking narcissism, by the petulance, the *moues* and the pouting that Lord Alfred shared with Dorian, with Mr. W. H., with the Infanta of the fairy tale, with Salome and with all those who, by their love, bring unhappiness, destruction and death to the lover whose inexorable sense of guilt demands that he pay such a heavy price for the happiness of being loved. In *Sexual Inversion*, Havelock

Ellis, who illustrates many of the tastes and beliefs of Wilde's era, quotes the case of a homosexual who generally recognized other homosexuals by their pouting lower lip; together with a preference for green, as a color, this belief or taste apparently belonged to the fin-de-siècle style of emotional or sexual esthetic which, like more conscious fads and fashions, changes from generation to generation. In Wilde's writings and life, the artistically trivial detail of the pouting lip is certainly a significant theme; it recurs as frequently, in both, as the writer's belief that "each man kills the thing he loves." In his own life, Wilde indeed sought love only from those whose love could be proved by their destroying him, only from creatures who, like Salome, were soulless dolls, "set in motion by some pitiless destiny," if not by the poet's own self-destructive impulses.

In his more mature works, and in his life too, Wilde thus began, at first unconsciously, to pursue the " shameful secret guests" of his vision of the Sphinx, though he had banished the beast from his poetry. And while the source of much of his poetry seemed to run dry, Wilde's prose still flowed freely for a while, and his whole life seemed to surge toward a high tide of sensual pleasure. He indeed pretended, both to himself and to the world at large, that his pleasures were still but the pursuit of the innocent and sexlessly hermaphroditic ideals of his earlier poetry; and this was the lie that distorted his whole ethic. Wilde began to justify, on esthetic grounds, actions which he did not have the courage to justify on the ethical grounds of a less Victorian or more revolutionary philosophy. In *The Portrait of Mr. W. H.*, for instance, the whole moral and emotional problem of Shakespeare's passion for the young actor to whom he is supposed to have dedicated the *Sonnets* is veiled in discussion of this relationship's esthetic significance, and in the superficially iconoclastic hints that the "divine" Shakespeare was not free from sin, or that his "immoral" homosexuality might have been the source of his inspiration. In *The Picture of Dorian Gray*, no direct reference is made to the actual forms of Dorian's debaucheries and depravities, except when he unintentionally causes Sybil's death or later murders Basil; and the hero's wickedness is thus veiled in much esthetic theory concerning the value of experiencing sensation, as if Dorian's emotional life were but an extension, in realms of passion or of sex, of his sensuously handling and collecting ancient coins, rare perfumes or rich brocades. In his own life, when entertaining male prostitutes and potential blackmailers to elegant champagne suppers, Wilde often pretended, to himself and to his esthete friends, that these corrupt boys, for whom his passion could be but physical, were the modern counterparts of the young Greek athletes, beautiful and good, whose beauty and moral or intellectual virtues had once inspired the love of a Socrates. Even in court, Wilde thus denied, at first, his homosexuality; and his counsel had accepted to handle the case only on the assumption that the Marquis of Queensberry's remarks about Wilde were slanderous and that the poet, in proclaiming his innocence, was speaking the truth. But as the evidence quoted in court by Queensberry's counsel piled up, it became impossible for Wilde, in the face of all the underworld witnesses who testified to having had sexual relations with him, to deny his homosexuality any longer. And then Wilde sought refuge in a transcendental interpretation of "The love that dare not speak its name," proclaiming to the packed court that his love for Lord Alfred Douglas was "such a great affection of an elder for a younger man as there was between David and Jonathan, such as Plato made the very basis of his philosophy, and such as you find in the sonnets of Michelangelo and Shakespeare . . . that deep spiritual affection that is as pure as it is perfect" and that "dictates and pervades great works of art."

But this fine and blameless ideal of a relationship between an "elder man" who "has intellect" and a "younger man" who "has all the joy, hope and glamour of life before him" was a far cry from the reality of Wilde's debauchery with male prostitutes, from the unbridled sensuality and endless quarreling of his love for Lord Alfred, and from the orgies in which they had indulged together, as André Gide reports, in Algiers. Because Wilde could not bear to admit the moral degradation of his own life, he began to seek esthetic justifications for it, long before his trial, in which few "guilty" men, in any case, would have had the courage to admit the "crime"; and Wilde thus tried to persuade himself, except in moments of frankness and lucidity of which some of his unpublished letters give ample evidence, that his unorthodox love-life was the expression of an ideal that was esthetically more lofty and pure than that of the majority of his contemporaries.

Not that Wilde's way of life was unequivocally immoral. Many a heterosexual dandy's equally salacious relations with servant-girls and street-walkers had been generally condoned. But such a way of life requires, to justify it, an ethic which Wilde had neglected to formulate. He might have chosen an ethic of predestination or of privation of grace, such as the Jansenist ethic of Racine's *Phèdre* or of the Abbé Prévost's *Manon Lescaut*; or one of self-degradation and redemption through a descent into the deepest inferno of sin, such as that of Baudelaire or Dostoievsky; or a Satanic or Dionysiac ethics, as in the philosophies of Stirner or Nietzsche at their lower levels of interpretation, where the expression of a super-man's personality justifies in itself all its possible effects on others; or a cynically hedonistic or a mechanistic or materialist ethics, such as that which the Marquis de Sade had borrowed from the *Système de la Nature* of Holbach and illustrated in the philosophic novel *Aline et Valcour*, where pleasure or self-knowledge through pleasure are all that matters.

Wilde himself, in his more philosophical moments, must indeed have been aware of the need to formulate an ethic more consistent with his way of life. In different works or different parts of one work, he thus proposes different approaches to the one problem of good and evil. Long before his bitter experience of Nemesis in his trial and imprisonment, from which he returned with *The Ballad of Reading Gaol* and its prudential moral of predestination according to which "Each man kills the thing he loves," and with the penitent admissions of folly or guilt of *De Profundis*, Wilde had made Salome cause beloved Iokanaan's death and narcissistic Dorian Gray kill himself. But Basil Halward, in the novel, had also proposed the more conventional ethics of moral duty, and Lord Henry had expounded a third ethics, which Dorian had interpreted as that of cynical hedonism. The novel thus illustrates, with its merely prudential moral, Basil's standards, Lord Henry's doctrines and Dorian's interpretation of them, four approaches to the one problem of good and evil. For Lord Henry's doctrine should more properly be interpreted as the Taoist ethics of quietistic self-knowledge and *ataraxia* which, as Cyril Connolly writes, is "so dangerously exposed to the corruption of laisser-faire," indeed to Dorian's misinterpretation of it, because "no one can achieve Serenity until the glare of passion is past the meridian," and because "there is no certain way of preserving chastity against the will of the body." But Wilde returned to Lord Henry's ethical doctrines in *The Critic as Artist*; and the dialogue, which required no plot or moral such as that of the novel, clearly advocates inaction and contemplation as the sole aim of "the elect."

In a letter to an inquiring reader, Wilde once paraphrased Flaubert's remark that *"Madame Bovary, c'est moi,"* and explained that, in his own novel, Lord Henry, Basil Halward, and Dorian Gray were all three self-portraits. Many critics or readers had already identified either Lord Henry or Dorian as portraits of the author; but no critic has yet recognized, in Basil, the embodiment of the conscience which later prevented Wilde from escaping abroad to avoid arrest at the time of his trials, and which then dictated to him many of the penitent passages of *De Profundis*. It might thus be argued psychoanalytically that Dorian, Wilde's Id, is driven to self-inflicted death by his misinterpreting, in too selfishly literal a manner, the doctrines of beauty and pleasure which are preached by Lord Henry, Wilde's Ego; and that Basil, the author's Super-Ego, is killed when his warnings and reproaches might frustrate Dorian in his unbridled pursuit of sensual satisfactions.

Taoists and Freudians alike would affirm that none of these three characters was right, or that all three are right in that rightness resides in achieving harmony among them, through self-knowledge, and in transcending, by contemplative inaction, the strife of their conflicting purposes. In *The Critic as Artist*, Wilde affirms, as a disciple of Chuang Tzu, that "it is to do nothing that the elect exist. Action is limited and relative. Unlimited and absolute is the vision of him who sits at ease and watches, who walks in loneliness and dreams." But the true sage or dandy can attain this inaction only by transcending both desire and conscience; and he is always in danger of eliminating a particular desire or temptation merely by succumbing to it and stifling his conscience, as Dorian did, or by denying and repressing desire as Basil Halward did. Lord Henry's destiny, in the novel, is indeed easy: he is disturbed neither by desires nor by conscience, and he is able to achieve inaction mainly because he is never tempted, it seems, to act.

In his tragedies, Racine had illustrated analogous problems in conflicts of will and predestination, of passion and duty, all within one character. In his novel, Wilde required a different character to illustrate each of three attitudes toward the problem of good and evil; his doctrine of character or of the passions, it seems, was too simple to allow any great conflicts of passion within one character. In his lyrical dramas, Wilde had already presented a type of tragic character whose single ruling passion often excluded all other passions and even assumed the nature of an obsession. Such a character's experience, as a constant, of the infinite variables of life almost necessarily took the form of sensations of the body, more physical or psychological than moral, rather than of passions of the soul. But sensations can only stimulate or weary, whereas experience of passions may purge, educate or otherwise transform a character which, if constant, allows of no such change. Hence the emphasis, in Wilde's life and in many of his works, on sensations and pleasure: the elect, as a constant, has no need of works or of passions.

But the philosophers of antiquity, with a few exceptions among the more mundane hedonists, had all emphasized, in their various ethics or philosophies of character, some doctrine of the passions and of their purging, or of self-restraint and of the education or shaping of character. Nor did they identify, as Wilde tended to do, the passions of the soul with physical sensations, love with sexual pleasure or with the orgasm, for instance. Experience of a passion was not considered, in antiquity, identical with experience of any particular sensation toward which this passion might tend; and a passion, as an experience, could have a moral value which did not necessarily reside in the sensations which might accompany it. Wilde's hedonism would thus have appeared, to representative Hellenic thinkers, a veritable heresy; and in nineteenth-century England, such a misinterpretation of Greek thought, on the part of the apostle of a "New Hellenism," can be traced only to the very confusing influences of both Christian Puritanism and the experimental or empirical science of the Enlightenment. Christianity, by placing such strong taboos on physical sensation, had indeed led many agnostics who resented these taboos to identify the freedom of pagan philosophy with a cynically mundane hedonism, a true Sybaritism; and empiricism, by emphasizing the importance of individual experience of the physical world rather than of metaphysical or ethical thought or tradition, had led, beginning with the age of Descartes, to a confusion of the passions of the soul with the sensations of the body.

The earlier Romantics, until the age of Byron, had still distinguished, to some extent, passions from sensations. When they emphasized the value of experience, they thus thought in terms of passionate living, such as Byron's fighting for Greek freedom, rather than in terms of physical sensations, such as those of Byron's love-life; and their more energetically virile or soldierly attitudes are well illustrated by Alfieri, Stendhal, Byron or Lermontov, in real life, and by Fabrice del Dongo or Henry Pelham in fiction. Only later, as opportunities for experience of the passions became more scarce in the staid and peaceful bourgeois world of the middle of the century, did Romantic esthetes and dandies begin to adopt, in the age of Musset or of Chopin, more languorous attitudes toward life, and to advocate extreme or rare sensations such as addiction to drugs or to sexual perversions.

In these attitudes of the consumptive esthete or of the dandy who has become a "tired hedonist," the influence of new theories in the natural sciences can be detected. Among German Romantics, for instance, the use of opium had first been adopted as part of an ethical or an esthetic creed in the circle of Schelling, who had studied medicine at Bamberg under Roschlaub, from whom Novalis also obtained the miracle-drug. The drug was believed to liberate the unconscious and, by releasing one from the artificial constraints of society or of the individual, to unite one with nature, the supreme good. From Germany, "opium-eating" spread, with German Romantic thought, to the England of Coleridge and De Quincey, who advocated the drug for the treatment of tuberculosis, and to the France of Nerval and Baudelaire; and one need but read the works of Havelock Ellis to see how much German medical and psychological science contributed, throughout the Nineteenth Century, to our understanding of sex and of its anomalies, and must have thus influenced German Romantic thought and then the Romantic thought of England and of France.

In his more consciously philosophic writings, such as the dialogues or *The Soul of Man under Socialism*, Wilde was fully aware of the deep ethical implications of his hedonism. An ethic dominated by an esthetic where art must please or charm leads necessarily to an affirmation of the supremacy of art over behavior or nature; and this implies conclusions diametrically opposed to those that we generally associate with Greek thought. In *The Decay of Lying*, Wilde thus agrees with Plato when he insists that art begins where "lying" or the imitation of nature begin, but opposes him in affirming that "lying" is a virtue, not a vice, of poetry; and in *The Soul of Man under Socialism*, the Utopia which Wilde proposes will be wholly peopled by those artists or liars whom Plato excludes from his Republic. The dandy's transcendental anarchism thus extends from Wilde's politics to his ethics, whenever the latter is systematically formulated; and the good life, in *The Decay of Lying* and *The Critic as Artist*, resolves itself as the "Christlike" life of the pure individual who, by being an esthetically perfect artist, is also an ethically perfect man and a politically perfect citizen.

Wilde thus re-examined, in the light of a trenchant new critique of political, ethical and esthetic values, all the accepted doctrines of past and present, whether pagan or Christian. His "New Hellenism" was no mere return to the opinions and standards of Greek thought and art, but a frontal attack on all Western beliefs, from the age of Plato to our own; and he made this attack with the dialectical weapons of Greek thought, though to reach different conclusions. In one of his *Poems in Prose, The Doer of Good*, he indicates that evil may arise from a good action; in a fairy-tale, *The Young King*, he affirms that "out of the luxury of the rich cometh the life of the poor," out of an evil, some good. The charitable actions of *The Happy Prince* or of *The Young King* are thus beautiful rather than good gestures, and true good resides in the contemplative and beautiful *ataraxia* or inaction of the artist rather than in any action which is generally believed to be good.

In his defense of art, Wilde turned their own weapons against the heirs to the tradition of the Byzantine Iconoclasts who had attacked and destroyed all art as pagan or evil; and Wilde attacked all that was considered Christian or good as being morally ambivalent and just as pregnant with evil consequences as with good. In *Pen, Pencil, and Poison*, Wilde thus set out to prove that an artist's failure to be great is in no way due to his morally evil character, so that Wainewright's being a criminal made him no better and no worse as an artist. In *The Portrait of Mr. W. H.*, he attacked the traditional and unthinking respect for the sacrosanct figure of Shakespeare: The National Bard of the *Sonnets* is no worse as a poet for having perhaps been homosexual and "immoral." In some of his *Poems in Prose*, Wilde was even led, by his inverted Iconoclasm, to parody the *Bible*, that other sacred text of the Philistines, and to propose parables whose moral is diametrically opposed to those of the Gospels.

But one cannot honestly claim, as some fascists have done in democratic nations, protection under the laws of a system whose principles one flouts habitually in word or in deed. Wilde himself admitted finally the folly or dishonesty of his dual standards when he wrote, in *De Profundis*, that "the one disgraceful, unpardonable and to all time contemptible action" of his life had been to allow himself "to appeal to society for help and protection," when the Marquis of Queensberry attacked him, and thus to invoke the very laws in defiance of which he himself had lived and against which he had always protested. In the same confession, Wilde also faced at last the full moral implications of his sexual habits; expanding his earlier esthetics of mere "charm" or "delight," he thus admitted the nature of the relationship of horror or evil to beauty. As an excuse for associating with them, Wilde had once compared Clibborn, Atkins or other male prostitutes, who later reappeared to testify against him at his trial, to Charmides or Alcibiades. But they had really been to him, Wilde now wrote, "the brightest of gilded snakes," whose "poison was part of their perfection" and whose mixture of beauty and evil rather than of beauty and good had actually fascinated him.

By extending his definition of beauty, as a source of emotion, to include fear or horror as well as more generally pleasurable emotions, Wilde broadened the scope of his whole philosophy. In *De Profundis*, he thus admitted that the best of his earlier works, such as *Salome* or some of the fairy-tales or the dialogues of *Intentions*, had already revealed, at times, insights into this ambivalent relationship of pleasure to pain, of good to evil, and of sorrow to joy; but Wilde insisted that his new wisdom must lead to an entirely new art, and went on to discuss, in a new tone, the esthetics of Christianity as a perfect expression of the Romantic spirit. In this argument, Wilde identified ethics absolutely with esthetics and the beautiful absolutely with the good. But his new conception of the beautiful or good, as in some of the writings of Baudelaire or of some Catholic mystics, included "sin and suffering as being in themselves beautiful holy things and modes of perfection," stations in the progress of the predestined who must necessarily see the light of salvation in the darkness of sin. The perfect man was thus, as in *The Soul of Man under Socialism,* the true individualist who lives "completely for the moment" and is saved from his sins "simply for beautiful moments" in his life.

It is in the confessions of *De Profundis,* with their fragmentary elements of a new philosophy which is not yet fully formulated, that the resolution of Wilde's dualism of word and deed or of art and life or nature is finally resolved. In this new philosophy, whose scope had been vastly broadened by the artist's bitter sufferings, one finds an extension of Wilde's earlier paradoxical doctrine rather than a revision or a refutation of it. Here, the paradox at last attains its loftiest meaning as a device that symbolizes the simultaneous being and no-being of all things. To a classicist such as Settembrini in *The Magic Mountain,* the paradox is, of course, "the poisonous flower of quietism." But in Wilde's ultimate doctrine of the identity of contraries, where everything both is and is not, the paradox as a truth falls at last under its own law: that which is true is also not true, the contraries which are identical are also not identical, and the truth which is expressed in the paradox is also not expressed in it. In the writings of his maturity, Wilde had repeatedly emphasized his belief, for instance, that art is not autobiography; but *De Profundis* now illustrated the new truth that autobiography is art and that "Art begins where Imitation ends," that is to say that nature is art and that art is either mere nature, on this side of imitation, or else, beyond imitation, is a transfigured nature.

Plato had similarly faced, in his dialectic, an ultimate paradox. When he condemned all art as imitation or "lying," he yet condemned it in a dialogue whose Socrates was but a "lying" imitation of the real Socrates. The philosopher who had condemned all art and the artist who had condemned all but art thus finally agreed, in an abandonment or a transcending of art if not in a condemnation of it. Plato condescended to imitate nature, in the art of his dialogues, only in order to communicate his doctrines; and Wilde returned to art, in *De Profundis* or *The Ballad of Reading Gaol*, only to testify that art, in his expanded philosophy, was now identical with nature as was literature with autobiography or esthetics with ethics.

But the new art to which such a philosophical attitude must lead is ambiguous in its very nature, even more ambiguous than all other art: it is no longer an alternative to action but has become action itself, and is therefore subject to both ethical and esthetic critiques. Such an art can no longer be content with the forms of imitation but must adopt those of nature and of life. Plato's *Letters*, especially the Seventh, if they can be considered authentic, would thus illustrate the philosopher's ultimate doctrine more directly or explicitly than the art of any of his dialogues; and, in Wilde's case, *De Profundis* and the conversations and letters of his last years* would represent the ultimate flowering of both his art and his life. But various editors have cut or tampered with the text of *De Profundis*, Wilde's conversation is always more or less reliably reported, and we still have no complete or reliably edited corpus of Wilde's letters; so that his ultimate doctrine and the art of his last years cannot yet be subjected to a thoroughly critical examination. This very impotence of criticism is also a symbol, in a way, of the ambivalence of an art which has become completely identified with nature and, in the case of Wilde's last years, with the physical as well as the moral weaknesses of nature, with the disease that finally killed the artist and with all the details of a life that must now be examined and judged according to a diversity of standards, esthetic, moral, biographical or medical, none of which is in itself adequate or sufficient as a critique of the whole man.

But Wilde has thus made the ethics of the dandy, as in Baudelaire's essay on dandyism, finally become almost a theology. Transcending the degradations and follies of his own past and present, the dandy had been hypostatized or transfigured in eternity by the "beautiful moments" of his life which are recorded in *De Profundis*; and he is now analogous to the great artist, the great hero or the

---

*For further discussion of Wilde's letters, see "Wilde's Art in His Life," a new chapter on page 173 prepared for this edition.

saint, as Baudelaire suggested, and perhaps even identical with them and also with the supreme revolutionary. He has accepted his sorrows and sufferings as the just price or punishment for his pleasures and his sins. For art, he now has but one use, as in Rimbaud's *A Season in Hell*, which is to correct or complement his past, whether as an imperfect artist or as a sinner. In *De Profundis*, Wilde therefore writes: "I remember that I was sitting in the Dock on the occasion of my last trial listening to Lockwood's appalling denunciation of me . . . and being sickened with horror at what I heard, suddenly it occurred to me, *How splendid it would be, if I was saying all this about myself.*" In this ultimate testament which is both autobiography and art, imitation and nature, Wilde does at last say it all about himself. But the religion of art in which he thereby proves himself a saint is only analogous to Christianity in general or to Catholicism in particular, not identical with them. No Christian theologian can ever condone the artist's fundamental heresies, and the Fowlies and Fumets and other Catholic apologists of literature only fool themselves and their readers when they try, as they have already done for Baudelaire or Rimbaud, to interpret such a transfiguration as that of a Catholic saint. Their apologetics can lead, in such cases, but to one conclusion: that all the roads of genius lead inevitably to Rome, if the artist's prestige can serve the purposes of the Church, so that those of us who are blessed with genius need never trouble ourselves with trying to avoid sin.

The Esthetics of the Dandy

It is difficult to evaluate Oscar Wilde's art, and especially his poetics, exclusively in terms of philosophical principles and not historically too. His writings, like those of any artist, represent a contribution to an existing controversy whose very history determined many of Wilde's arguments and principles. The leading

English poets of the Nineteenth Century, long before Wilde's advent, had generally rejected many of the basic critical principles which had been inherited from antiquity. Surviving almost unconsciously in the poetry of the Middle Ages, these principles had been slowly elucidated by Humanist poets and critics till they had been formulated again in full by the artists of our Augustan Age, when poets had known once more, with some clarity, what they sought to achieve, and all conscious artists had again possessed an intelligent and intelligible doctrine of art. But writers of the last decades of the Eighteenth Century had begun to lose faith in such rational and accessible perfections, and to lean toward theories of the sublime or of a chance felicity of expression rather than of a more studied imitation of known perfections, or toward doctrines of self-expression or invention rather than of the imitation of nature or of art. The emotional vagueness of the thought of Shelley and Keats had then propagated further doubts concerning the validity of rational principles for the appreciation of a poem's conceptual content; Wordsworth, and his friends, had finally formulated a new poetics of self-expression, in the preface to the *Lyrical Ballads*, which is best illustrated in Wordsworth's *Prelude*. The subject of this poem is indeed never objectified in any myth or central incident, as in Dante's *Divine Comedy* or Gray's *Elegy*; it is "the Growth of a Poet's mind," as if the very poem were the record of it, like that contained in a section of a tree-trunk, and not an imitation of this growth in terms of art. Only Byron, among the innovators of that age, had protested against these poetics, on grounds of taste and common sense, and ridiculed the new preference, illustrated most clearly in much of Southey's poetry and in *The Idiot Boy*, for even the stupidities of nature as opposed to the rational selectiveness of art.

Blake had already written that "Rome and Greece swept Art into their maw and destroyed it," but Tennyson was perhaps the first major English poet to throw overboard nearly all the classical principles of both narrative and dramatic poetry. In *Maud*, a "monodrama" or dramatic poem to be recited by one actor, though on no known stage, the poet expects his listener or reader to gather the plot or action only from a few obscure hints that are scattered at random in the course of lamentations and lyrical outbursts occasioned by these happenings. *Maud* is almost devoid of what Aristotle would have called plot or character, the latter being represented at a minimum in the drama's one actor, so that little or no argument or *dianoia* is possible; and the poem has likewise been stripped of the musical element of ancient tragedy's chorus, and of all the element of staging or spectacle. As a drama, *Maud* had thus been reduced to lyrical poetry and must subsist on its diction and on what elements of plot, character, or spectacle this diction may suggest.

But can such a poem still claim legitimately to be dramatic? And on what principles had the poet decided to break with all traditions and practices of drama? What did he understand the nature and purpose of his art to be?

The poetry of Robert Browning illustrates another aspect of the same problem, though other illustrations of it can be found in other works of Tennyson, such as *Rizpah*, and even in his more traditional verse-dramas. Browning's *The Ring and the Book* has generally been acclaimed as "the triumph of the dramatic monologue," a genre to which belong a large number of his more important poems: *Johannes Agricola in Meditation, Rudel to the Lady of Tripoli, My Last Duchess, The Laboratory, The Confessional, The Glove, The Italian in England, Pictor Ignotus, The Bishop Orders his Tomb at Saint Praxed's Church, Saul, Fra Lippo Lippi, Andrea del Sarto, Abt Vogler, Caliban upon Setebos*, etc. The plot of *The Ring and the Book* is derived, Browning explains, from a collection of old legal documents which have been transformed by the poet's imagination into something that can be shaped into a work of art much as a baser metal is mixed in an alloy that can be shaped into a beautiful ring. This plot is dramatic, in a novelistic or historically picturesque way, and illustrates violent conflicts of interest and murderous passions in a colorful age; but it offers little possibility of a tragic *catharsis* and no truly dramatic resolution. Instead of shaping this material into a tragedy, Browning has therefore told his story in a series of dramatic monologues where various characters reveal themselves, the plot, and their own views concerning the plot. But if there is no real drama, why these monologues which employ the rhetoric proper to dramatic speeches, though without their purpose, that of determining the actions and replies of the other characters as well as the spectator's responses? Why did Browning thus complicate his telling of the plot, with so many repetitions of one sort or another, when a straightforward narrative poem might have told it all with a more striking economy and more intelligibly? And why, in the metrics of this and of so much Victorian poetry of a quasi-narrative nature, these adaptations of Shakespearean blank verse rather than of Miltonic verse?

The answer to these questions is that the monodrama or dramatic monologue, with its greater lyrical freedom, seemed to offer the Victorian poet more scope for self-expression. He needed but to "put himself in the shoes" of an imagined character and then think aloud; but, the price of this was the loss of many of the devices of a more complex narrative or dramatic poetry which had helped poets of the past to communicate to readers or listeners, whether by rational exposition or by the more mysterious means of *catharsis*, the basic moral values of the actions which they imitated in their art. Among modern poems, W. H. Auden's *The Sea and the Mirror* and Delmore Schwartz' *Coriolanus* indicate that the Victorian genre of the poetic drama which is no drama offers the same advantages to the poets of our own age.

Romantic poets such as Tennyson or Browning were indeed bent upon changing the course of all Western literature, from the age of Homer to that of Byron. The great Victorian poets did not hesitate, in their devotion to self-expression, to be stupid rather than intelligent, if the use of intelligence threatened to halt the flow of their "sublime" thoughts and verse; and a surprising percentage of their verse was sublime or at least melodious, colorful or interesting. Only habit, it seems, or some sense of how their public still expected poetry to sound or to look, yet restrained them from scrapping other hindrances too, such as rhyme, scansion or poetic diction. Browning did abandon, however, the rhyming verse of his earlier monologues in favor of an ever looser dramatic blank-verse; and he relaxed his diction ever further as the years went by. Logically, many nine-teenth-century poets were ripe for the dictaphone or the trance-like utterances of the medium. They had confused artistic expression with natural expression, much as Trissino had done, in the Six-teenth Century, when he explained that he had chosen blank-verse as the medium of his tragedy because it approximated the natural expression of characters in real life more than rhyme did. But might not the prose diary, such as that of Pepys or Amiel, or the form of Confessions, such as those of Rousseau, have served Wordsworth's purpose better than the very artificial scansion and diction of his *Prelude?* If the artist's self-expression must approximate natural expression as closely as possible, then his art must reject all the devices of artistic verisimilitude in favor of the forms of factual "truth" and of natural thought or speech.

With such models before them, many lesser Victorian poets rushed, with the enthusiasm of Gadarene swine, to their final annihilation as artists. It is difficult for us now to imagine any less intelligent poetry than that of Thomas Edward Brown, except the verses published in our mass-produced "pulps" and "slicks," or those of a few neo-primitivists of the schools of William Carlos Williams or of Kenneth Patchen:

> A garden is a lovesome thing, God wot!
> Rose plot,
>   Fringed pool,
> Ferned grot—
>   The veriest school
>   Of peace; and yet the fool
> Contends that God is not—
> Not God? In gardens! When the eve is cool?

But this poem is still included, as a significant example of Victorian poetic achievement, in most anthologies; and its author was much admired and praised by W. E. Henley and by other representative poets and critics of his age. Had these poets and critics preserved any clear notion of the real nature of poetry and of criticism?

Even some of the better poems of Dante Gabriel Rossetti make us likewise wonder on what principles the poet indulged in his affected refrains, inspired by an amateurish knowledge of medieval poetic forms and repeated *ad nauseam* in poems which, by their very length, already tended to be tedious:

> It was Lilith, the wife of Adam;
>   (*Eden's bower's in flower.*)
> Not a drop of her blood was human,
> But she was made like a soft sweet woman.
>
> Lilith stood on the skirts of Eden;
>   (*And O the bower and the hour!*)
> She was the first that thence was driven,
> With her was hell and with Eve was heaven.

In the ear of the snake said Lilith:
(*Eden's bower's in flower.*)
To thee I come when the rest is over;
A snake was I when thou wast my lover.

I was the fairest snake in Eden;
(*And O the bower and the hour!*)
By the earth's will, new form and feature
Made me a wife for the earth's new creature.

There are forty-nine such stanzas to this poetic vision whose ideas
and imagery belong almost to the world of William Blake and
might well deserve the praise of a Surrealist. But the poem is marred
by many fads and affectations of Pre-Raphaelitic estheticism; of
these, the most offensive is certainly the use of the two refrains, each
of which appears twenty-five times.

As we now read some Victorian poems, with their incredible
refrains, we are often tempted to burlesque them:

Then said she, "I am very dreary,
He will not come," she said;
She wept, "I am aweary, aweary
O God, that I was dead!"

But "Ave Mary," made she moan,
And "Ave Mary," night and morn,
And "Ah," she sang, "to be all alone,
To live forgotten, and love forlorn."

This is one of the aspects of Tennyson's poetry that Lewis Carrol
and even the Laureate's friend Edward Lear burlesqued; and it is
significant that the age which produced so much solemn poetry was
also peculiarly fruitful, from *The Ingoldsby Legends* and Canning's
Needy Knifegrinder to *The Hunting of the Snark* or the limericks of
Edward Lear, in all sorts of nonsense-verse which ridiculed, and
continue to ridicule in our own age, the devices and tones of any
loftier poetry. Even to contemporaries, much of the loftier poetry of
Tennyson, however subtle its metrics and rhymes, however fine its
imagery and melodious its verse, must have seemed erratic, in its
rational content; indeed it could not avoid, as it rushed blindly
ahead in self-expression, tripping every once in a while over some

utter absurdity. Some of the serious poetry of the Victorian era is thus barely distinguishable from its nonsense-rhyming:

> Are you ready for your steeple-chase
> Lorraine, Lorraine, Loree?
> Barum, Barum, Barum, Barum,
> Barum, Barum, Baree.

These are the opening lines of a poem in which Charles Kingsley told, in 1874, the sad tale of the victim of a brutal husband's cruelties. It is one of the later and more mature poems of the much respected artistic exponent of "muscular Christianity" and "Christian Socialism"; and young Oscar Wilde was then on the eve of writing his first poems and of entering a world of Victorian letters whose most eminent and respected artists had nearly all tried desperately to rid themselves of any devices or principles which might guard them against absurdity or stupidity.

Though the much vaunted perfection of Tennyson's rhythms and rhymes does not always outweigh the nonsensical nature of their content, Elizabeth Barrett Browning on the other hand had admired and imitated, in her youth, the more rational poetry of Pope, and had retained in later years an epigrammatic brilliance of which G. K. Chesterton wrote: "These epigrams . . . were never so true as when they turned on one of the two or three pivots on which contemporary Europe was really turning. She is by far the most European of all the English poets of that age; all of them . . . look local beside her. Tennyson and the rest are nowhere!" But if the rational content of Elizabeth Barrett Browning's poetry is so far superior and more generally acceptable or less local in its appeal, her versification often betrays a curious insensitivity to the nature and purpose of her poetic forms. Leaving aside its title's absurd meaning, in later American idiom, *The Dead Pan* illustrates, in its metrics and rhymes, how crude and slovenly the author's art could be. Hellas, tell us; silence, islands; roll on, the sun; glory, evermore thee; flowing, slow in; know from, snow-storm; for us, glories, these are but a few of the more offensive rhymes of her poem. They are of a kind which we are prepared to accept, for their very drollery, in a satirical poem such as Butler's *Hudibras*, but for which Pope and all critics since his age have condemned the metaphysical poet Edward

Benlowes, simply because such rhymes tend to introduce, into a loftier poetry, an inappropriate element of the comic or of the grotesque.

In much of their poetry, we now find good reason to wonder what Tennyson, Rossetti or Swinburne really thought they were doing, and whether Robert Browning and his wife, when her work betrayed his metrical influence, or Walt Whitman were not really, as George Santayana has pointed out, the apostles of a new barbarism or Philistinism rather than representatives, in their age, of the eternally civilizing mission of art. Only Matthew Arnold and William Morris, among the major poets, seem to have constantly maintained art's traditional principles in their age; and their work, though never or hardly ever absurd or stupid, now seems more dull or diffuse, at times, than that of many equally gifted poets of earlier ages whose critical standards were more classical.

Significantly, young Wilde listed William Morris, in one of his poems, among his masters, together with Rossetti, whose more foolish devices he avoided; and he proclaimed, in critical articles, his admiration for Elizabeth Barrett Browning, whose crude metrics and rhymes he never imitated. Wilde claimed no other eminent Victorian poets as his masters, however much he may have borrowed ideas or minor devices of diction from Tennyson or Swinburne. His other immediate masters were Byron and Keats, champions of an art which was intellectually less irresponsible than that of Tennyson or Browning, and Shelley and Wordsworth who, though already committed to somewhat uncritical doctrines of self-expression, had not yet pursued them as far as later poets did. It is curious, however, that Matthew Arnold should not be mentioned in the invocations where, in his earlier poetry and criticism, Wilde lists the votaries of the Spirit of Beauty whom he would emulate; but Wilde calls Matthew Arnold, in his later criticism, "one whose gracious memory we all revere, and the music of whose pipe once lured Proserpina from her Sicilian fields, and made those white feet stir, and not in vain, the Cumnor cowslips."

Of Robert Browning, Wilde wrote, in *The Critic as Artist*, that he was "inarticulate" and "incoherent," but "great." Browning "did not survey," and "but rarely . . . could sing." Wilde also noted that Browning "passed not from emotion to form, but from thought to chaos. . . . It was not thought that fascinated him, but rather the processes by which the thought moves," so that "the method by which the fool arrives at his folly was as dear to him as the ultimate wisdom of the wise." And Wilde concluded that language, in Browning's opinion, was "an incomplete instrument of expression," and that "Meredith is a prose Browning, and so is Browning."

Of Tennyson, Wilde wrote nothing. Of Swinburne, he wrote that the author of *Songs and Ballads* had "once set his age on fire by a volume of very perfect and very poisonous poetry," but had turned revolutionary and pantheistic, invented Marie Stuart and inflicted Bothwell on his readers, then "retired to the nursery" whence he had finally returned "extremely patriotic" and with "a strong affection for the Tory party." Though "a great poet," Swinburne thus had "his limitations . . . the entire lack of a sense of limit. His song is nearly always too loud for his subject" and "conceals rather than reveals." In fact, Wilde's review of *Songs and Ballads*, with its unpleasant truths and its ironical banter about "the ballad in sham Scotch dialect," was politely and wittily contemptuous.

Wilde's knowledge and appreciation of Latin and Greek literatures and of their critical principles had probably allowed him, from the very start, to develop more intellectually critical tastes than most Victorian poets of an earlier generation. Some of these poets, such as Swinburne, had indeed been as familiar with their classics as Wilde; but their masters, at Oxford or Cambridge, had not always been equal, in some respects, to the more methodical scholars under whom Wilde had later studied, so that Romantic theory and tradition, among poets of the generation of Tennyson or that of Swinburne, had still blurred much of their sense of the intellectual's or the artist's obligations. Not that these obligations imply, as Yvor Winters now acrimoniously suggests, any stern ethics of art, but simply that it is the duty of any performer, if he appears before his public, to reveal his art at its very best, its most beautiful and most intelligent, so that the artist who is not prepared to accept this obligation actually forfeits his right to a public.

The estheticism of Wilde's youth was a doctrine of tastes, however, rather than of clearly coordinated principles. It is true that the poet proclaimed, in his very earliest critical work, his belief in the need to distinguish clearly between art and morality, esthetics and ethics, the beautiful and the good. Of how little this basic principle was generally understood, even many years later, we have evidence in a preface which John Cowper Powys wrote for a reprint of *The Soul of Man under Socialism*: "It may be an 'absurd idea' that art should deal with the abysmal difference between good and evil," suggests Powys, answering Wilde's plea against the absurdity of ethical appreciations of art, but "you cannot separate art from moral valuations, because . . . if art is to 'justify the universe as an aesthetic spectacle' . . . it must recognize, as an inevitable part of the material with which it has to deal, these very customs, traditions and habits from which . . . it turns away with rebellious distaste." Yet Wilde fully understood that the moral problems of life are one of the necessary ingredients of art, without which we can have no drama or fiction, and very little poetry; he insisted, however, that the whole could not be judged according to standards which are peculiar to the part, and that a whole work of art whose "moral" part might be "immoral" was not necessarily a bad work of art, since esthetic standards alone are applicable to the whole.

The tastes and principles of Wilde's youth are rather clearly illustrated in his poems; and he expounded them as a doctrine in the lectures which he delivered in America, in the preface to Rennell Rodd's *Rose Leaf and Apple Leaf,* and in several early essays and book-reviews. In an ugly age, Wilde believed that art should not imitate life but art, even the art of less ugly ages. Hence, his neo-antique manner and his Pre-Raphaelitism; hence, too, his interest in the William Morris theories of interior decoration, in the lilies and sun-flowers of a nature which had remained beautiful enough to be imitated by art. But Wilde associated beauty, in much of the thought of his youth and even of his maturity, too closely with pleasure and happiness rather than with sorrow or pain, and generally with more hedonistic pleasures or happiness than with any transcendental conception of pleasure as *ataraxia* or contemplation. He thus defined the purpose of art as to charm or delight. Though unable to avoid sorrow or pain as subject matter in much of his poetry, of his lyrical drama or his poetical prose, Wilde yet insisted, in his preface to Rennell Rodd's poems, that "the most joyous poet is not he who sows the desolate highways of this world with the barren seed of laughter, but he who makes his sorrow most musical, this indeed being the meaning of joy in art." This joy of art, Wilde believed, came from what Keats called the "sensuous life of verse"; it was an "incommunicable element of artistic delight . . . the element of song in the singing, made so pleasurable to us by that wonder of motion which often has its origin in mere musical impulse, and in painting is to be sought for, from the subject never, but from the pictorial charm only—the scheme and symphony of the colour, the satisfying beauty of the design."

The purpose of art, in the esthetics of Wilde's youth, was thus to gild the pill of sorrow and pain so as to disguise, under a surface of pleasure, all unavoidable unpleasantness. As a disciple of Walter Pater or of Théophile Gautier rather than of Ruskin, Wilde objected to the latter's belief that "perfection of workmanship seems but the symbol of pride." Nor were Pater's tastes and beliefs the appanage only of immoral or decadent esthetes in Victorian England. Even such a stern moralist as Mark Rutherford, whose novels describe the respectable lives of religious dissenters, was in some ideas one of Pater's disciples. Cardew's tale of Charmides, in Rutherford's *Catherine Furze*, thus has much in common, in spite of its Christian moral—which can also be derived, moreover, from *Marius the Epicurean*—with the more fleshly poetry of Wilde's Oxford years. But to Wilde and his friends of the English Renaissance, "the transcendental spirit is alien of the spirit of art," so that a painting, for instance, has no "spiritual message or meaning" but is "a beautifully coloured surface, nothing more, and affects us by no suggestion stolen from philosophy, no pathos pilfered from literature, no feeling filched from a poet, but by its own incommunicable artistic essence—by that selection of truth which we call style, and that relation of values which is the draughtsmanship of painting, by the whole quality of the workmanship, the arabesque of the design, the splendour of the colour. . . ."

Nor should a work of art merely conform to the fashions and "aesthetic demands" of its age; it should also bear "the impress of a distinct individuality" and must therefore "rest on the two poles of personality and perfection." But we attain a "pure and passionate devotion to Art" only "when the harsh reality of life has too suddenly wounded" us, "marring" our youth "with discontent or sorrow"; and "one's real life," in art, is "often the life that one does not lead," so that the personality revealed in art need not be the same as the personality revealed by the artist in his life. The artist's true "sincerity and constancy" express themselves in "plastic perfection of execution," and the artist cannot be constant to "any definite rule or system of living." But a "purely artistic effect," Wilde affirms, "cannot be described in terms of intellectual criticism." The element of personality, in art, is presumably something sublime; it transcends all merely intellectual cognition and, in the scene of nature which the artist describes, there need not necessarily be "much beauty." The artist's personality, like "some little breaking gleam of broken light" may thus "lend to the grey field and the silent barn a secret and a mystery that were hardly their own," so as to "transfigure for one exquisite moment" the world of nature.

From Pater, Gautier or Whistler, Wilde had indeed inherited tastes and principles which allowed him to progress, beyond the moralizing and often maudlin esthetics of Ruskin or the Pre-Raphaelites, to a doctrine of art for art's sake which respected only perfection of workmanship and allowed no ethical considerations to interfere in its appreciations. But such an emphasis on the display of individual skills rather than on the imitation or attainment of more generally accepted models or ideals soon leads to a conception of art as sheer virtuosity or showmanship, that of Paganini on the concert platform, of Edgar Allan Poe or Thédore de Banville in the perfection of metrics and rhymes exhibited by their *funambulesque* poetry, that of William Harnett in the *trompe l'oeuil* magic of his paintings. The impassive artist who makes such a brilliant display of his art before an astounded audience must rely on a great variety of technical devices, many of which belong to the realm of nature or life rather than to that of art, much as the dandy, in his life, relies on many of the devices of art; and in this confusion of art and life, the artist becomes a dandy whose life illustrates esthetic beliefs whereas ethics are excluded from his art and almost from his life too. Théophile Gautier's flamboyant waistcoats, Baudelaire's impeccable austerity of dress, Whistler's conversational wit, Wilde's own sartorial extravagances and paradoxical remarks, all these are illustrations, in the artist's life, of his esthetic beliefs. Barbey d'Aurevilly's and Baudelaire's studies of dandyism are thus important contributions to the esthetics of art for art's sake, just as Théophile Gautier's poems, quoted in *Dorian Gray*, or Huysmans' *A Rebours* became gospels of taste among decadent dandies; and when, much as Lautréamont did in the preface to his unwritten later poems, Wilde distorted proverbs and commonplaces, when he said that "divorces are made in Heaven" or discussed "washing one's clean linen in public," he was but practicing, at the level of social conversation, the theories of the sublime, as an element of sheer surprise or of dazzling virtuosity, which he illustrated more loftily in the descriptive prose-poetry of *Salome* or of *A House of Pomegranates*.

On his return from his American lecture-tour, Wilde began to revise his esthetics considerably in their application to dandyism, especially when his sojourn in Paris offered him an opportunity to become better acquainted with the theories and works of French artists and writers of later Romanticism or of the *Parnassien* or *Décadent* groups. Bulwer Lytton, some sixty years earlier, had similarly returned from Paris to write *Pelham*, where he bitterly criticized English tastes in food and dress and formulated fastidiously austere principles of sartorial elegance. And Vivian Grey, with his new recipes for punch, had made the gourmet's art one of the tools of his social success.

In the more flamboyant years of his youth, Wilde's affectations and effeminacies, his knee-breeches and lilies, had violated many of the canons of Bulwer Lytton's or Baudelaire's taste. When he returned from Paris, Wilde began, however, to preach more consistent or fastidious doctrines of sartorial or culinary elegance. Nor was his dandified interest in sauces and embroideries of the same order as Frau Stoehr's absurd boast, in *The Magic Mountain*, that she knew the recipes for twenty-eight sauces to be served with fish. Whereas Frau Stoehr intended to display in this manner the full splendor of her refinement and knowledge of art or of the world, the dandified artist, in his essays on food or dress, intends only to illustrate the application of his lofty esthetic principles to the more lowly arts of civilized living. When he reviewed "Wanderer's" *Dinners and Dishes* for *The Pall Mall Gazette* or discussed dress in *The Woman's World*, Wilde was thus preaching his estheticism to readers who might not be interested in loftier applications of it and to a Frau Stoehr who might be able to understand its importance only if he stated it in the language of the linen-room or the kitchen. But even in trivial matters, Wilde was careful to argue as wittily and seriously, as convincingly and learnedly, as when he reviewed *The*

Renaissance in Italy, by John Addington Symonds, or the William Morris translations of Homer; and in these intellectually more lofty reviews, Wilde displayed an unusually scholarly knowledge of Italian History or of Greek, and did not hesitate, for instance, to correct the great historian's errors of detail.

Of the artist's or the dandy's self-assurance in his meticulous perfecting of detail, Wilde gave an ironical illustration in the self-satire of *An Ideal Husband,* where Lord Goring, "The first well-dressed philosopher in the history of thought," explains to his man-servant, while discussing a buttonhole, that "fashion is what one wears oneself . . . what is unfashionable is what other people wear . . . just as vulgarity is simply the conduct of other people" and "falsehoods the truths of other people." Elaborating on the French moralist's *"Décidément, je n'aime pas les autres,"* Lord Goring thus concludes that "other people are quite dreadful," that "the only possible society is oneself" and that "to love oneself is the beginning of a life-long romance." Returning to the problem of the button-hole, Goring then decides to wear "for the future a more trivial buttonhole . . . on Thursday evenings"; and the man-servant explains that a loss in the florist's family may account "for the lack of triviality your lordship complains of" in the offending buttonhole.

No loss in the artist's own family, no private sorrow or woe, according to such a doctrine, must ever mar the relatively trivial details of an impassive art whose perfection of form should make even sorrow seem beautiful and delightful, though with a beauty that is superimposed rather than distilled from the sorrow itself. But a paradox resides in this very doctrine, which encourages the skill of the individual while discouraging the expression of his emotions, so that the artist must reveal his personality and express himself in the very devices which have been elaborated to conceal emotions and self. Self-expression is thus identified with all the perfections of form which the spokesmen of self-expression had once wanted to reject as hindrances to the expression of self. Wilde's two critical dialogues, *The Decay of Lying* and *The Critic as Artist,* accordingly set out to disprove most of the beliefs of the Romantics, but without reverting to the doctrines of classicism.

The general aim of both dialogues is to restore to art its traditional intellectual suzerainty over nature, and to criticism, its rights as a form of creativeness or of self-expression. Romantic rhapsodists and estheticians, from the age of Thomas Gray or Rousseau to that of Walter Scott, had so rapturously praised the beauties of nature that every Philistine of Wilde's generation felt himself entitled, once he had viewed the Swiss Alps or the Trossachs, to demand of art that it merely reproduce nature or life with the photographic truth of Frith's *Women and Children First* or his *Saint Pancras Station.* Wilde therefore shocked the journalists of America and their smug readers by declaring that the Atlantic Ocean had disappointed him, that Niagara Falls were not beautiful and that nature was "a bore." Similarly, Romantic theory had so consistently praised uncritical artistic self-expression to the detriment of any criticism of art, that Wilde now felt the need to reassert the creative nature of criticism as perhaps the intellectually loftiest form of art and of self-expression.

In his dialogues, Wilde thus returned to many of the fundamental problems of Western poetics or esthetics and to the great controversial issues of ancient criticism. To the Greek critical spirit, wrote Wilde, "we owe the epic, the lyric, the entire drama in every one of its developments, including burlesque, the idyll, the romantic novel, the novel of adventure, the essay, the dialogue, the oration, the lecture, the epigram . . . in fact, everything, except the sonnet, American journalism . . . and the ballad in sham Scotch dialect." In discussing again the esthetic problems which Plato had investigated, Wilde therefore tried to formulate his own dissenting opinions, whenever he disagreed with the Platonic Socrates, in the same dialectical form of the philosophical dialogue. But in a brief appeciation of Aristotle's *Poetics, The Critic as Artist* praises unreservedly this "One perfect little work of aesthetic criticism"; Wilde admits that the *Poetics* may not be perfect in form, that "it is badly written, consisting of notes jotted down for an art lecture, or of isolated fragments destined for some larger book," yet he found it "in temper and treatment . . . perfect absolutely." Plato, Wilde felt, had discussed "the ethical effect of art, its importance to culture, and its place in the formation of character" all quite amply enough; and in Aristotle, art was at last treated "not from the moral, but from the purely esthetic point of view."

In his aims, if not yet in his methods, Wilde was thus a rare Aristotelian among the many Platonists and Neo-Platonists of nineteenth-century esthetics. On Aristotelian grounds, he rejected Ruskin's confusion of ethics and esthetics, and likewise saw the limitations of Pater, an "intellectual impressionist" who was doomed to be "least successful" when his subject was abstract and therefore more an artist than a thinker. But of Matthew Arnold's theory of the critic's "serious" and objective concern with the work of art "in itself," Wilde was just as critical: "it is a very serious error, and takes no cognisance of Criticism's most perfect form, which is in its essence purely subjective, and seeks to reveal its own secret and not the secret of another." Here, however, Wilde strayed from his Aristotelianism into Neo-Platonic pastures; in a similarly transcendental manner, Wilde elsewhere defined the critic's faculty as his "soul," though he did not thereby mean, it seems, an ecstatic soul divorced from all intelligence, but rather the individual's highest faculty, spiritual, moral or intellectual. In rejecting Arnold's theories, Wilde was moreover aware of their fatal weakness: an acceptance of much of nineteenth-century art "in itself" commits the critic to an acceptance of its unintelligent aims, and thus to a negation of criticism and of the critic's right to formulate intellectual or moral judgments.

In *The Decay of Lying*, Wilde sets out to contradict Plato's assertion that poetry or *mythopoeia*, because it is a form of lying, must be condemned on moral grounds. Wilde protests that art is not necessarily inferior to nature merely because art's truths do not generally coincide with the truth, whether with that of the "real things" of nature or with that of the philosopher. "Art," Wilde insists, "never expresses anything but itself. It has an independent life, just as thought has, and develops purely on its own lines. . . . In no case does it reproduce its age. To pass from the art of a time to the time itself is the great mistake that all historians commit." The dialogue's second argument is that "All bad art comes from returning to Life and Nature, and elevating them into ideals," instead of using them "as a part of Art's rough material." Thirdly, Wilde argues that "Life imitates Art far more than Art imitates Life"; even "external Nature" imitates Art, so that "the only effects that she can show us are effects that we have already seen through painting." Finally, Wilde concludes that "Lying, the telling of beautiful untrue things" that are utterly convincing because delightful and charming, "is the proper aim of Art."

In *The Critic as Artist,* Wilde expands his doctrine of *mythopoeia* to include criticism as a form of art or of lying. It is impossible, within the necessary limits of this discussion, to summarize all the steps in Wilde's brilliant argument, surely the most important of his critical writings, if not of all his works. Though not always consciously, he seems to foresee here, at times, some of the truly novel doctrines which he was destined to formulate a few years later in *De Profundis.* In any case, the step from his doctrine of Taoist inaction, formulated in *The Critic as Artist,* to his renunciation of all art except as a mode of life, in *De Profundis,* was easy to take. "There is no sin except stupidity," wrote Wilde, as he discussed, in his dialogue, the "antinomian" nature of the artistic critic's task, so similar to the mystic's way of life: "Aesthetics, in fact, are to Ethics, in the sphere of conscious civilisation, what, in the sphere of the external world, sexual is to natural selection." On his release from Reading Gaol, in the open letters on prison life which he published in the London *Daily Chronicle,* Wilde protested against the inhuman stupidity of prison cruelties; as an artist whose esthetics had so completely resorbed all ethics that it had become an ethics and a politics too, Wilde condemned the unintelligent and the unbeautiful just as a moralist condemns the sinful, because the unintelligent, the unbeautiful, and the sinful or evil had become one and the same.

Before experiencing the apocalypse of *De Profundis,* Wilde had already been prepared, in *The Critic as Artist,* to abandon all art in favor of quietistic contemplation or Taoist inaction. When the *discipulus* of the dialogue summarized his *magister's* main arguments, he listed them, at the end, as follows: "You have told me that it is more difficult to talk about a thing than to do it, and that to do nothing at all is the most difficult thing in the world; you have told me that all Art is immoral, and all thought dangerous; that criticism is more creative than creation, and that the highest criticism is that which reveals in the work of Art what the artist has not put there; that it is exactly because a man cannot do a thing that he is the proper judge of it; and that the true critic is unfair, insincere, and not rational." Surely, it would be difficult to contradict more completely the common beliefs of Romantic or Pragmatist Philistinism; and the true critic of Wilde's unworldly esthetics must be none other than the ignorant Oedipus who was able to solve the riddle, the legendary *Puer senex* of mystical philosophy, the "white-haired boy," as Lao-tse himself was called, the apocalyptic babe who knows nothing and everything, out of whose inexpert mouth comes truth because his very innocence is proof of his true expertness and of his ability to avoid all the errors of a merely worldly knowledge which reveals itself ultimately as ignorance. A Franciscan theory of naive art such as some critics have developed to justify their love of modern primitives of the type of the Douanier Rousseau, Rimbaud's abandonment of all art in favor of life, Proust's creating a work of art out of his very inability to create or out of his criticism of all art, each of these is implied, as a doctrine, in the ultimate paradoxes of *The Critic as Artist.*

When absolute individualism is thus identified with absolute universality or impassivity as an individual, self-expression is almost identical with the mystic's self-defeat or loss of self; and an esthetics founded on these principles must inevitably lead either to the transcendental inaction of contemplation which *The Critic as Artist* advocates or, beyond it, to the final crisis, the loss of faith in both art and self, which Gérard de Nerval faced in *Aurélia,* Baudelaire in his *Intimate Journals,* Rimbaud in *A Season in Hell,* Lautréamont in the preface to the later poems which he planned but never wrote, Wilde in *De Profundis,* Mallarmé in every one of his mature poems, Proust in *Le Temps Retrouvé* and Scott Fitzgerald in *The Crack-up.* Beyond such a crisis, the artist then must either abandon all art in favor of life, as Nerval did when he rejected the dreams of art and chose the hallucinations of madness or as Rimbaud did when he abandoned the adventures of art for those of life; or else, expanding or rejecting his earlier esthetics, as Wilde did in *De Profundis* or Proust in the revelation described in the opening pages of *The Princesse de Guermantes Receives,* he must set forth in quest of a new art which the accidents of life allowed Mallarmé and Proust to find but which death prevented Baudelaire, Lautréamont, Wilde or Fitzgerald from ever finding, if they had all been equally capable of achieving it. To survive such a crisis as an artist, the writer who has lost faith in the art which he had always identified with his very self must indeed be endowed with the selfless fortitude of a saint; for beyond the actual recording of the crisis in the art of literary confession, there can be for him no art but one like that of Mallarmé, where each word is a victory over the horrors of no-being, of silence and of the blank page, or like the art of Proust, where "beautiful moments" of memory or of luminous insight suddenly transfigure the dreadful night of futility and despair into which the artist's life would else degenerate wholly.

Scott Fitzgerald, in *The Crack-up*, discovered that his anguish consisted in his having "developed a sad attitude toward sadness, a melancholy attitude toward melancholy and a tragic attitude toward tragedy." Instead of maintaining the pure artist's detachment which he had come to recognize as the expression of his own peculiarly dispassionate personality, Fitzgerald was shocked to observe that he had now "become identified with the objects of" his "horror or compassion." In *De Profundis*, Wilde had similarly discovered that his "nature" was "seeking a fresh mode of self-realisation," and that "sorrow, then, and all that it teaches one" were his "new world." Formerly, Wilde had lived "entirely for pleasure," shunning sorrow and suffering of every kind and concealing them, in his art, beneath a mask of beauty which did not express them but merely "sugared" the bitter pill. Now, however, Wilde knew that "truth in art is the unity of a thing with itself: the outward rendered expressive of the inward: the soul made incarnate: the body instinct with spirit." Sorrow must therefore be sorrowful in art as in life or nature, instinct with a sorrowful beauty of its own rather than disguised beneath any borrowed beauties of a dispassionate art. With art now resorbed within nature, Wilde could even conclude, concerning both art and nature, that there must be "pleasure for the beautiful body, but pain for the beautiful soul." In his almost theological new understanding of esthetics as identical with the ethics and the politics which they had absorbed, he saw that "every single work of art is the fulfilment of a prophecy" and "the conversion of an idea into an image," just as "every single human being should be the realisation of some ideal, either in the mind of God or in the mind of man."

But Wilde's new philosophy was no orthodox Christianity. Beyond religion, Wilde had discovered realms of absolute art, and declared that there were still but "two subjects on which and through which I desire to express myself." These subjects were

"Christ as the precursor of the romantic movement in life" and "the artistic life considered in its relation to conduct," that is to say two aspects of the total subordination of religion and ethics to an esthetic which has absorbed both.

The absolutely romantic artist no longer needed to express himself in works of art, in poems, paintings or music. His life had become his art and, in "living completely for the moment," he hoped yet to achieve, even in "sin and suffering" as "modes of perfection," some of those "beautiful moments" which can redeem a sinner's life. But Wilde had not yet understood, as he wrote *De Profundis*, all that his new philosophy implied. He still believed that into his art too, "no less than into my life," there might come "a still deeper note, one of greater unity of passion, and directness of impulse." But this "something . . . of fuller memory of words perhaps, of richer cadences, of more curious effects, of simpler architectural order, of some esthetic quality at any rate," this new quality was fated never to inform any new works of art, except the relatively artless *Ballad of Reading Gaol*. Wilde's life had indeed become his art, and his whole task was now to be beautiful, in soul if not in body, and even in sin, in illness and in sorrow, rather than to create things of beauty any longer. When Sebastian Melmoth, alias Oscar Wilde, at last died in his almost shabby Paris hotel, his landlord, who surely knew all the sordid details of the broken artist's debts and debauchery, revered him as a saint, a beautiful soul in whose frightful life moments of beauty had redeemed all ugliness and all evil.

Wilde's Life and Writings in the Perspective of History

Since the present book was first written and then published by New Directions, attitudes toward male homosexuality have changed very considerably in most of the major urban centers of the English-speaking world, and this evolution is even reflected to some extent in that of law enforcement. *The Kinsey Report,* among many other scientific studies, did much to reveal to an astonished public that male homosexuality, if not female homosexuality too, is far more widely prevalent and practiced in all classes of American society than had previously been suspected. A number of successful movies, plays, and novels also contributed to the emergence of a more objective or open-minded attitude to what had caused in England such an uproar and scandal at the time of the trials of Oscar Wilde. Only a few decades before these trials, arrested and condemned homosexuals had still been exposed in England to public savagery in the stocks and been pelted with refuse and stones until most of those who survived this ordeal were blinded or otherwise maimed for life.

By 1970, barely a quarter of a century after the first publication of this book, it was already possible to conduct a class, in the English Department of a reputable American University, on "Oscar Wilde and the Decadents" without seeing the whole campus invaded by indignantly protesting delegations of the local Chamber of Commerce, the American Legion, and a number of the more traditionalist or Fundamentalist Protestant Churches. A few years later, an overtly homosexual cultural publication could even obtain financial grants and other forms of support from official national sources. Were the mayor of a major American metropolis to make now the kind of snide remark that Mayor La Guardia once made about Noel

Coward and Oscar Wilde, he would probably be greeted with hoots of ribald laughter.

Nor is this evolution due to any appreciable extent to the relatively recent efforts and activities of the movement that calls itself Gay Liberation and is its spin-off rather than one of its causes, the latter having been certainly determined mainly by the psychoanalytical research and publications of Freud and his disciples. Little concerned with literature, the arts or even science, except insofar as great writers, artists or scientists of the past, such as Michaelangelo, Benvenuto Cellini or Giordano Bruno, are known to have been homosexuals and can still serve its propaganda purposes, Gay Liberation appears to be more active and effective in liberating many of its followers from their own maudlin self-pity, in fact in "bringing them out of the closet" and into the open forum of public life. Whether now being able to flaunt one's homosexuality more freely in mass demonstrations and parades is a sign of real progress remains, however, a moot point. Most people, whether homosexual or not, still consider that their loves belong in the domain of their private life and require, in order to be successful and happy, at least a minimum of discretion and secrecy. Many heterosexuals, for instance, practice with their partners some acts that are generally described as perversions, but refrain from advertising this overtly in parades of husbands and wives who regularly and merrily practice oral or anal intercourse together behind the drawn curtains of their home.

Any call-girl can testify to the fact that both these forms of heterosexual intercourse are frequently demanded of her in the daily practice of her profession. A recent court case in California thus involved a number of members of a local police force who had made such demands on girls recruited as partners for one of their drunken orgies, and it has been variously reported that even married members of the police force of some American cities have been known to subject arrested prostitutes or homosexuals to these practices. But no association of members of our police forces has yet staged a public demonstration demanding greater indulgence of such trifling pranks inspired by mere high spirits, claiming that a more democratically permissive society should certainly tolerate them. Nor have geese, ducks, sheep, donkeys, and other feathered bipeds or furred quadrupeds yet become sufficiently aware of their "civil rights" either to protest against being sexually assaulted by humans or else to demand greater freedom to commit such acts with adult and "willing" human partners. Of all these other varieties of sexual experience, so few examples are still brought to public attention that we tend erroneously to believe that they occur very infrequently. But a heavy veil of secrecy, discretion, prudence or mere prudery conceals most of them from our awareness of how widely they are actually practiced in private.

In the case of the private life of Oscar Wilde, this veil of secrecy was brutally torn by the very shocking and unsavory publicity of his trials, which deliberately sought to heap on him as much obloquy as possible by suggesting that even some of his less guilty associations with younger men had been thoroughly reprehensible, and by confusing some such associations of Lord Alfred, of which Wilde had borne the cost, with his own. These trials became overnight a significant event in English social and literary history, while public opinion reacted so violently to them that British publishers and editors felt obliged overnight to embark on a new policy of extreme caution. Wilde's own writings remained practically taboo for a number of decades as subjects of serious critical discussion, while his immensely popular and financially successful comedies were immediately withdrawn from the London stage. Only *The Importance of Being Earnest* then began, after a "decent" delay, to be performed again, almost as a kind of companion piece to an equally harmless and hilarious farce, *Charley's Aunt,* which can now be said with some justification to display in any case the influence of Wilde's incomparable sense of the absurd. Actually, the immediate and immense commercial success of *Charley's Aunt* had inspired Wilde, less than two years later, to try his hand at the writing of the same kind of farce, in the hope of earning, with *The Importance of Being Earnest,* the kind of royalties that Walter Brandon Thomas was already earning with *Charley's Aunt.* Wilde was indeed, in those years, so constantly plagued with pressing debts as a result of his own extravagance and the hysterical demands of Lord Alfred Douglas that he was becoming desperate in his hasty search for an even more popular and financially profitable form of literary expression than his social comedies, such as *Lady Windermere's Fan* or

An Ideal Husband, that attracted almost too exclusively upper-class audiences.

Attitudes towards Oscar Wilde's life and his writings have indeed changed very considerably since 1945, and a great deal of significant material on both has thus come to light since this book was first written and published, including the posthumous publication of some of Wilde's own unpublished writings, among which the first volume of his selected letters, numbering over one thousand pages and admirably edited by Sir Rupert Hart-Davis, is certainly one of the most important. To some of these letters preserved in the William Andrews Clark Library of the University of California at Los Angeles, I already had access, thanks to Lawrence Powell, in 1945, but was not yet allowed to quote from those that are of greatest importance, so many of which contain references to Lord Alfred Douglas, who was still living and opposed their publication. Sir Rupert later published a second volume, *More Letters of Oscar Wilde,* which includes a number of equally significant letters which had subsequently been brought to his attention.

Although the complete text of the long letter originally addressed by Wilde from jail to Lord Alfred Douglas and subsequently published by Robert Ross as *De Profundis* was not yet available in English, presumably because Robert Ross was anxious to avoid litigation with Lord Alfred, I had already been able in 1945 to read a controversial translation of it that had been published in German and that contained passages suggesting that Lord Alfred and his mother had given Wilde, at the time of his trials, certain financial assurances which they subsequently failed to respect, so that Wilde was declared a bankrupt and all his belongings were hurriedly seized and sold to pay his debts. Even some of Wilde's unpublished manuscripts appear then to have been lost in the course of the hasty dismantling of his London home and the dispersion of his possessions. From my readings of this more complete but still controversial German version of *De Profundis,* I already drew certain conclusions which are reflected, though somewhat discreetly, in one of the earlier chapters of this book. These conclusions have meanwhile been proven correct by the belated publication of the complete English text of Wilde's long letter to Lord Alfred, who appears to have opposed its full publication until his very death. The original publication of my book only in an American edition, and its very limited circulation in England, may even have saved me from litigation with Lord Alfred, who was a notorious legal pettifogger in such matters.

Montgomery Hyde's *The Trials of Oscar Wilde* has also helped, by the publication of the complete transcript of the three trials, to clear up a number of biographical or literary problems. Since we are concerned more exclusively with literary problems, the full published text of what was said in court has proven without doubt one point that deserves to be stressed again here: that Wilde was not, as I had already stated in the earlier edition of this book, the author of the somewhat mediocre and pornographic story entitled "The Priest and the Acolyte," which the Marquess of Queensberry and his lawyers had falsely attributed in court to Wilde's pen.

It is now quite clear, from the transcript of the trials as well as from one of Wilde's subsequently published letters, that this story, which had originally appeared in the same Oxford undergraduate publication, *The Chameleon,* as two poems by Lord Alfred and some aphorisms of Wilde, emanated from the circle of Lord Alfred's less reputable or more exhibitionistic young Oxford friends, and not from Wilde's circle of older or more responsible London literary acquaintances. Its author, John Francis Bloxam, was an undergraduate from Exeter College and the editor of *The Chameleon,* to the first and only issue of which Lord Alfred had persuaded Wilde to contribute his series of aphorisms entitled "Phrases and Philosophies for the Use of the Young," which are wittily cynical, but certainly not immediately conducive to any kind of immorality. In a letter addressed to his friend Ada Leverson, "the Sphinx without a Secret," some time before his trials, Wilde moreover described Bloxam as "an undergraduate of strange beauty" while disclaiming his own authorship of "The Priest and the Acolyte" and already condemning it as "to my ears too direct; there is no nuance; God and other artists are always a little obscure. Still, it has interesting qualities, and is at moments poisonous: which is something."

Later, when Wilde was asked in court whether he thought that Bloxam's story was immoral, he replied more cautiously, though still in terms of his own aesthetic philosophy: "It was worse; it was badly written. . . . it violated every artistic canon of beauty."

In many respects, another particularly informative publication of the last few decades has been *Oscar Wilde and the Queensberry Clan,* written in collaboration with Percy Colson, after Lord Alfred's death, by none other than a Marquess of Queensberry, in fact a grandson of the blustering "Scarlet Marquess" who had originally been responsible, as a consequence of his systematic persecution of Wilde, for the latter's unwise decision to sue him, which then led to the two subsequent trials, in the last of which Wilde was sentenced to jail. As co-author of this remarkably frank and well-documented book, the younger Marquess reveals in great detail and without any compunction the petulantly selfish and irresponsible character of his own uncle, Lord Alfred Douglas, and the disastrous manner in which, almost like a male prostitute, Lord Alfred exploited the infatuation that he inspired as "Bosie" in Wilde. However physically attractive Lord Alfred may have been in his youth, and talented and promising too as a writer, even according to the testimony of such contemporaries as George Bernard Shaw, who was certainly not homosexual, he emerges, from a reading of his own nephew's book, as well as of a number of other published sources, as a thoroughly vicious and unpleasant character.

Finally, one of Wilde's sons, Vyvyan Holland, author too of a collection of whimsical but very proper limericks, has published *Son of Oscar Wilde,* which offers us a few vivid insights into Wilde's family life, his relationship with his wife and children, and their fate after his trials and imprisonment. This book also contains a few of Wilde's previously unpublished poems and aphorisms, which are all, however, of much the same nature as those that were already widely known.

Much of the new material on Wilde that has been published in the past forty years reveals indeed that both the literary qualities of his writings and the circumstances of his private life can now be discussed much more openly and dispassionately than when the present book was first published. Wilde's writings, in particular, were then generally held in rather low esteem in most American intellectual circles, and a critic of the very open-minded *New Yorker* even felt that such an unexpectedly serious and objective critical appreciation of Wilde's writings as this was praiseworthy enough to deserve the week's full-page book review.

Hollywood had not yet had the courage or the initiative to launch on its public the first and very widely discussed of its movie versions of *The Picture of Dorian Gray*, the acting, sets, and costumes of which inspired a considerable revival of interest in Tiffany glass lampshades and other typical elements of Decadent or Art Nouveau styles of dress or of interior decoration that had long tended to languish in the dusty windows of thrift shops.

True, many of Wilde's writings were still being widely read, though mainly in secret by callow youths in cheap and often unreliable reprints. Only Paul Goodman and I, among American critics of the time, appeared to devote much attention to Wilde as a writer and especially as a critical theoretician of real distinction, while the Canadian poet and anarchist George Woodcock was destined to publish his excellent *The Paradox of Oscar Wilde* only in 1949 in London, without ever finding an American publisher to reprint it, much as I too never found an English publisher for the present book.

The low esteem in which Wilde's writings were generally held in that decade is revealed by the absence of any reference to them in a collection of critical appreciations of the art of Henry James, *The Question of Henry James*, that was then published in New York by F. W. Dupee, one of the regular critics of the influential *Partisan Review*. Not only did Dupee entirely neglect to quote any of Wilde's few but very pertinent references to James while nevertheless salvaging from oblivion the opinions of far less notable early critics such as Thomas Wentworth Higginson, Frank Moore Colby or Herbert Croly, but he also failed to mention Wilde at all in the bibliography that he reprinted there from the Henry James volume of the American Book Company's *American Writers Series*. Even more significant is the fact that not one of the later critics of James reprinted by Dupee had ever mentioned Wilde or appeared to have thought of consulting Wilde's writings on the subject of James.

This general neglect of Wilde must certainly be attributed to other causes than the fact that Wilde never devoted a full essay or book review to any aspect of the writings of James, whom he mentions only casually, as already pointed out in an earlier chapter of the present book, in a couple of his reviews of books by other novelists and also in a more general discussion of his own theories of fiction. Joseph Conrad likewise devoted no book review or essay to any of the writings of James, but a brief excerpt from his *Notes on Life and Letters*, where he mentions James quite casually, was nevertheless reprinted in full by Dupee, as was likewise an equally brief excerpt from Thomas Beer's *Stephen Crane: a Story in American Letters*.

The fact is that Oscar Wilde's life and writings, in that benighted decade between 1940 and 1950, were still considered dangerously compromising topics in most American literary circles, and some critics of the present book, such as the late Edward Dahlberg, even concluded that only a homosexual could have felt impelled to take up the cudgel on behalf of the author of *Dorian Gray*, as if all the bearded nineteenth-century scholars who had studiously pieced together the surviving fragments of the Greek poems of Sappho must likewise, to a man, have been lesbians.

Wilde's interest in Henry James and appreciation of his art and its novelty and significance are indeed revealed three times in writings that Wilde published in the course of the same Esthetic Era as the earliest critical opinions reprinted in Dupee's book. Within the general context of the Esthetic Movement, these references to James represent Wilde's attitude, as one of the recognized hierophants of the Cult of Beauty, the *Reich der Schönheit* as the German philosopher Dolf Sternberger has called it, towards another. Wilde thus regretted, in his review of Lady Augusta Noel's *Hithersea Mere*, the absence, in England, of "any schools worth speaking of." The Brontës, Dickens, Thackeray, and Trollope, he seemed to think, had left no followers as Balzac or Flaubert had in France. Who could hope to reproduce the art of Meredith, whose energy Wilde praised while expressing, for his cumbersome techniques and confused thinking, the same distaste as James later expressed to Sir Edmund Gosse? But Wilde then admitted that "it is only fair to acknowledge that there are signs of a school springing up among us," and he went on to observe, as already pointed out, that "this school is not native, nor does it seek to reproduce any English master. It may be described as the result of the realism of Paris filtered through the refining influence of Boston."

Though Wilde avoided mentioning James here by name, it is clear that the author of *The Bostonians* was the only novelist to whom such remarks could then apply. In *More Letters of Oscar*

Wilde, first published in 1985, one now discovers somewhat belatedly that Wilde, as early as November 1886, had written a letter to Edward Tyas Cook, who was on the editorial staff of *The Pall Mall Gazette*, suggesting that he would gladly review there *The Bostonians*, which James had just published. Although it appears that Wilde never had occasion to review this or any other novel by Henry James in *The Pall Mall Gazette* or elsewhere, he referred covertly to James later in his review of Lady Augusta Noel's *Hithersea Mere*, then again in his review of Harriet Weston Preston's *A Year in Eden*, when he found occasion to refer briefly to "the elaborate subtlety of the American school of fiction"; and it must have become quite clear to Wilde's more perceptive readers that he could only have had James in mind in both these book reviews when he finally mentioned James by name and discussed his art at slightly greater length in *The Decay of Lying*. In this critical dialogue, published in 1890 in *Intentions*, Wilde expounded, with passing references to other novelists too, his own esthetics of fictional realism.

Frustrated in his original desire to review *The Bostonians*, Wilde thus appears to have expressed later in three different contexts the main considerations that his reading of this novel had suggested to him. Many of Wilde's other readings, like those of any good critic, likewise found their way, along equally devious channels, to appear ultimately as such *obiter dicta* in the very different contexts of his other writings. This whole episode of Wilde's variously expressed views on the art of Henry James is not only significant as early testimony in the general history of James criticism, but above all as evidence of the workings of Wilde's own critical mind, a mill to which all his readings could be grist.

However pertinent Wilde's brief remarks on the art of Henry James may be, many of those that he expressed on the writings of other English or American contemporaries, whether in his numerous book reviews or else in the equally numerous references to his readings that one finds in his letters, can now pose serious problems concerning his judgement and taste. These prove to have been exceptionally reliable in his appreciations of contemporary French literature, since nearly all the French authors whose writings he praised are still recognized in France, almost a hundred years later, as remaining of considerable importance. In his appreciations of the writings of some of his English contemporaries, Wilde proves, however, to be less reliable. Whether for purely social or other equally frivolous reasons, he repeatedly praised as "charming" or "delightful" a great deal of merely fashionable English fiction or of verse that nobody today, except perhaps such a militant postdated decadent from the Antipodes as the almost legendary and self-styled Count Potocki de Montalk, would still be capable of reading with much interest or pleasure.

Most of the supposedly decadent English poets of Wilde's generation or immediate circle, such as Lord Alfred Douglas, Ernest Dowson, Lionel Johnson or Richard Le Gallienne, whom Wilde appears to have admired or encouraged, are now considered, at best, rather minor. Nor were some of Wilde's choices of contemporary English fiction more felicitous. Only a few years after Wilde had praised highly the merely fashionable novels of his witty and loyal friend Ada Leverson, a judicious critic of London's *Times Literary Supplement* was already comparing one of them very unfavorably with *Dolores*, the first and still immature novel of young Ivy Compton-Burnett, most of whose later fiction now continues to be reprinted and widely read several decades after her death. With the one exception of Henry James, Wilde thus proves not to have been a very reliable judge of the lasting value of most of the new English or American fiction that he discussed in his critical writings.

Wilde's passionate commitment to the kind of English literature that was already known in his own lifetime as decadent or "Fin-de-Siècle" is well illustrated in a letter written in 1894, addressed to Leo Maxse, a diehard Tory journalist and political writer who claimed that Wilde had written a "slashing" article condemning "all that is known by the term Fin-de-Siècle." Wilde then replied: "I never write 'slashing' articles: slash does not seem to me to be a quality of good prose. Still less would I feel inclined to write an article attacking all that is known by the term 'Fin-de-Siècle.' All that is known by that term I particularly admire and love. It is the fine flower of our civilization: the only thing that keeps the world from the commonplace, the coarse, the barbarous. But perhaps your letter was intended for someone else. It seems to be addressed to a journalist, not an artist."

Again and again, whether in his published writings and public utterances or in private letters that were never intended for posthumous publication, Wilde deliberately taunted individual journalists or the press in general with such contemptuous references to their profession and habits of thought. But this appears to have been part of his very personal policy of public relations. He knew that by thus provoking journalists he could rouse them to serve his own purposes by publicizing his appearance, his activities, and his opinions at least with ridicule, and ridicule, above all in the popular middle-class satirical journal *Punch,* was already an effective means of achieving some kind of celebrity in the public eye.

Like Beau Brummel in the past and, in our own century, the novelist Ivy Compton-Burnett or the cartoonist Osbert Lancaster, Wilde was an expert at playing the merry English social game of seeking to appear, often with some success, as if one had been born in a more aristocratic environment than that of one's parents, perhaps even in one of those stately country homes of the hereditarily landed gentry rather than in urban Dublin, suburban Hove or some other even less prestigious neighborhood. In his dealings with those whom he believed to be his inferiors or whom he intended to impress with his lordly manner, Wilde could thus be either haughty or condescending. With journalists, even with his devoted brother William Wilde, he was almost invariably haughty. To many of the working-class boys with whom he appears, as was revealed in his trials, to have had homosexual relationships, he gave silver cigarette cases in a condescendingly and unnecessarily lordly manner.

At the same time, Wilde was well aware of the risks inherent in what is now generally known as "the cult of personality." The January 1895 issue of *The St. James Gazette* thus published "Mr. Oscar Wilde on Mr. Oscar Wilde; an interview." Sir Rupert Hart-Davis suggests that, although anonymous, it had actually been compiled by Wilde himself, in collaboration with young Robert Ross. Whoever the author or authors of this text may have been, Wilde declares there that "the personality of the artist is not a thing the public should know anything about. It is too accidental." Later, in the same interview, he refers to his own new play, presumably *The Importance of Being Earnest,* as "exquisitely trivial, a delicate bubble of fancy, and it has its philosophy . . . That we should treat all the trivial things of life very seriously, and all the serious things of life with sincere and studied triviality."

It was Wilde's paradoxical fate that the public should ultimately know far more than he intended about his personality and some of the more accidental aspects of his private life, and should take far too seriously those details of his private life that more dispassionate historians and critics might now consider relatively trivial, such as his lavish distributions of silver cigarette cases to unworthy young men who later appeared in his trials, prompted by the Marquess of Queensberry or the latter's detectives and lawyers, as witnesses against him.

Fate appears to have been, in this respect, as paradoxical in Wilde's life as he himself could be in his art, whether as a conversationalist or as a writer. He considered himself indeed, above all, an artist, in fact a poet, yet his poetry, with the exception of *The Ballad of Reading Gaol* and perhaps *The Sphinx, The Harlot's House* and a few other pieces, has long ceased, and quite rightly, to deserve much consideration. The early and rarely consulted English poems of the Portuguese poet Fernando Pessoa, especially *Antinous, Epithalamium* and some of his Shakespearean sonnets that Aleister Crowley considered uniquely skilled and inspired, are far better examples of English decadent poetry than Wilde's *Charmides* or any of the sonnets of Lord Alfred Douglas that inspired Wilde's passionate admiration.

By later generations, Wilde is thus respected mainly as the author of comedies such as *Lady Windermere's Fan*, and of one farce, *The Importance of Being Earnest*, which he wrote very consciously as pot-boilers, aiming mainly at their commercial success; or else, as the author of *De Profundis*, a truly remarkable confessional text that was apparently never intended for publication. As for the lasting success of Wilde's *Salome*, it is certainly due mainly to its continued performances as an opera. Without the musical score of Richard Strauss, it might by now have suffered much the same fate as Wilde's other lyrical dramas, such as *Vera, or the Nihilists, The Duchess of Padua* or *A Florentine Tragedy*, none of which is ever performed or even widely read.

Wilde had proclaimed, as already stated, that "the personality of the artist is not a thing that the public should know anything about," but his many biographers have pried by now into every possible nook and cranny of his personality and private life, often without paying much attention to the possible literary sources of some of his writings, such as the French plays of Alexandre Dumas

Fils and Emile Augier as sources for his comedies, as well as for those of Henry A. Jones, Arthur Pinero, and even young George Bernard Shaw in *Mrs. Warren's Profession,* among Wilde's contemporaries. Nor has anyone yet suggested Thomas de Quincey's *Suspiria de Profundis* as the possible source for the title of Wilde's *De Profundis.*

Oddly enough, in our age of Gay Liberation, Wilde even appears to be belatedly achieving the status of a kind of "Lesbian Dandy," as Aleister Crowley once described himself in the inscription on one of his autographed photographs. No other English writer of distinction, except Lord Byron and Dame Edith Sitwell, has ever taken such pains as Oscar Wilde to inspire, by his activities, style of dress, public utterances or other activities, what is now known as "the cult of personality." In American literature, only Ezra Pound, Gertrude Stein, and Truman Capote likewise appear to have deliberately achieved the same kind of almost legendary status.

Books on Oscar Wilde, alone among male writers known to have been homosexual, now sell as well as biographies of such famous Lesbian writers as Vita Sackville-West, Gertrude Stein, Natalie Barney, Djuna Barnes or Jane Bowles, and one even begins to regret that Lord Alfred Douglas failed to distinguish himself, like Alice Toklas, as the author of a cook-book.

Wilde's name remains indeed, however undeservedly, a symbol of sorts. In spite of his many affectations of manner, dress, and wit that were often those of a dandy rather than of a homosexual, and that had all been previously displayed in England by such other dandies as Brummel, Bulwer Lytton or young Disraeli, who were never accused of homosexuality, we can now see, close on a hundred years after Wilde's trials, that his homosexuality was scarcely more flamboyant or scandalous than that of a number of other major English or American writers, such as Christopher Marlowe, Lord Byron, Algernon Charles Swinburne or Walt Whitman. It was Wilde's misfortune, however, to become entangled in the family quarrels of the powerful and vindictive Marquess of Queensberry with his estranged wife and children and, once the antagonism of the Marquess had been aroused, to mishandle the various incidents and trials that ensued.

Had Wilde never become involved with Lord Alfred, he might even have been able for many more years, although a married man, to lead on the side a more discreet homosexual life, leaving puzzled scholars to quarrel now, as in the case of Lord Byron, and without the irrefutable evidence of Wilde's trials, about whether he was homosexual or not and, if he was, how important or exceptional his homosexual relationships were in a life in which he is also known to have had heterosexual relationships and even to have married and fathered two sons.

In a number of letters that are now famous and of other utterances that are quoted by Henry Abelove in an article, "Freud, Male Homosexuality, and the Americans," published in New York in the Winter 1986 issue of *Dissent*, Sigmund Freud stressed again and again, and quite rightly, his firm belief in the existence of a latent element of homosexuality in all men, if not in all women too. Several other nineteenth-century English poets are known to have perhaps been more exclusively homosexual than Wilde. Among others, Swinburne, Thomas Lovell Beddoes, the Honorable Roden Berkeley Wriothesley Noel, perhaps Wildred Scawen Blunt, and certainly Edward Carpenter. But none of these has yet attracted the attention of as many biographers and apologists as Wilde, although the life of Beddoes, who may even have been murdered in Zurich in circumstances similar to those that attended in England the death of Marlowe, was certainly more mysteriously adventurous than Wilde's, and the life of Blunt, who also served a term in prison, though apparently for political reasons, remains similarly fraught with a great deal of mystery.

But how many editors even of America's gay press have ever heard of Beddoes, Roden or Blunt, and suggested to one of their more scholarly contributors that he undertake the necessary research for even a brief article on any one of them? And would the dubious attribution of the authorship of an anonymous and relatively undistinguished pornographic novel, such as *Teleny*, which has again and again been falsely attributed to Wilde's pen, to any of these other writers now sell such a book to any extent? True, Edward Carpenter has in recent years attracted some attention in the gay press as a pioneer apologist for a very idealized form of male homosexuality, in fact like Hans Blüher in German literature, as a kind of namby-pamby Walt Whitman.

Were an unwise author now to start peddling his typescript

biography of Beddoes, Noel, Blunt or Carpenter up and down and in and around Madison Avenue, no commercial publisher would be likely to rise like a trout to the fly and swallow such a biography, hook, line and sinker, while expecting it to sell well on his coming Fall list. Yet the life of Beddoes was fraught with suspense, obscure political intrigue and violence, and he is even suspected of having associated in Germany or Switzerland with Georg Büchner, the revolutionary German author of *Danton's Death*, of *Wozzek*, and of a kind of Communist Manifesto that preceded that of Karl Marx, as well as with other pre-Marxist political activists.

A biography of Wilfred Scawen Blunt, who was a fine poet—at least in "The Desolate City"—the husband of Byron's grand-daughter, a breeder of Arab horses, an ardent champion of Irish independence, a pioneer critic of British colonialism, and, in his sympathies for the Arabs, a kind of precursor of T. E. Lawrence, would also yield a great deal of interesting information, especially if the full transcript of the political trial that led to his imprisonment were, like the transcript of Wilde's trials, still available. Actually, Wilde's letters reveal that he was at least superficially acquainted with Blunt and expressed great respect for him.

Of the relatively withdrawn life of the Honorable Roden Berkeley Wriothesley Noel, who was also related to Byron and thus to Blunt too by the latter's marriage, relatively little, I admit, is known, and even the most intense research is never likely to lead to any sensational revelations. Many of his poems, including those that one finds in *The Oxford Book of Victorian Verse*, suggest that his mind was haunted by the same kind of idealized love of male adolescents as Wilde too expressed, some years later, in *Charmides*, though Noel's imagery is less lush than Wilde's and refrains too from Wilde's spectacular displays of classical erudition.

But even a meticulous analysis of the poetry of Beddoes, Noel or Wilde is unlikely ever to reveal anything as ambiguously compromising as the love for Hallam expressed in Tennyson's *In Memoriam*. In this respect, poor Wilde has proven to be, as a result of the unfortunate publicity of his trials and also of his own improvident handling of his public relations with the press of his age, a pioneer victim of the kind of cult of personality that has become so typical now of the activity of our mass media. In the minds of Mayor La

Guardia and of many others who may never have read a single page of Wilde's writings, he thus survives, as a homosexual, much larger than he ever was in real life, in fact more famous for the more trivial aspects of his personality and private life than for any of his major achievements as a writer.

Was Oscar Wilde a "Shy Pornographer"?

The history of the various published editions of *Teleny*, a pornographic novel on a very overtly homosexual theme, and of the suppositions of those who have published, edited or prefaced it concerning its original authorship, has been well related by Winston Leyland in his excellent preface to his 1984 Gay Sunshine Press edition of this book that has so often been attributed to Oscar Wilde's pen. But this history, however factual and free from fanciful suppositions, remains very confusing, if only because the book's original London publisher, Leonard Smithers, appears to have insisted that its author or authors should tamper considerably with the original manuscript, which the bookseller Charles Hirsch had already had occasion to read in 1890, so as to transfer the story's action, in its first edition, published by Smithers in 1893, from London to Paris.

Charles Hirsch later obtained possession of the original manuscript, which has now disappeared, and translated it faithfully into French, thus producing a French version of *Teleny* that he published in Paris in 1934. The present Gay Sunshine Press English-language edition of *Teleny* is thus a skillful compilation of passages from the original Smithers edition or its various English or American reprints and of exact translations from the French text of the edition published by Hirsch. Some of the anomalies that can now be noted in the action of the novel in its Gay Sunshine Press edition may therefore be due to overlapping of the English and French versions or to contradictions between them that escaped the otherwise careful attention of Winston Leyland.

The attribution of the authorship of *Teleny* to Wilde rests mainly on gossip and rather vague and flimsy circumstantial evidence concerning the early history of its original manuscript, which now appears in any case to have been lost, and certainly not on a careful analysis of the style and structure of the book in its various available published versions. But this circumstantial evidence is scarcely of the kind that might stand the test of presentation before an impartial court of law, and is moreover belied by the only reliable witness who appears to have examined carefully the original manuscript before it was published by Smithers in a tampered version. In his introduction to the Gay Sunshine Press edition of *Teleny*, Winston Leyland quotes this testimony at length, but fails, for reasons of his own, whether as publisher of the book or as propagandist for Gay Liberation, to grant this testimony the importance that it deserves and that even leads Patrick J. Kearney, who compiled on the basis of all reliable evidence and testimony of experts *The Private Case*, an annotated bibliography of the erotica preserved in the British (Museum) Library (London, Jay Landesman Limited, 1981), to conclude: "Despite claims of authorship by Wilde, this appears to be a collective work by several hands."

Montgomery Hyde had already explained, in his introduction to the 1966 English reprint of *Teleny*, that this reliable witness, Charles Hirsch, was a French dealer who owned at one time a bookstore where Wilde frequently purchased French books. Hirsch had previously sold to Wilde a copy of the 1881 edition of *The Sins of the Cities of the Plain*, an anonymous fictional or partly autobiographical account of a male homosexual's experiences in London, when Wilde, towards the end of 1890, one day entrusted to Hirsch a sealed package, declaring: "A friend of mine will call for this package and will show you my card." Some days later, a young man whom Hirsch had already seen in Wilde's company came and collected this package.

This procedure was repeated three times, all in all by four such callers, the last of whom was less careful and returned the contents of the parcel, a manuscript, unsealed and unwrapped. Charles Hirsch was then tempted to read it, and the manuscript proved to be that of *Teleny*. What particularly struck Hirsch was "the extraordinary mixture of different handwritings, erasures, interlineations, corrections and additions made by various hands." It was thus evident to Hirsch that "several writers of unequal literary merit had collaborated in this anonymous but profoundly interesting work." Later, Hirsch told a friend that *Teleny* was "undoubtedly written by various friends of Wilde, who had himself supervised and corrected the manuscript, adding touches of his own here and there."

Such is the only circumstantial evidence of Wilde's presumed authorship of the book. Without the manuscript, it is not possible to prove how much Wilde added "here and there" to the original text, or how much he corrected it. The testimony of Charles Hirsch, who knew Wilde personally, could recognize his handwriting, and saw the original manuscript with his own eyes, should in any case carry more weight than other presumptions concerning the book's authorship such as those expressed by Winston Leyland and other critics, editors or publishers, such as Maurice Girodias, of various published editions of *Teleny*, so many of whom continue to attribute the book to Wilde.

Another important fact should also be considered in this context. We know that Oscar Wilde was in 1889 and the following years in constant financial straits. Had Wilde really been the author of *Teleny*, he would almost certainly have sought ways and means of publishing it, if only anonymously and abroad, so as to raise some ready cash. But no mention of this is made in any of the allegations concerning Wilde's presumed authorship of *Teleny*, and nothing in Wilde's many letters that have so far been published suggests that he ever attempted to undertake such a clandestine publication, nor can one find, in any of these letters, any admission of his awareness of the existence of *Teleny*, nor any reference to its possible author or authors.

Had Wilde written *Teleny*, he would almost certainly have mentioned it in letters to Robert Ross or some other close friend, especially after his release from prison, when he began to refer far more overtly and frequently to his own homosexuality. Nor does he admit in any such letter that he had ever corrected the manuscript of *Teleny*, so that one is led to conclude that he may have accomplished this task rather hastily and as a relatively unimportant favor for a friend. Even when Wilde, after his release from prison, was always so short of money and constantly writing from his self-imposed exile in France to various close friends or to publishers, often begging them desperately for small sums of money, he never refers there, even in his letters to Smithers, the original London publisher of *Teleny*, to any possible reprint of the book as a possible source of income. If only from this last fact, one can conclude that Wilde never considered himself author or co-author of *Teleny* and may even have very soon forgotten his own involvement in suggesting improvements of the book's original text.

In addition to apparently correcting this manuscript, which in any case displays "here and there," in both the text with which Smithers had tampered and in the French translation by Hirsch or the excerpts from the latter that Winston Leyland has translated back from French and inserted in his own edition of *Teleny*, some very obvious and sometimes rather crude imitations of various passages of *The Picture of Dorian Gray*, Wilde was already exerting in 1890 a considerable literary influence on a number of his younger English friends and readers. Under his guidance, several of these were discovering the writings of important French authors of the Parnassian, Symbolist, Decadent, and Realist schools. Even as respectable a writer as George Moore, who expressed on several occasions his antipathy for Wilde and the latter's ideas and way of life, was thus destined to reflect in his own works, at least partly under Wilde's direct or indirect influence, that of his own readings of Huysmans' *A Rebours* in *The Confessions of a Young Man*, of *Germinie Lacerteux*, by the Goncourt Brothers, in *Esther Waters*, and of various works of Flaubert in *The Brook Kerith* and elsewhere.

From Wilde's published letters, we know how much he admired Flaubert, that he likewise admired Jules de Goncourt and even corresponded with him after meeting him, and that he often expressed, though with some critical reservations, his interest in the writings of Huysmans. Like George Moore in *The Confessions of a Young Man* and, many years later, Carl Van Vechten in *Peter Whiffle*, the mysterious author or authors of *Teleny* had also been influenced by readings of *A Rebours*.

It would thus appear to be rather rash to attribute to Wilde's own pen every detail in the style of *Teleny* that might reflect only his direct or indirect influence on its author or authors, since his influence was already very extensive, even on younger writers whom he had never met, at the time of the first recorded appearance of this novel's lost manuscript in the Hirsch bookstore in London. Too many details too, in the style and structure of *Teleny*, are so characteristic of immature, hasty, slovenly, confused, pretentious or even imitative writing that one should hesitate to attribute such a hodgepodge to as skilled and fastidious an artist as Wilde had proven to be in all but a few of the more callow productions of his youth. Many of these flaws, in the original London edition of *Teleny*, however, may be the result of the tampering that the manuscript underwent at the hands of Smithers before its publication.

The task of listing here in detail all the affected archaisms in *Teleny*'s English and all the pretentious and unnecessary interpolations of French words by its real author or authors would be too fastidious for our present purposes. One major flaw, in the novel's construction even in the Gay Sunshine Press edition, nevertheless deserves more detailed discussion.

Several incidents, including *Teleny's* first concert in London's Queen's Hall, revealed clearly, in the original manuscript which Hirsch later translated into French, that London should constitute the background of most of the action of the novel, excepting a few minor scenes, such as its young protagonist's trip to Eastbourne (which, by the way, constitutes no valid proof of Wilde's authorship, although evidence quoted in the course of his trials proved that he had visited Eastbourne on several occasions with Lord Alfred Douglas or had been involved in other homosexual adventures there). A number of other descriptive details likewise continue, throughout the book, to suggest that the setting of its action is London. The painter's studio where the homosexual orgy takes place nevertheless owes much of the decadent exoticism of its elaborate decorative finery to descriptions of the home of des Esseintes in *A Rebours*; but one can still find a few such opulent late-Victorian artist's studios also in London, including the former home of the painter Lord Leighton that is now preserved as a museum in Holland Park and a few others too in the St. John's Wood area, where James Tissot and other successful artists were living in that age.

One whole important episode in *Teleny* appears, however, to have been lifted from another novel that had Paris as its setting and then been clumsily grafted onto the novel's London setting, either in the Smithers edition or else in Winston Leyland's compilation of the Smithers edition and the Hirsch translation, without most of the necessary adjustments. Suddenly, in the course of the jealous young protagonist's pursuit of Teleny and Bryancourt through the streets of London, he reaches the river's embankments. But the scene revealed to him there is one that could occur only in Paris, on the embankments of the Seine and not in London on those of the Thames.

Homosexuals, of course, may well haunt by night the embankments of both rivers. But, had I been a member of the charmed circle of Wilde's friends who were privileged "around 1890" to read the original manuscript of *Teleny*, I would have challenged its author to find me, along the embankments of the Thames, a single typically Parisian *vespasienne* such as the one that is described in both the Smithers and the Gay Sunshine editions of *Teleny*, or likewise a bridge in London beneath the arches of which homosexuals can withdraw in sheltered privacy beneath the embankments, as one finds all along the Seine in Paris but not along the Thames in London.

Had the author or authors of *Teleny* then been able to convince me that such typically Parisian architectural details can also be found in London, I would then have condemned him or them to haunt the London Embankments night after night in order to meet there and bring back to me, bound hand and foot if necessary, a young Zouave sub-lieutenant, a "slim and swarthy youth, apparently an Arab," wearing the full uniform of this colorful North-African regiment of the French Army which, in any case, recruited in those days mainly Algerians of European or Jewish origin rather than Arabs.

What would a French Zouave have been doing in uniform in London, unless he were attached to the French Embassy as a guard, although Zouaves, as far as I know, have never been attached to it? As Big Ben would be striking midnight from the tower of the House of Parliament on Hallowe'en, the author or authors of *Teleny* might even have found, on the Embankments of the Thames, a mandrake root with child more readily than a Zouave in full uniform.

Had Wilde really been the author of *Teleny*, he would certainly have eliminated from its original manuscript all such structural or stylistic flaws, had they been there in the first draft of its original version, as well as all the other solecisms or absurdities that abound in it, before displaying it even to his closest friends, and he would certainly never have allowed Smithers to tamper with its text before even publishing it anonymously. In any case, had he been the anonymous author of such a text that Smithers had undertaken to alter so radically before publishing it with so many additions, eliminations or alterations that cannot be attributed to as fastidious an artist as Wilde, he certainly would not later have entrusted to Smithers the publication of *The Ballad of Reading Gaol*, which was first printed anonymously under Wilde's mere number as a prisoner, though very soon too under his own name.

But the personal tastes of at least one of the possible authors of *Teleny* are revealed elsewhere in the novel, when a Syrian boy and a Spahi are described among the guests at Bryancourt's homosexual orgy. Yet we know, from André Gide's account of his meeting with Oscar Wilde in Algeria, that Lord Alfred Douglas rather than Wilde displayed there a homosexual interest in Arabs, Zouaves or Spahis, and it became quite clear, in the course of Wilde's trials, that his own homosexual tastes, apart from his passion for Lord Alfred, were almost exclusively for working-class English adolescents.

Teleny certainly emanates from the circle of some of the less reputable literary friends of Wilde and Lord Alfred. Perhaps, like "The Priest and the Acolyte," it was even written by one of Lord Alfred's more exhibitionistic or provocative Oxford undergraduate friends, and then Wilde, out of sheer kindness or under pressure from Lord Alfred, did his best to correct and review it hurriedly in view of its ultimate publication, which he nevertheless appears to have refrained from sponsoring in any way.

The real authorship of *Teleny* thus remains a mystery that might be solved, if at all, only by a careful analysis of all the other anonymous homosexual pornography written and published in English between about 1880 and 1900, and after a meticulous study of the style and the apparently fetishistic fixations, such as on Arabs, Zouaves or Spahis, of each one of these anonymous authors. But is such a mediocre novel as *Teleny* worthy of so much trouble? And is it so necessary to solve, nearly a hundred years later, the problem of its authorship? Let it suffice to affirm here that its author cannot possibly have been Oscar Wilde, but may well have been one of his enthusiastic and less gifted imitators, some of whose flaws of style Wilde was apparently kind enough to correct in his own hand in the manuscript that Hirsch had occasion to read and later translated into French.

Had Wilde been the author of *Teleny*, the Marquess of Queensberry, who spared no expense in employing detectives to collect compromising evidence about Wilde's life and activities in the years that immediately preceded the trials, would probably have found ways and means of worming this information out of Leonard Smithers, Charles Hirsch or some other member of Wilde's immediate circle. The Marquess did indeed claim, in the course of the trials, that Wilde had been the author of "The Priest and the Acolyte," and Wilde then replied, when asked whether he considered this story "immoral," that "it was worse; it was badly written." Had he been questioned in the course of his trials about the authorship of *Teleny* and the quality of its writing, he would most probably have denied being its author and have condemned it in much the same terms as "The Priest and the Acolyte."

But over-ambitious or irresponsible publishers can be expected to continue to reprint *Teleny* from time to time as "a novel attributed to Oscar Wilde," if only because Wilde's name can still be expected to sell the book fairly successfully.

Wilde's Art in His Life

In the two volumes, *The Letters of Oscar Wilde* (London, Rupert Hart-Davis Ltd., 1962) and *More Letters of Oscar Wilde* (London, John Murray Ltd., 1985, and New York, Vanguard Press, Inc., 1985), that Sir Rupert Hart-Davis has now published with excellent editorial comments, one already finds slightly less than two thousand letters that have been considered worthy of publication. Most of those that I might have quoted in the earlier edition of the present book were inaccessible to me in 1945, and, as already stated, I was not yet allowed to quote from most of those that I had been able to consult in manuscript in Los Angeles.

Much that these published letters contain will make it at last possible to write a well-documented biography of Wilde in which the main focus might no longer be on his homosexuality, his trials, and his imprisonment. What I might have chosen to quote in the earlier edition of this book would only, in most cases, have corroborated what I had already observed or concluded from my readings of Wilde's published writings and had therefore presented in the various earlier chapters of this book, or else in an article, *Oscar Wilde and Henry James*, that I published in 1948 in the University of Kansas City's *University Review*. Most such pertinent quotations from Wilde's letters might even appear rather redundant in these new chapters added to the present edition of my book. A few of these letters and of the material published in Montgomery Hyde's *The Trials of Oscar Wilde* or elsewhere since 1945 might nevertheless justify here some additional critical comment, although the latter may well seem to repeat what had previously been stated in the various chapters of the original edition of this book. But my own evaluations of the literary significance of some of Wilde's writings have also undergone, in close on half a century, an evolution that is reflected, however subtly, in such apparent repetitions. *Habent sua fata libelli*, the Roman poet Horace once complained, and Oscar Wilde's writings continue to experience, in my own mind as well as in the minds of others, the fate of all published books.

According to André Gide, Wilde once admitted to him in Algiers, perhaps in a moment of despondency while Lord Alfred Douglas was busy pursuing young Arabs, Zouaves or Spahis at Wilde's expense, that he had put his genius in his life, but only his talent in his writings. As in many of Wilde's other quips, there is some truth here, but also a heavy dose of self-disparagement. According to all those who knew him, Wilde was indeed a conversationalist of genius, "larger than life and twice as natural" in the spontaneity and brilliance of many of his utterances. He even managed, on one extraordinary occasion in London's Café Royal, to charm his own

arch-enemy, the very obtuse and prejudiced Marquess of Queensberry. But conversations, unlike poetry that, according to Horace,
can outlive stone or bronze, evaporates very fast, even in our age that
enjoys the benefit of tape-recorders.

To the ancient Greeks we owe the invention of two literary forms
in which some of the brilliant conversation of the past two and a
half millennia could be preserved: comedy, in which the wit and
repartee of an author's often anonymous contemporaries can be
mounted like precious stones in their setting, and the philosophical
dialogue, in which Plato taught us how to embalm and preserve,
within the corset of a strict dialectic, some of the profound opinions
that had been expressed more freely in serious discussion.

Wilde was a very conscious heir to these two great traditions
inherited from ancient Greek literature, with which he was remarkably familiar as a former student of Classics at both Trinity College
in Dublin and at Oxford. In his own writings, he had recourse to
both the dialogue and to comedy, though to both in modernized
forms that are no longer those of Plato or Aristophanes, but rather
those of the Neo-Platonic dialogue of the Italian Renaissance and of
the so-called New Comedy of Menander and, in Latin, of Plautus
and Terence. Much of his conversational wit has indeed survived in
both his dialogues and his comedies, like fossil flies preserved in
amber, but also in his fiction. More of it has also survived in the
published recollections of a few of his friends, though perhaps with
flaws that are due to the tricks and lapses of individual memory. As
one now reads the brilliant conversation of the characters in Wilde's
dialogues, fiction and plays, one occasionally feels that he must
almost certainly have tested many of these quips and paradoxes in
his own conversation before using them in his writings.

One of Wilde's later disciples, the novelist Ronald Firbank, was
reported to me in conversation, by either Ivy Compton-Burnett or
her friend Margaret Jourdain, to have made a practice of using, in
the dialogues of his novels, much the same procedure, but conversely by preserving there the remarks of other people rather than
his own. When he returned home from a social gathering, his
pockets were always full of scraps of paper where he had secretly
noted any absurdities that he had overheard, and these he then
stored near his desk in brown paper grocery bags from which he

retrieved, as he wrote, many of the remarks of his fictional characters, so that their conversations were composed like a kind of mosaic
of materials salvaged from real life.

Wilde may well have had recourse in much the same way in his
writings to his memories of his own conversational quips, stored in
his memory instead of in brown paper grocery bags. Some of these
quips or paradoxes he used again and again, often in slightly
different forms and each time in a different context, whether in his
fiction, his dialogues, his comedies or his few collections of epigrams. They were his social stock in trade as a dandy as well as his
professional stock in trade as a writer, and his published letters as
well as the published memoirs of some of his friends tend to prove
that many of them originated in his life rather than in his art.

Like every other dandy, Wilde was an exhibitionist or narcissist,
always on display at his best when he felt that he faced an audience.
Above all, his exhibitionism was verbal, especially when, as the years
went by and his looks and figure became increasingly gross, he
began to realize that he could no longer lay claim to the good looks
of his youth. He then enjoyed more and more displaying in public
his virtuosity in words and ideas, with which he could still charm as
he had once charmed with his mere looks. Even under the stress of
his appearances in court, he was unable to resist the temptation, at
least throughout the first trial and much of the second, to put on a
show of his ready wit for which he was justly famous. Montgomery
Hyde, in his introduction to the published transcripts of the three
trials, thus writes that Wilde "managed to keep up a running fire of
banter, whether it was a question of his preference for iced champagne, contrary to his doctor's orders ('Never mind your doctor's
orders, Sir,'—'I never do.') or the time it took to walk from his house
in Tite Street to the abode of one of his young male friends ('I don't
know, I never walk.')"

All this ready repartee and paradox, recorded even in the official
transcripts of his trials, was intended by Wilde to highlight his
persona as a dandy and artist who was at all times more concerned
with style in his own life and that of others, as well as in art, than
with morality in art or life. Because he lived in a society that very
hypocritcally overstressed the importance of morality both in life
and in art while at the same time tolerating the lowest forms of
prostitution in its slums and the most brutal kinds of political

repression in Ireland, India and elsewhere, Wilde very firmly adopted the stand that art and morality share no common ground, and he chose personally to be a champion of art as opposed to morality. All this comes out clearly in the passages of *The Picture of Dorian Gray* where he describes, with much the same horror as Thomas De Quincey or Dickens, the sheer degradation of life in Victorian London's slums, or else later in *The Soul of Man under Socialism*. Finally, after his imprisonment, in such texts as *The Ballad of Reading Gaol, De Profundis*, and the few letters to the London press on the conditions that prevailed in English prisons, or to such friends as Reginald Turner, he becomes in turn an indignant and more humane champion of morality, although always, in a way, in the name of art and in order that life and morality should at last conform with his lofty conceptions of art. Wilde's respect for this kind of idealism, however impractical it may appear to be in real life, is also expressed briefly in a couple of his letters to Wilfred Scawen Blunt or where Blunt is mentioned. In a letter addressed in 1890 to Herbert Vivian, who had published an article quoting one of Wilde's letters without Wilde's permission, Wilde even suggests Blunt, the poet and anti-imperialist champion of what were then considered lost causes but have by now all been won, as an arbiter, in Wilde's dispute with Vivian, of both taste and morality.

Whether in his conversation, his writings intended for publication or his private correspondence, Wilde's defense of art as opposed to morality, or else, after his imprisonment, of a more humane morality in the name of art, constantly surfaces as one of his main concerns. He was well aware of the fact that he thereby antagonized the majority of his middle-class English contemporaries and, above all, London's daily press that flattered their prejudices and never missed an opportunity of ridiculing him. But Wilde also knew that he owed to this antagonism and publicity much of his ambiguous popularity which, until his trials, served him well by selling his books to a broader public and attracting record audiences to the performances of his comedies. Up to a point, his contemporaries even seemed to enjoy being shocked. With his trials, however, the point of no return was reached. He had gone too far.

In most of his letters to editors of the London press, Wilde had long been deliberately offensive, as already stated, on the subject of journalists and journalism, if only to rouse their ire enough to serve his own purposes by acting unwittingly as his unpaid publicity agents. Such affectations of contempt for journalism and journalists was part of his stock in trade as a dandy and public figure and should be interpreted as a tacit admission of his awareness of the power of the press. But the press ultimately avenged itself on him, at the time of his trials, for all his past expressions of contempt.

With the exception of what is preserved in his own writings, in the transcripts of his trials and the published memoirs of some of his friends, much of Wilde's conversational virtuosity is irretrievably lost, however much it may once have delighted or shocked his listeners. With the relatively recent publication of the majority of his letters that have survived, we can nevertheless recapture much that had long remained inaccessible to us. Of the close on two thousand letters that Sir Rupert Hart-Davis has deemed worthy of publication in the two volumes of Wilde's correspondence that he has so far edited and published, the majority, of course, are of more strictly biographical than literary interest, casting new light on various events in Wilde's life or helping us to date more accurately some points that still remained vague or controversial. Commenting in his introduction to the first of these two volumes on Wilde's famous remark to Gide on his own life and writings, Sir Rupert writes that "the art of the talker, like that of the actor, dies with the artist and can seldom be recaptured from the written word. Perhaps the nearest approach to it is by way of letters."

In our age of rarely written or hastily dictated letters, recordings can also preserve for posterity some of the utterances of virtuoso talkers. Although texts that have been retyped from such recordings without careful editing can prove to be somewhat repetitious, the speaker at least steers clear, in a recording, from those spelling mistakes that mar a too hastily scribbled letter and can be found, as Sir Rupert points out, even in some of Wilde's letters.

In an interview published some years ago in New York in *Antaeus*, Gore Vidal deplored the decline of the art of letter-writing in our age of long-distance phone conversations. He suggested that an enterprising publisher should undertake the publication of an edition of the selected phone conversations of Truman Capote. But one shudders at the mere thought of how many more books our great libraries would be destined to preserve if the phone conversations and other *obiter dicta* of all our more brilliant talkers were thus recorded and published as religiously as the often rather mediocre utterances, letters, and other papers of some of our Presidents. In the seventeenth century, Oxford's Bodleian Library was one of Europe's greatest, with only some five thousand volumes. Robert Burton, the author of *The Anatomy of Melancholy*, spent ten years there, systematically reading all the authors of the past whose works could provide him with the many curious facts, such as how Bishop Hatto allowed himself to be devoured by rats, that he then quoted in his masterpiece. Now the library of the University of California at Los Angeles can already boast of storing a good five million volumes. Like Alice's thirty maids with thirty mops who would never be able to sweep away the sands of the seashore, no scholarly bookworm, even endowed with the proverbial nine lives of thirty cats, would ever be able to emerge from the stacks of the libraries of the University of California at Los Angeles with as comprehensive a harvest of available and pertinent facts and anecdotes as one finds in *The Anatomy of Melancholy*.

Wilde too was a voracious reader, though perhaps not as systematic as Burton. Even at the height of his career as an unusually successful writer, lecturer and man-about-town, a welcome guest too in many exclusive London homes, he still found time to read a great deal, to review a remarkable number of books, and to write many letters where he refers to his other readings. Many of these letters reflect to some extent his art as a conversationalist, and some few, especially the long letter addressed from prison to Lord Alfred and later published as *De Profundis*, are documents of rare and intense human interest. Others are rich in critical insights concerning his readings, which cannot be found in any of the writings that he published.

In a brief letter of 1890 addressed to the American writer Edgar Saltus, Wilde thus admits that the latter's "strange book, so pessimistic, so poisonous and so perfect," gave him a *"nouveau frisson."* This admission is of particular interest because Saltus is known to have given Wilde a copy of his *Mary Magdalen*, published in 1891. Saltus also published much later, in 1917, a pamphlet, *Oscar Wilde: An Idler's Impression*, in which this letter is preserved together with some personal memories of Wilde, whom Saltus had met in London. Although poor Saltus is now rarely read, his wit often had much in common with Wilde's, and the influence of the writings of both Saltus and Wilde as well as of Thomas Beer's *The Mauve Decade* can now be detected in some of the early writings of Djuna Barnes.

In a letter addressed in 1893 to the English actor Edward Hamilton Bell, Wilde asks him, in particularly kind terms, to encourage another American writer, Jonathan Sturges, who was a cripple from childhood and spent most of his life in England, to send him some of his "brilliant, vivid, jewelled stories." Sturges had just published *The First Supper and Other Episodes* and was a friend of Whistler and Henry James, who is reputed to have used him as model for the character of Little Bilham in *The Ambassadors*. Sturges had met Wilde in London, in the company of the poet Stuart Merrill, in 1890. In 1895, Merrill drew up a petition to Queen Victoria begging for Wilde's release from prison and asked Sturges to approach James to sign it too. Sturges then wrote back to Stuart Merrill: "I do not think he will sign the petition, though I know he feels sorry for Oscar." The petition came to nothing, for lack of signatures of a sufficient number of prominent French or English writers. However grateful Sturges may thus have proven to be for Wilde's encouragement as a writer, his claims to literary celebrity now rest mainly on his friendships with other writers and artists and, above all, with Henry James.

But one should not attach too much importance to some of the critical appreciations and other forms of encouragement that Wilde lavished in many of his letters to younger writers whose works he found "charming" or "brilliant." Other letters, however, are rich in valid critical insights. In a letter hastily written from prison in Reading to Robert Ross and without much visible concern about his own style, Wilde states, about the *Vailima Letters* of Robert Louis Stevenson, that "I see that romantic surroundings are the worst possible surroundings for a romantic writer. In Gower Street, Stevenson could have written a new *Trois Mousquetaires*. In Samoa, he wrote letters to *The Times* about Germans. I see also the traces of a terrible *strain* to lead a natural life. To chop wood with any advantage to oneself, or profit to others, one should be able to describe the process. In point of fact the natural life is the unconscious life. Stevenson merely extended the sphere of the artificial by taking to digging. The whole dreary book has given me a lesson. If I spend my future life reading Baudelaire in a *café* I shall be leading a more natural life than if I take to a hedger's work or plant cacao in mud-swamps."

True, the author of *Treasure Island, The New Arabian Nights* and *The Dynamiters*, all of them romantic tales of action written in an unromantic environment, failed pathetically to produce anything as colorful and dramatic after withdrawing to the kind of Polynesian setting that could inspire Melville or Gauguin. But Wilde neglects, in applying his strictures with some justice to poor consumptive Stevenson, to take into consideration the latter's failing health and desperate fight for survival, which probably prevented him from achieving the right kind of adaptation to the romantic environment of Samoa, where he was seeking, by leading "the natural life" and through physical labor, to recover his lost health and strength. To Melville, a romantic writer if there ever was one, Wilde's strictures would not be applicable, nor to W. H. Hudson.

The same letter to Robert Ross contains a more pertinent condemnation of the style of the much-admired French novelist Joris Karl Huysmans: "*En Route* is most over-rated. It is sheer journalism. It never makes one hear a note of the music it describes. The subject is delightful, but the style is of course worthless, slipshod, flaccid. It is worse French than Ohnet's. Ohnet tries to be commonplace and succeeds. Huysmans tries not to be, and is. . . ." Georges Ohnet was in those days a very popular French novelist whose style Wilde had good reason to despise, and whose works are now remembered in France, if at all, only as proverbial examples of a truly obsolete kind of *Kitsch*. But as one now reads Wilde's critique of Huysmans, one might well wonder whether, had he survived long enough, he would have perceived the music of Vinteuil's fictional sonata from a reading of Proust's prose description of it.

Wilde's letters contain many other perceptive critical appreciations of French writers, especially of those who were his personal friends, but also of others, whether of the past or his own contemporaries. Alexandre Dumas Père, Baudelaire, Flaubert, and Gautier, among French writers of the past, are perhaps those whose works he praised most frequently and enthusiastically; among his contemporaries, Edmond de Goncourt, Mallarmé, Hugo, Verlaine, Pierre Louÿs, Anatole France, Marcel Schwob, to whom he dedicated *The Sphinx,* and young André Gide, among others. Of the latter's *Les Nourritures terrestres,* Wilde nevertheless wrote that the book failed to fascinate him and that "the egoistic note is, of course, and always has been for me, the primal and ultimate note of modern art, but *to be an Egoist one must have an Ego.* It is not everyone who says "I, I" who can enter the Kingdom of Art. But I love André personally very deeply." Although one might be tempted to agree with Wilde that much of Gide's writing is self-important, solipsistic or precious, one begins to wonder what Wilde would have thought of the far more solipsistic poetry that we now see published in such great quantities in England and America. Compared with Robert Duncan, Gary Snyder or Allen Ginsberg, for instance, André Gide now seems to have concealed his Ego with almost modest reticence.

As a literary critic, Wilde had within easy reach his remarkably clear memories of a broad range of previous readings, and a vision that allowed him to focus immediately on essentials. Like a hawk hovering high up in the sky, he could survey a broad field and swoop down unerringly on his prey. Few critics in our "journalistic age," to misquote slightly Hermann Hesse's *Glasperlenspiel,* can display these rare qualities that I could admire so often in the critical writings of my friend Kenneth Rexroth.

But volumes of collected letters, even if as brilliant, informative or varied as those of Wilde, no longer enjoy, like volumes of collected sermons too, the kind of popularity with the reading public that they enjoyed a hundred or more years ago, although volumes of recorded interviews appear now to be beginning to enjoy much the same kind of success. The two volumes of Wilde's collected letters include, as previously stated, slightly less than two thousand of those deemed worthy of publication, so that he is likely to be remembered among the few most prolific English letter-writers. His published correspondence amounts indeed to about a third of that of D. H. Lawrence and slightly less than that of Horace Walpole, and the importance, number and variety of Wilde's correspondents surpass those of either Lawrence's or Walpole's, so that Wilde may yet rank among the very greatest English letter-writers of all times and certainly well above, for instance, James Joyce.

Wilde's correspondence not only casts light on many important aspects of his complex private life and his often misinterpreted public life, but it also contains valuable revelations concerning the social life of his age and many critical appreciations of his extensive readings that cannot be found in the writings that he published in his lifetime. Because it is being more and more widely recognized that Wilde was one of the greatest and most perceptive English literary critics of the nineteenth century, these many appreciations might deserve to be extracted from the mass of his correspondence and made more readily accessible in a separate volume.

American readers may well be particularly impressed by the variety of Wilde's interests as it is illustrated in a letter that he wrote in French in 1891 to the French novelist and diarist Edmond de Goncourt. As early as 1883, Goncourt had referred in his *Journal* to the possibility of extracting hydrogen from the atmosphere in order to create "a terrible destructive device." This section of Goncourt's *Journal* was then published in Paris in the daily *Echo de Paris* of December 17th 1891, together with Goncourt's inaccurate report of some statements that Wilde had apparently made to him about Swinburne on April 21st 1883. In his letter protesting to Goncourt against these inaccuracies on the very day of their publication, Wilde refers also to Goncourt's speculations about the possible invention of a hydrogen bomb. In Wilde's opinion, such an invention would be "a masterpiece, if not of science, at least of art."

I now regret not having had access to some of Wilde's critical observations contained in many of his letters when I was first writing this book, long before the publication of the two available volumes of his correspondence. Had I known, for instance, the long letter that Wilde wrote from Paris on March 23rd 1883 to the American actress Mary Anderson concerning the proposed production of his lyrical drama *The Duchess of Padua*, I might have considerably expanded my discussion of this play in order to include quotations from Wilde's letter where he explains how he feels that it should be performed and what his intentions were in shifting its mood so constantly back and forth from or to different levels of comedy or of tragedy. A careful reading of this letter might even lead one to conclude that Wilde, in writing *The Duchess of Padua*, may have been unconsciously more Jacobean than truly Elizabethan in his intentions, in fact emulating some of the effects of Webster's *The Duchess of Malfi* rather than those of any Shakespearean tragedy, such as *Romeo and Juliet* or *Othello,* that likewise has an Italian Renaissance setting.

But the evolution of literary taste nearly always produces this kind of curious hybrid when it comes to what is known as "imitation of the ancients," in fact the emulation of classical models. Whether in Italian, French, English or later too in German, no major neo-classical dramatist such as Tasso, Alfieri, Corneille, Racine, Dryden, Addison, Schiller or Kleist has ever produced anything that can truly be said to follow exactly the pattern of the tragedies of Sophocles. In nineteenth-century English verse drama, a similar metamorphosis of Elizabethan or Jacobean models can be observed. Whether in Shelley's *The Cenci,* Byron's *Manfred,* Tennyson's *Harold* or Wilde's *The Duchess of Padua,* one discerns those ingredients of typically Romantic rhetoric that also produced, in *Death's Jest-book* by Thomas Lovell Beddoes, the somewhat self-conscious imitation of, for instance, the utterances of the Fool in *King Lear* which strikes one in the speeches of Homunculus Mandrake. What had once been more spontaneous baroque rhetoric became, after a lapse of time, a learned imitation of a style of the past that can still offer us interesting readings, but that generally renders such nineteenth-century English verse dramas quite unfit for production on any stage. For reasons too complex to be discussed here, this kind of romantic rhetoric has proven to be dramatically more felicitous in nineteenth-century French verse drama: Victor Hugo's *Hernani* and Edmond Rostand's *Cyrano de Bergerac* can still be performed successfully on the stage and attract enthusiastic audiences.

Wilde may have been influenced to some extent, in his lyrical dramas, by the example of contemporary French verse drama, since he expresses in many of his letters his passionate admiration of Sarah Bernhardt as well as of other French actors, dramatists, and theatrical producers. His detailed explanations, in his letter to Mary Anderson, of how almost every character and scene of *The Duchess of Padua* should be performed goes indeed a long way towards explaining why nineteenth-century English verse drama followed this peculiarly rhetorical evolution. Like many nineteenth-century academic painters of historical scenes, the authors of such plays were too much concerned with a kind of learned reconstruction of the past which they conceived almost in terms of operatic stage-craft. In the particular case of the authors of verse drama, they were attempting to revive a form that the Augustan era, in the tragedies of Dryden or Addison, had long eschewed. Viewing their Elizabethan or Jacobean models from such a distance in the perspective of history, Romantic or Post-Romantic English poets exaggerated the rhetoric of Shakespeare and his contrasts between the tragic and comic scenes of his histories. Above all, they lacked his spontaneity. In the particular case of Wilde's early lyrical dramas, his youth and relative inexperience of the stage were also responsible for his excessive reliance on the kind of rhetoric and other devices that mar all nineteenth-century England's other examples of an "Elizabethan Revival" of drama, so that even its masterpieces have much in common with the earlier architecture of Horace Walpole's and William Beckford's attempted "Gothic Revival" in the architecture and decoration of Strawberry Hill and of Fonthill Abbey.

Wilde also states, in his letter to Mary Anderson, proudly and with no hesitation, that *The Duchess of Padua* "is the masterpiece of all my literary work, the *chef d'oeuvre* of my youth." Although it already displays considerable improvements on the pretentious immaturity of *Vera, or The Nihilists*, it still lacks the uniquely Symbolist quality of *Salome, A Florentine Tragedy* and his project of *La Sainte Courtisane*, which Wilde himself described in *De Profundis* as "beautiful coloured, musical things." In these later and more mature lyrical dramas, Wilde no longer sought to imitate the Elizabethans, but had struck out on his own under the influence of contemporary French lyrical drama, and was already managing to create, at least in *Salome*, a work in which the "coloured" and "musical" qualities of his writing lend themselves to the scenery, costumes and music that ultimately transformed it, as an opera, into the kind of "total work of art" which had been Wagner's aim. Such a concept of "synesthesia," of a synthesis of poetry, music and visual art that would appeal simultaneously to several senses, had already haunted the minds of many Romantics, above all of Balzac and Baudelaire.

Wilde's letters are rich in such expressions of his esthetic beliefs and intentions. A whole book of commentary on his *obiter dicta* could thus be compiled from a careful reading of many of his letters, and one hopes that the English Department of some university will soon encourage one of its more industrious and perceptive graduate students to devote his doctoral dissertation to this task, which might cast considerable light on the whole controversial subject of the esthetics of English so-called Symbolist or Decadent literature. Through the example of his own published writings, of his conversation and of his letters to friends or to the London press, Wilde exerted a very considerable influence in his lifetime and for many years after his death, often on writers or artists, such as Natalie Barney or Djuna Barnes, who had never known him personally. Among his letters to the press, his replies to criticism of *The Picture of Dorian Gray* that had been published in *The Scots Observer, The Daily Chronicle,* and *The St. James Gazette* are particularly brilliant and informative as *ex post facto* declarations of his esthetic intentions in writing the novel, but scarcely lend themselves to more detailed discussion here, since they reiterate very clearly and firmly the distinction that Wilde always insisted on making between art and morality, between esthetics and ethics.

His esthetics were, in general, those of all English Symbolist or Decadent literature, of which he remains the main spokesman, whose theories, formulations and tastes influenced those of most of the other writers of this school. But Wilde himself derived many elements of his esthetics not only from the Pre-Raphaelites, William Morris, Walter Pater and Ruskin in an earlier generation, but also from his very extensive readings of contemporary French literature and his personal friendships, conversations and correspondence with a number of outstanding French writers, above all with Mallarmé, Pierre Louÿs, Marcel Schwob, Edmond de Goncourt, and André Gide.

Wilde's knowledge of French was quite remarkable, and the few letters that he wrote in French are grammatically and stylistically almost impeccable, their few flaws being generally of the kind that one can also find in letters written rather hastily by some French writers. The eminent American-born French Symbolist poet Stuart Merrill, together with the rather minor French Symbolist poet Alfred Retté, nevertheless took the trouble of checking and correcting Wilde's French in his original French version of *Salomé*. In his memoirs that he wrote and published later in French, Stuart Merrill remarks that it had not been easy to persuade Wilde to accept all their corrections, and that Wilde wrote French as he spoke it, with an imaginative quality that could be colorful in conversation but would have produced, in a theater, a deplorable impression. In the letters that he wrote in French, Wilde's vocabulary and style are indeed, from time to time, quite colorful, but more often rather formal.

On French literature too, Wilde exerted in turn some influence, mainly on younger writers with whom he associated after his release from prison in his self-imposed exile in Paris. Two of these younger French writers deserve to be specially mentioned here: André Gide, who later exerted so very great an influence on even younger writers in France, Germany and elsewhere, and Ernest La Jeunesse, a gifted and curious eccentric with whom Wilde associated a great deal in Paris, but who is now remembered, if at all, only as a colorful character who haunted the cafés of the Boulevards. Wilde's influence can even be detected in most of the writings later published in French by the American expatriate author Natalie Barney, who appears never to have actually met him, but to have deliberately set out in Paris to be, both in her life and published aphorisms or paradoxes, a kind of opulent lesbian version of Oscar Wilde.

The letters selected for publication by Sir Rupert Hart-Davis are not, of course, all of equal literary interest, as has already been suggested. Many of them reveal the vast and complex network of Wilde's friendships, associations and enmities, whether in England, France or the United States. One may thus be surprised to discover that he corresponded briefly, in the course of his American tour, with Oliver Wendell Holmes, Joaquin Miller, Walt Whitman, Charles Eliot Norton, Samuel Ward, who was the brother of Julia Ward Howe, the pioneer American expatriate journalist and poet Theodore Tilton, the sculptor William Westmore Story, whose biography Henry James published in 1903, and more extensively with the American actress Mary Anderson; later too with the American painter Albert Sterner, among others.

Other letters prove that several of Wilde's closest London friends were Jews: among others, Ada Esther Beddington, who was married to Ernest David Leverson, the son of a diamond merchant, the family of the German-born banker Leo Schuster, one of whose descendants is the poet Sir Stephen Spender, the pioneer English

Impressionist painter William Rothenstein, and the musician and translator Felix Moscheles. A close friend of Leonard Montefiore from their common Oxford days, Wilde became likewise a friend of his younger brother Claude and of their sister Charlotte, to whom Wilde even proposed marriage. When she rejected his proposal, Wilde wrote her: "With your money and my brain we could have gone far."

With the very wealthy young Russian-born writer André Raffalovich, who wrote in both English and French and sometimes under a pseudonym, Alexander Michaelson, Wilde had occasion to quarrel, though without any hint of anti-Semitism. From Wilde's letters and from other sources, Raffalovich appears to have been a rather tactless busybody. With Princess Alice of Monaco, who was *née* Heine and closely related to the poet Heinrich Heine, Wilde corresponded briefly, as well as with her protégé, the composer Isidore de Lara, *née* Cohen.

From Frank Harris' otherwise often unreliable *Oscar Wilde: His Life and Confessions*, one gathers that several of Wilde's Jewish friends were among the few who rallied most spontaneously to his assistance both during his trials and imprisonment and after his release from jail, perhaps unconsciously because Jews still felt that their position in English society that was so fraught with prejudices, was in a way as marginal and precarious as that of homosexuals, a fact that Proust later remarked again and again about the position of Jews in French society too.

It was indeed, according to Frank Harris, an unnamed Jewish yacht-owner who offered to convey Wilde secretly to France aboard his craft between Wilde's second and third trials, when Wilde could only expect, under England's barbarous laws, to be sentenced to jail, and it was in Ada Leverson's home that Wilde's few most faithful friends foregathered to greet him when he was at last released from prison, and Adela Schuster, the banker's daughter, who generously provided him with a thousand pounds of sorely needed funds when he was declared a bankrupt and already in jail.

Later, at the time of the Dreyfus Affair in France, Wilde associated in Paris mainly with French friends who believed firmly in the innocence of Dreyfus and who attended regularly the salon of Madame Straus-Bizet, the real-life original of Proust's Madame Verdurin, according to the writer Maurice Sachs, whose grandmother's second husband had been the son of Madame Straus-Bizet by the latter's first husband, the composer of *Carmen.* After meeting Esterhazy, the notorious adventurer who had forged the compromising document on the basis of which Captain Dreyfus was falsely accused and condemned as its author and a traitor, Wilde reported to a French friend that Esterhazy had actually admitted to him his own guilt. But Wilde couldn't then refrain from adding one of his typical quips, which is reported only in French: "Esterhazy is much more interesting than Dreyfus. It's always wrong to be innocent. To be a criminal, one needs imagination and courage." Should this now be interpreted as a sly admission, after his own associations with criminals in jail, of his own guilt?

In a letter written from Paris, around the same time, to Robert Ross, Wilde nevertheless describes his indignation over the behavior of his friend Sherard, who was Wordsworth's great-grandson and had made a violently anti-Semitic scene in Campbell's Bar. In this whole context, Wilde thus proves to have been far more openminded than, in the next generation of English writers, G. K. Chesterton and Hilaire Belloc, both notorious and vicious anti-Semites, or Virginia Woolf who was so absurdly intolerant of her devoted husband's Jewish family.

Wilde's earliest published letters, addressed in his boyhood and adolescence mainly to his mother between 1868 and 1878, are of no literary interest except a few that were written in 1875 or later during his Oxford years, above all those where he describes his impressions of Venice, Florence, Padua, and Milan on the occasion of his first trip to the European continent. These impressions are still couched in a self-consciously Ruskinian style, and one feels that he is here trying his hand as a writer of "artistic" prose. Only after his return early in 1883 from his American lecture tour does much of his correspondence begin very rapidly to display the very personal style and wit for which he so soon became famous.

For our more strictly literary than biographical or psychological purposes, by far the most interesting of these letters of Wilde's heyday in London society are those in which, after his return from America, he expressed critical opinions on his readings, on art, on the plays that he had seen, on personalities of the worlds of literature and the arts, and on his intentions in his own writings, as in the previously mentioned long letter to Mary Anderson about how, in his opinion, *The Duchess of Padua* should be directed or acted; or else, as in his various letters to the London press on his intentions in writing *The Picture of Dorian Gray*. In this general context, it is interesting to note that Wilde wrote, some nine years after writing to Mary Anderson, an enthusiastic short letter about a London performance of Webster's *The Duchess of Malfi*, but we have no evidence other than what a reading of *The Duchess of Padua* and its very title might suggest, that Wilde was acquainted with Webster's masterpiece when he wrote what he considered the *chef-d'oeuvre* of his own youth.

Many of the letters that Wilde wrote during his trials, from prison and, after his release, from his self-imposed exile abroad, above all the long letter known as *De Profundis*, are of profound human interest. While still including frequent and often pertinent remarks on his readings, several such later letters to a few of his closer friends are far more frank about his homosexuality. In a letter written to Robert Ross from Nice in February 1898, he declared quite bluntly: "A patriot put in prison for loving his country loves his country, and a poet in prison for loving boys loves boys." Many of these later letters from abroad are full of complaints and pleas on the subject of money; others, on his efforts to be of assistance to the few men who had been his friends in prison, or to a jailor who had been particularly kind to him, are truly touching, in an almost childlike manner. Wilde had indeed become, after his release from prison, much more humane, in fact less haughty and pretentious.

The literary opinions that one finds scattered in so many of Wilde's letters are far too numerous and varied to be quoted and commented on here in greater detail. Some of them, of course, are of a very superficial nature, dictated by his social obligations, when he writes to thank an author for a book that he has received and read, others too by sheer kindness, when he wishes only to encourage a younger writer, as was probably the case when he suggested that Jonathan Sturges send him more stories. Wilde is at his best, however, in those longer letters where he quite frankly expresses his opinion of the writings of one of his more important English contemporaries, as in a letter of 1897 to the painter William Rothenstein in which he discusses the work of W. E. Henley, an English poet and prose-writer who was then considered of some consequence although he is now but rarely read: "When I said of

W.E.H. that his prose was the prose of a poet, I paid him an undeserved compliment. His prose is jerky, spasmodic, and he is incapable of the beautiful architexture of a long sentence, which is the fine flower of prose-writing, but I praised him for the sake of antithesis; 'his poetry is the beautiful poetry of a prose-writer;' that refers to Henley's finest work: the *Hospital Poems*, which are in *vers libres*, and *vers libres* are prose. The author by dividing the lines shows you the rhythm he wishes you to follow. But all that one is concerned with is *literature*. Poetry is not finer than prose, nor prose finer than poetry. When one uses the words poetry and prose, one is only referring to certain technical modes of word-music, melody and harmony one might say, though they are not exclusive terms, and though I praised Henley too much, too extravagantly, when I said his prose was the beautiful prose of a poet, the latter part of the sentence is a subtle appreciation of *vers libres*, which W.E.H., if he had any critical faculty left, would be the first to appreciate! You seem to me to have misunderstood the sentence. Mallarmé would have understood it." The opinions expressed here on Henley's *vers libres*, those of a literary Realist, leave one wondering whether Wilde would have formulated the same strictures concerning the far more overtly poetic *vers libres* of some of his French friends, such as Pierre Louÿs and André Gide.

With the exception of *The Ballad of Reading Gaol*, Wilde's only writing entirely conceived after his trials and imprisonment are his numerous letters from prison and later from his years of exile on the Continent. Many of these, above all *De Profundis*, are truly great literature, although of a strictly confessional nature. These belong in a different literary category than most of his earlier letters, while others, where he reverts to literary criticism, as in the letter to William Rothenstein on Henley's writings, are of much the same literary quality as anything that Wilde wrote for publication in the heyday of his successes.

Wilde's shocking prison experiences and his few later years of poverty and illness in Normandy and Paris certainly affected his whole philosophy of life, including to a great extent what I have called his esthetics, ethics, and politics of the dandy. Had his health and morale still allowed him to produce any new work of fiction, it is indeed unlikely that he would then have written anything like *The Picture of Dorian Gray* or been able to imagine, in the field of drama, as carefree and frothy a farce as *The Importance of Being Earnest*. In one of the many book reviews written in his literary heyday, he had observed that "the object of most modern fiction is not to give pleasure to the artistic instinct, but rather to vividly portray life for us, to draw attention to social anomalies and social forms of injustice. Many of our novelists are really pamphleteers, reformers masquerading as story-tellers, earnest sociologists seeking to mend as well as to mirror life."

Elsewhere, Wilde likewise condemned scientific or psychological exactitude in fiction, which should possess over fact the supreme advantage that "it can make things artistically probable; can call for imaginative and realistic credence; can, by force of mere style, compel us to believe." The collapse of the macabre building at the end of Poe's *The Fall of the House of Usher*, the landslide which annihilates the ledge where live the fatal rattlesnakes at the end of Oliver Wendell Holmes' *Elsie Venner*, the fire which destroys the house and its treasures in the last pages of James' *The Spoils of Poynton*, are all, like the death of Wilde's hero at the end of *The Picture of Dorian Gray*, far more artistically than scientifically or factually probable. But Wilde, as a dandy, had long preferred this type of artistic probability to the pedestrian psychological probing of the French novelist Paul Bourget, who, according to Wilde, "commits the error of imagining that the men and women of modern life are capable of being infinitely analysed for an innumerable series of chapters." All this, in Wilde's poetics of fiction, is indeed a far cry from the shape of such major novels to come in the twentieth century as those of Marcel Proust or Robert Musil, and Wilde concluded his objections to most of the fiction of his contemporaries by declaring that "what is interesting about people in good society . . . is the mask that each one of them wears, not the reality that lies behind that mask," because, behind that mask, "sooner or later one comes to that dreadful universal thing called human nature." Too scientific an analysis of psychological motivations, he concluded, would reduce all characters to an inartistic monotony. Although he expressed such great admiration for Flaubert, Wilde appears never to have understood the originality of Flaubert's psychology in *Madame Bovary* or *L'Education sentimentale*, where the great French novelist contrasts the masks that his characters assume with the reality that these masks conceal, in fact what his characters assume that they are with what they are. Since Wilde formulated these views about fiction, Freud and his school have taught us, however, that the masks imposed on us by society and our Super-ego can be far more monotonous than the infinite variety of the Ids that they conceal.

Wilde appears to have begun to become aware of this as a result of his prison experiences, and some of the letters that he wrote from jail and after his release suggest that he too might then have sought, in any later fiction, "to mend as well as to mirror life." In *The Soul of Man under Socialism,* he had already displayed his idealism as a social or political reformer. What he preached there in prose and later in some of his letters to the press on the subject of prison reform, he was beginning to practice in the more realistic poetry of *The Ballad of Reading Gaol.* But there is too little available evidence to suggest to us what other major works Wilde might have written on his release from prison, had his morale, his failing health, and his financial worries not kept him in an almost constant state of humiliation and despair.

Although Wilde's brief literary heyday began close on a hundred years ago, all sorts of legal and other considerations postponed for many decades after his death the publication of the bulk of his letters that have survived, and nearly all the letters that he received, if he ever kept them, disappeared long ago. Most probably, those of importance in the years that preceded his trials were destroyed or wantonly scattered, together with other papers and manuscripts, when he was declared a bankrupt and the contents of his London home were seized and sold. Wilde later lamented on several occasions the loss of his library, which appears to have been extensive and valuable. Yet no catalogue of it was ever printed, like that which Maggs Brothers had published earlier for the auction of the magnificent library of Horace Walpole, so that we now know the titles of only a few of the books that Wilde possessed. Much that concerns his private life, whether his friendships and loves or his readings as the source of some of his writings, must probably remain for all times a mystery. The prudery that prevailed in England in his age led to the interpretation of much of his extravagance as proof of his homosexuality. Even in the course of his trials, the evidence produced against him proved only his homosexual associations and mannerisms, without describing any of his sexual acts. His gifts of silver cigarette cases to a number of boys of dubious character did not constitute sexual acts of the kind that might be analyzed in greater detail in a *Psychopathia sexualis*.

As late as 1954, seven years after the publication of the original edition of the present book, Montgomery Hyde, a member of the British Parliament for Ulster, a barrister-at-law of London's Middle Temple, and author of *The Trials of Oscar Wilde* which had already been published in 1948, tried in vain to obtain access, for purposes of further research, to official documents concerning Wilde's imprisonment. The British Government, however, was still so squeamish on the subject that the following discussion then occurred in the House of Commons, as reported in the London *Times*, on June 24th 1954.

OSCAR WILDE PAPERS

Mr. Montgomery Hyde (Belfast, North, U.U.) asked the Home Secretary why access to the official correspondence in his department relating to the imprisonment of Oscar Wilde continued to be restricted; and whether he would deposit those papers in the Public Record Office, and why the Home Secretary had refused to allow him to see the papers.

Sir David Maxwell Fyfe (Liverpool, West Derby, C.): Papers relating to ex-prisoners are withheld from public inspection until sufficient time has elapsed to diminish the possibility of their disclosure giving pain to living persons. I do not think I would be justified in making an exception to this practice in the case of Oscar Wilde.

Mr. Hyde said the correspondence was of considerable interest to students of English penal history and of prison conditions last century, and it concerned matters which occurred about 60 years ago. Would the Home Secretary conform with his predecessors in the attitude that departmental papers down to 1900 should be made available for public inspection?

Sir D. Maxwell Fyfe said he could not think that the aspect of the matter mentioned in the first part of the question would be the primary motive for disclosure of the documents. He must maintain the position he had stated.

Mr. Shinwell (Easington, Lab.) asked if the Home Secretary realized that Mr. Hyde was a prolific writer of articles and books on the subject and that he was only anxious to augment his income. (Ministerial cries of "Oh!")

Mr. Hyde said that his request for access to the documents was for purposes of genuine historical research. Access to papers later than 1897 had been granted to other applicants.

Sir D. Maxwell Fyfe said he had given a perfectly reasonable explanation.

And there the whole matter appears to have rested for the past thirty years and more, since no new publications on Wilde's imprisonment have yet quoted these papers. On their restricted nature and the need to refuse access to them, a pompous member of England's Conservative Party and a notoriously snide member of its Labour Party seem to have almost miraculously agreed.

Conclusion

Critics or apologists of modernism in literature often discuss the ideas of Baudelaire, of Rimbaud or of Proust rather than their forms, as if these writers had been philosophers rather than artists. Our examination of Wilde's ideas has now indicated that he followed, in much of his thought if not in his more technically artistic achievements, paths very similar to those of Poe or Baudelaire, of Rimbaud or Lautréamont, of Proust or Mallarmé; and Wilde was conscious of his aims, since he wrote, in *De Profundis,* that he had "made art a philosophy and philosophy an art." His failure to be accepted, in our age, as a great and important writer is thus a reflection of our own failure to understand his ideas, and of our tendency to evaluate him only as a technician, in terms of the perfection of art-forms which Wilde stressed in all his writings, though these forms may now seem to us, at times, imperfect or obsolete.

But the very forms of Wilde's art are also of considerable technical interest, in our age, if we analyze them properly. As one of the rare nineteenth-century poets who understood at least some of the fundamental principles of tragedy which Aristotle had investigated and defined, Wilde wrote a lyrical drama, *Salome*, which could be staged and can still fascinate an audience. Returning from the aberrations of Swinburne or Browning, whose dramas can be staged today even less easily than when they were first published, Wilde thus progressed toward a new kind of Senecan tragedy, if not yet toward a revival of true tragedy. As a poet who relied to a great extent on intelligence and on critical rather than intuitional taste, Wilde was able to skirt, in much of his poetry, most of the major pitfalls of absurdity, confusion, stupidity, affectation or argumentativeness where many of the greater Victorian poets often floundered. In such poems as *Hélas*, *Taedium Vitae* or *Humanitad*, Wilde indeed expressed an uncritical, confused or unworthy self; and he never achieved the Virgilian sweetness of Tennyson's metrics and dictional texture. But as a writer of prose poetry, Wilde surely ranks among the greatest and most creative in English literature, especially in some of his fairy-tales, in the myths of his dialogues, and in the prose of *Salome*. As a writer of fiction, hasty and imperfect though much of his work may be, he left us, in *The Portrait of Mr. W. H.*, as perfect a "story of an artist" as any of those of Henry James; and his understanding of the nature of the work of art was so much clearer than that of Henry James that the work of art, in Wilde's story, is properly integrated within the plot, though the "imperceptible points of view" give to the fiction of James more psychological verisimilitude. In *The Picture of Dorian Gray*, moreover, in spite of hurried writing, Wilde has left us English literature's most perfect example of that by-product of *Wilhelm Meister*, the *Erziehungsroman* of dandyism, in fact a novel whose dialectical structure illustrates an ultimate philosophical meaning which nearly all other such novels, too formless or too merely fashionable, generally failed to convey. Finally, as a critic, Wilde ranks among the greatest of the formal exponents of the poetics of Romanticism, though of a later and more sophisticated Romanticism, closely allied to that of many "moderns," than the less organized doctrines of the early Nineteenth Century which histories of literature still propose as having been "revolutionary."

Nor are these minor achievements, in terms of "modern" literature. T. S. Eliot, as poet or dramatist, was indeed more successful,
though his progress had been made easier by Wilde's work and by
the general clearing of the literary fog since 1880. But as critic and
esthetician, Eliot failed signally to offer us an organized doctrine.
Few of his essays read as well as Wilde's best critical writings, where
specific analysis of an artist's work, as in *Pen, Pencil, and Poison*,
serves to illustrate clearly one of the fundamental problems of the
philosophy of art. In his analysis of Eliot's views on Dante, Yvor
Winters ably indicated that Eliot's basic critical principles are as
confused as any Pre-Raphaelite's; but Wilde possessed a more
conscious philosophy of art, both more sound and more modern,
unless modernism consists in unsoundness.

If we agree that Wilde is modern, what modern literature has he
helped to shape? The forms of Wilde's art have no longer been
imitated to any appreciable extent by important English or American writers of the last few decades. In France and Germany, Gide,
Stefan George, and Huge von Hoffmansthal were considerably
influenced by Wilde's ideas and forms; Proust in his early stories,
where the seeds of his later masterpiece can already be detected,
followed much the same course as Wilde, though Proust may have
borrowed forms and ideas from Robert de Montesquiou, the original
of des Esseintes in *A Rebours*, rather than from Wilde; and *Salome*
and *The Ballad of Reading Gaol* were widely read and much
admired in pre-revolutionary Russia, in circles where Blok and
Essenin were perfecting their art.

But the ideas of Wilde's art have been much more fruitful than its
forms. Wilde's esthetics have been, among younger thinkers, the
starting-point of a constant discussion of art and literature, to which
we now owe types of literature as varied as the novels of George
Moore and those of Virginia Woolf. George Moore's doctrine of art
for art's sake stems from Wilde's interpretation of Flaubert's philosophy of art, and Virginia Woolf's fictional impressionism from the
esthetics of Clive Bell and Roger Fry, both of whom took up the
discussion where Wilde had left it in *The Critic as Artist*. Much of
the English or American literature of recent decades which, without
reverting to classicism, has formulated stricter disciplines of self-

expression than those of the Victorian Romantics, stems in fact from the discussion of the nature of art which Wilde once provoked. Our age has thus been, in the best of its literature, to a great extent the heyday of an artistic individualism which, uniting the contraries of subjectivism and objectivism in a self-examining impressionism, has sought to record experience scrupulously as the individual artist sees and feels it. To Oscar Wilde we owe much of the theory of this individualism and, in our adolescent readings, the stimulus which first led many of us to investigate its possibilities and our own natural gifts as artists. Finally, to Wilde's satirical wit and paradox we owe a whole tradition of literature, though its basic seriousness has not yet been fully appreciated. Some of the masters of this school have been Ronald Firbank, Carl Van Vechten, the completely forgotten novelist Max Ewing, and Evelyn Waugh, Juvenals of our corrupt and decadent café societey who have achieved, in their novels, what Wilde set out to do in the dialogue of his comedies.

Of his own importance Wilde was signally aware, as any important artist must be: "I was a man who stood in symbolic relations to the art and culture of my age. I had realised this for myself at the very dawn of my manhood, and had forced my age to realise it afterwards. Few men hold such a position in their own lifetime, and have it so acknowledged. It is usually discerned, if discerned at all, by the historian, or the critic, long after both the man and his age have passed away. With me it was different. I felt it myself and made others feel it. Byron was a symbolic figure, but his relations were to the passions of his age and its weariness of passion. Mine were to something more noble, more permanent, of more vital issue, of larger scope." Of this larger scope, this nobility, permanence and vitality, our discussion set out to indicate the measure.

Appendix I (Biographical)

Oscar Fingal O'Flahertie Wills Wilde was born in Dublin on the 16th of October, 1854, the second son of Dr. William Robert Wills Wilde, noted ear and eye specialist, Irish antiquarian and philanderer, and of Jane Francesca Elgee, Irish patriot, Byronic poetess under the name of Speranza, mediocre novelist under the name of John Fenshawe Ellis, and imperturbable wife in the midst of her husband's scandalous amorous intrigues. After the birth of her first child, William Wilde, who later became a London journalist and typically genial Irish raconteur, Speranza had hoped to be blessed with a daughter. Instead, Oscar was born, then raised for some years almost as if he were a girl, till Isola Wilde was born. In 1864, Oscar's father was knighted. Sir William Wilde's two sons were then being educated at the Portora Royal School, whence Oscar went, with an "exhibition" scholarship, at the age of seventeen, to Trinity College, Dublin. An outstanding student of Greek and Latin, he was there elected to a Queen's scholarship. In 1874, Oscar Wilde won the Berkeley Gold Medal for Greek, established by Bishop Berkeley, the eighteenth-century philosopher, and was awarded also a scholarship to pursue his studies at Magdalen College, Oxford, where he attended Ruskin's lectures and became a regular disciple at Walter Pater's gatherings.

In 1876, Sir William died. Oscar invested a part of his modest inheritance in a trip to Italy and Greece, where he went, early in 1877, with John Pentland Mahaffy, one of his Trinity College instructors. Oscar was already writing poetry, and this trip inspired many of the earlier poems which he published, four years later, in his first volume. The ancient world and Renaissance Italy became, moreover, a living ideal which from then on never ceased to haunt Wilde, the one with its paganism which he considered joyfully hedonistic, the other with the pomp and pageant of its Catholicism. In Rome, too, Wilde visited the tomb of Keats, "Priest of Beauty" and "divine boy." On his return, he began to discover the intellectual and social life of London, whither Lady Wilde had moved now that Dublin, after her husband's and her daughter's death, suggested too many sad memories. In Lady Wilde's transplanted salon, Oscar met some of those who belonged to more august circles and later introduced him to their friends. James McNeill Whistler, for instance, opened new vistas of elegance, taste and wit for the young poet whose esthetic creed was still that of a modified and neo-pagan Pre-Raphaelitism, of Ruskin and Pater in esthetics, of Rossetti and Swinburne in poetry, of Burne-Jones and Sir Lawrence Alma-Tadema, or Lord Leighton, in painting. And Willie Wilde was already on the staff of *The World*, where he printed some of his younger brother's poems and began to display toward the poet that unquestioning loyalty to which Oscar, in later years, owed so much useful publicity.

In 1878, Wilde was awarded, at Oxford, the coveted Newdigate Prize for poetry: his poem, *Ravenna*, commemorated his discovery of Italy, but significantly chose, rather than pontifical Rome or Humanistic Florence, the epigonic capital of Byzantine Exarchs as its cherished symbol of a glorious past. His studies now completed, Wilde set out to establish himself in London as Professor of Esthetics and Art critic. He began by courting, in an ostentatious and passionately Platonic manner, Lily Langtry, the reigning beauty of the day, as well as Helena Modjeska, a Polish actress one of whose poems he translated in 1880, and Sarah Bernhardt. The young poet's extravagant costumes and affectations soon attracted so much attention that he became identified with the Esthetes satirized in *Punch's* cartoons, and especially with Bunthorne, the absurd poet of the operetta *Patience*, by Gilbert and Sullivan. And it was indeed as an advance poster for his American Production of *Patience* that D'Oyly Carte sent Wilde to America, on a lecture tour, in 1882, shortly after the publication, in London, of the young esthete's *Poems* which, though wryly reviewed by nearly all critics, had been a success with the curious public.

Oscar Wilde landed in New York on the 2nd of January, 1882, and was whisked on a coast-to-coast tour in a tornado of brash journalism and publicity. The details of this tour have been ably told, by Lloyd Lewis and Henry Justin Smith, in *Oscar Wilde Discovers America* (New York, 1936). While in America, Wilde met most of the leading American men of letters and even visited Whitman, for whose ideals he had early inherited, from Speranza, a passionate reverence. In his lectures, Wilde expounded the principles of the English Renaissance and of "the New Hellenism," with special emphasis on their application to interior decoration and dress-reform. He illustrated the latter by wearing, during most of his lectures, knee-breeches which fast became legendary, and by flaunting long hair and other sartorial extravagances for which he remained famous. And in New York, he ambitiously peddled his earlier dramas, *Vera, or The Nihilists* and *The Duchess of Padua*, among Broadway producers and leading ladies, though with no immediate success.

He returned from his American triumphs much chastened, it seems, more conscious of his real talents, wise to most of the tricks of journalism and publicity, and convinced of his own showmanlike ability to impose himself on his public and thus earn a living. In emotional matters, however, he was still a remarkably pure young man, though he had proved himself able to impress Western toughs with his physical strength and courage and his ability to drink and bluff at poker as well as most. Speranza's London salon had meanwhile become the hub of Parnell's Irish Nationalism and of Oscar's own estheticism. In quest of an atmosphere more conducive to writing, Wilde soon left for Paris, in January, 1883, and immersed himself in that city's many artistic and literary movements. He studied the art of Balzac, Théophile Gautier, Huysmans, Baudelaire, Barbey d'Aurevilly, Puvis de Chavanne, and Gustave Moreau, imitating many of their mannerisms of dress, speech, and behavior and imbibing the doctrines of dandyism and of decadent hedonism. During this period, he finished writing *The Duchess of Padua*, began rewriting *The Sphinx* and toyed with other projects, perhaps already with *The Harlot's House*, though this poem, the most perfect example of Wilde's mature art as a poet, was not published till 1885. In Paris, Wilde also renewed his friendship with Sarah Bernhardt, met Victor Hugo, Edmond de Goncourt, Coquelin, and many others, and established numerous lasting friendships.

Returning to London, Wilde immediately sailed for New York, to supervise the production of *Vera*, which proved a flop. Soon back in England, he began lecturing to provincial audiences, though with little of the fanfare of his American tour and far less successfully or profitably. In Dublin, he became friendly with Constance Lloyd, whom he married in London, in May, 1884. It was a select society wedding, after which the young couple honeymooned in Paris before setting out to find and decorate, in London, the home which was to be the illustration of all Wilde's esthetic theories.

This ideal home was finally established in Chelsea, at number 16 Tite Street; and Wilde soon began, in spite of Constance's small capital, to describe the money-situation there as "tight." Other tensions were soon felt too. Wearying of the limitations of conjugal bliss and, after the birth of Cyril Wilde, in 1885, and of Vivian Wilde, in 1886, of the tender joys of fatherhood too, Wilde allowed himself to develop the habit of going out ever more frequently without Constance, whose shadowlike devotion and uncritical approval may have bored him. At first, he had indeed seemed content to establish himself as a fashion-expert, with Constance as his model and the whole of Mayfair as his following; and for his children he had begun to write the fairy tales of *The Happy Prince*. All this led to his being offered, in 1887, the editorship of *The Woman's World*, a fashions and society monthly; for two years, he devoted much of his taste and energy to editing it, and was rewarded, for his efforts, with great success. But this very success allowed Wilde to indulge the passion for pleasure, whether esthetic or sensual, that seemed to grow more imperious as he became aware of the illusory nature of his happiness. And he began, during these years, to become fully conscious of his homosexual desires and to succumb to them as to all other desires. At first, this self-discovery was artistically most fruitful: between 1887 and 1891, Wilde wrote or published a large number of book reviews for *The Woman's World* and other magazines, all the tales of *The Happy Prince* (1888) and *A House of Pomegranates* (1890), all the essays and dialogues of *Intentions* (1890), the stories of *Lord Arthur Savile's Crime* (1890), his novel *The Picture of Dorian Gray* (1890), his Utopian essay on *The Soul of Man under Socialism* (1890), and the French version of *Salome*.

But he met, in the summer of 1891, Lord Alfred Douglas, a young wastrel endowed with great nobility of appearance and birth, and with unusual poetic talents and skills which, had he but submitted to the sterner disciplines of the artist's life, might have assured him an outstanding position in the literary world of his age. Twenty-one years old and a younger son of the prize-fighting Marquis of Queensberry, Lord Alfred, as a homosexual, was apparently no novice. Nor was Wilde, for that matter: as his marriage had become more and more of a failure, he had drifted rapidly into habits of pleasure, until he now exhibited his homosexuality with the ostentatious insouciance which seemed to be the hall-mark of his every action. Wilde had picked up, for instance, a young clerk in his publisher's office, and brought him home to meet Constance and the children. Lord Alfred likewise became a regular visitor at Tite Street, and Constance accepted him as unquestioningly as she did all her husband's whims. But the reports of the orgies in which Wilde and Lord Alfred became involved began to spread rapidly; and Wilde's life grew increasingly irregular, with frequent pleasure-trips abroad, wild week-ends in the hotels of London and of the South-Coast resorts, and a heavy load of debts incurred to satisfy his own extravagances and those of Lord Alfred, the petulant loved one who would accept his devotion only if it were offered in an aura of amusements and luxuries.

It was in this atmosphere that Wilde turned again to the stage. His comedies, from *Lady Windermere's Fan*, early in 1892, to *The Importance of Being Earnest*, in 1895, proved to be a veritable goldmine. During these years, apart from completing *The Sphinx*, putting final touches to *Salome* and dickering with a few minor poetical works, Wilde seems to have devoted all his talents to the commercial drama, though there may have been more serious projects among the manuscripts that were scattered and lost at the time of his trial. He was at the peak of his career: all London applauded his wit, whether in his comedies or in his conversation. And all London seemed content to whisper about his vices while pretending to ignore them, much as a tyrant ignores or forgives a court-jester's irreverence.

But there was one man whose neurotic purposes Wilde's scandalous life could be made to serve. Ever since his divorce, the Marquis of Queensberry had madly sought to persecute his former wife and her children, especially Lord Alfred who was the mother's favorite. In morality, the Marquis displayed indeed but a superficial interest, and he was not at all afraid of a public scandal. He began to persecute Wilde and Lord Alfred with open taunts, threats, and insults; and the climax came, on the 18th of February, 1895, when he left, with the porter of Wilde's club, a visiting-card on which was scrawled: "To Oscar Wilde, posing as a Sodomite."

Lord Alfred and his brother had long been urging Wilde to sue their father in order to put a stop to his persecutions. Assured of their support, Wilde now consulted lawyers, swore that Queensberry's accusation was untrue, and went to court. But the Marquis spared no expense in accumulating evidence. In court, only Wilde's writings were at first criticized, especially his unfortunate contribution to *The Chameleon*, an undergraduate Oxford periodical edited, with a distinctly homosexual flavor, by a friend of Lord Alfred. Later, as the case progressed, Wilde's life also became the topic of discussion: male prostitutes with whom Wilde had had sexual relations were produced as witnesses, and one of Wilde's friends, Alfred Taylor, who acted as host in a kind of homosexual call-house, was dragged into court too. Queensberry's insults were thus found to have been justified, and Oscar Wilde's prosecution, under laws which punished homosexuality, became inevitable now that his guilt had been made manifest in court.

Wilde could expect to be arrested at any moment, as a common criminal to be prosecuted by Her Majesty Queen Victoria. His friends urged him to escape abroad, and Speranza began supervising the packing and shipping of his baggage. But he was arrested, it seems, before any definite plan for escape had been formulated. The details of the two ensuing trials have been scrupulously told, by Frances Winwar, in her well-documented biography: *Oscar Wilde and the Yellow 'Nineties* (New York, Harper and Brothers, 1940). The expense and publicity of prosecuting Queensberry had already ruined Wilde. All his goods, in the Tite Street ideal home, were seized and sold at auction, most of them fetching absurdly low prices. *The Importance of Being Earnest* was withdrawn from the stage of the St. James' Theater, and no publisher or producer, for the next few years, dared handle any of Wilde's works. Constance and a few friends were unaffected in their devotion, but nearly all those who had applauded and flattered Wilde in his heyday now failed him, and foremost among the faithless, as soon as the first trial began, was Lord Alfred, who fled to Paris.

The jury, at the first trial, failed to agree. The prosecution followed shameless tactics in its anxiety to shield some of Wilde's friends, Lord Alfred, for instance, and a nephew of the Solicitor-General, who had been proven, in the evidence unearthed by Queensberry, as guilty as the accused. Bail was finally granted, and Wilde's friends again besought him to flee to Paris. But he seemed either listless or intent, under the pressure of guilt-feelings, on drinking the cup of degradation and retribution to its dregs; besides, he seemed to believe that it was his duty to shield Lord Alfred by bearing the full brunt of the scandal.

At the second trial, the jury again began to wonder why only Oscar Wilde was being prosecuted. The Solicitor-General's nephew's name was again mentioned several times by witnesses, and the foreman of the jury expressed dissatisfaction with the proceedings; it seemed almost, at times, as if Wilde might be acquitted. But the summing up was stern, and the jury finally returned, after having again disagreed and then again deliberated, a verdict of guilty on all counts but one. Wilde was condemned to two years, hard labor.

It was in Reading Gaol that Wilde now experienced the extremes of physical and mental misery, of solitude, undernourishment, callous routine, intellectual privation and spiritual anguish, from which he distilled *De Profundis* and *The Ballad of Reading Gaol.* When he was released, in May, 1897, he signed a deed of separation from his wife, and now went to live abroad, under the name of Sebastian Melmoth. From France, he sent the *Ballad* to his publisher and wrote, to *The Daily Chronicle,* two letters on prison reform. He tried to resume work on his unfinished *Florentine Tragedy,* and toyed with several other projects. But he soon realized that he had been stripped, by adversity and suffering, of the energy or faith that art generally demands. He drifted to Paris and made several fruitless attempts to revive the passion of his earlier relations with Lord Alfred, who had little use now for an aging, fallen, and impoverished lover; then Wilde settled down to die beyond his means, on the charity of his friends and in a routine of joyless drinking and debauchery.

Speranza had died while her son was still in prison. Constance had died a year after his release, and his brother William died shortly after her. Only a few close friends now remained, among them Frank Harris and Robert Ross, to whom Wilde had become "a sort of adopted prodigal baby." When death at last came to Oscar Wilde, it was in an inexpensive Paris hotel room, on the 30th of November, 1900. And it was the same angel of death as had once visited Heine and Baudelaire and was yet to visit the Hungarian poet Ady: syphilis, the "mal sacré" of poets whose experience of love has been so bitter that only this crowning agony of love's retribution is still lacking.

Appendix II (Philological)

In *De Profundis*, Wilde wrote that he had "disgraced" his name "eternally" and "made it a low byword among low people." The limited edition of Renier's somewhat journalistic Wilde biography thus begins with an anecdote where an unfortunate homosexual falls into the clutches of a blackmailer who calls him insultingly an Oscar Wilde. In the course of the year when this book was being written, further evidence of the disgraceful meaning of the byword was unearthed in the incident which set Noel Coward at odds with Brooklyn. In an unsurprisingly fatuous little book of impressions and memories of a tour of Mediterranean battle-fronts, the idol of Café Society snobs, stage-door swooners, and Tin Pan Alley crooners had made some slighting remarks, whose anti-Semitism, though veiled, was none the less obvious, about the endurance and courage of wounded service-men from Brooklyn. Immediately, united Brooklyn, "irrespective of race, creed or color," as so many texts of that oratorical year say, was up in arms. And New York's parental Mayor La Guardia delivered himself, in his weekly radio talk, of one of his most ambiguous diatribes: "I can understand the indignation of the good people of Brooklyn, for they know their own boys. Perhaps they do not know the gentleman. You see, it is understandable if you do know him, because I do not think Mr. Coward knows much about

American he-men. They are not the kind of bed-fellows he is accustomed to associate with. I received a letter about him the other day, and they said he was really a talented man. He is, yes. They said he was an actor and a musician and a poet. He is a poet, and so was Oscar Wilde."

But Oscar Wilde's name can still suggest other and less sordid thoughts to the Philistine mind. "How the ideas of Oscar Wilde can help you," suggests the prospectus of Wm. H. Wise & Co., New York publishers, announcing a twelve-volume Connoisseurs Edition of Wilde's Complete Works: "Wilde had singular gifts of ease, grace, poise, understanding and tact. He had the faculty of solving problems with a witty phrase and laughing off discomforts and annoyances with words that cheer and restore. From his writings, you acquire—unconsciously—his happy skill of making every contact, business or social, comfortable, easy, helpful, stimulating. Wilde communicated this art of getting on with people in every paragraph." One can well imagine Edith Wharton's Undine Spragg, in the sucker days of her brash New York début, flying to Brentano's to subscribe to this miraculous set of books, just as she rushed to the Opera when she thought that her being seen there might open to her the doors of Fifth Avenue society. Whether as a symbol of glittering Dale Carnegie success or of sordidly criminal degradation, Oscar Wilde's ambiguous name still means more than that of almost any other writer.

Appendix III (Bibliograpical)

To list a bibliography for a book of this sort is necessarily an arbitrary and fruitless task. For two or three lines devoted to the taste for medieval Latin poetry displayed by such later Romantics as Baudelaire, I might quote some fifty sources which I have consulted for a more ample and scholarly discussion of this topic, and well over a hundred sources to justify the interpretations of sixteenth-century Italian poetics and lyrical drama to which I owe the principles of my discussion of Wilde's lyrical dramas. A book of this sort is the product of many years of general reading rather than of a few months of specific research. The critic's authority thus resides in his methods or principles, or in the persuasive quality of his arguments, far more than in an infinite regress of sources or authorities listed in a bibliography of works which generally refer to each other and which an unskilled critic can always misinterpret.

Bibliographies on Oscar Wilde are already numerous and confusing. That of the William Andrews Clark Memorial Library of Los Angeles, to which I am much indebted, is certainly the most detailed. Published in several volumes, it examines critically, and with unusual acumen, a large number of items from the Library's unique collection of Wilde editions, of books and articles on Wilde, and of Wilde manuscripts. Most of the other Wilde bibliographies are more or less unreliable: much unmitigated gossip and sheer nonsense has been published about Wilde, and even critical bibliographies accept most of it at its face-value, while other bibliographies make no attempt to pilot the reader through these shallows.

Many older editions of Wilde's writings are unreliable, except Methuen's. Some of them include works that appear to have been selected at random, others exclude whole passages from poems they have reprinted, others are full of typographical errors or claim to be complete works while making no mention of some of Wilde's published writings. Of the biographies, let it only be said that those of Wilde are generally as sensational and unreliably biased as those of Arthur Rimbaud, and that Frances Winwar's *Oscar Wilde and the Yellow 'Nineties* stands out among the more carefully documented just as Enid Starkie's more intellectually perceptive *Arthur Rimbaud* is the best biography of the equally controversial French poet. Most of the other Wilde biographers have busied themselves with proving that he was a homosexual but not a sodomite, or that he was neither, or that the author of the biography was neither, or that the whole scandal was truly scandalous, or that there was no scandal at all. Few other works on Wilde, apart from books of personal reminiscences which contain anecdotes about him, can stand a very thorough critical analysis. *Oscar Wilde in America*, by

Lloyd Lewis and Justin Smith, is unusually well documented; readers of *The Bostonians* will rediscover in it the journalistic world of Matthias Pardon which Wilde hated and despised as much as did Henry James, and for the same reasons.

New Directions Paperbooks—A Partial Listing

Walter Abish, *In the Future Perfect.* NDP440.
How German Is It. NDP508.
Alain, *The Gods.* NDP382.
Allman, John. *Scenarios for a Mixed Landscape.* NDP619.
Wayne Andrews, *Voltaire.* NDP519.
David Antin, *Talking at the Boundaries.* NDP388.
Tuning. NDP570.
G. Apollinaire, *Selected Writings.*† NDP310.
C. J. Bangs, *The Bones of the Earth.* NDP563.
Djuna Barnes, *Nightwood.* NDP98.
Charles Baudelaire, *Flowers of Evil.*† NDP71.
Paris Spleen. NDP294.
Benn, Gottfried, *Primal Vision.* NDP322.
R. P. Blackmur, *Studies in Henry James,* NDP552.
Wolfgang Borchert, *The Man Outside.* NDP319.
Johan Borgen, *Lillelord.* NDP531.
Jorge Luis Borges, *Labyrinths.* NDP186.
Seven Nights. NDP576.
E. Brock, *Here. Now. Always.* NDP429.
The River and the Train. NDP478.
Buddha, *The Dhammapada.* NDP188.
Bulgakov, M., *Flight & Bliss.* NDP593.
The Life of M. de Moliere. NDP601.
Frederick Busch, *Domestic Particulars.* NDP413.
Ernesto Cardenal, *In Cuba.* NDP377.
Zero Hour. NDP502.
Cary, Joyce. *A House of Children.* NDP631.
Second Trilogy: *Prisoner of Grace.* NDP606;
Except The Lord. NDP607; *Not Honour More.* NDP608.
Hayden Carruth, *Asphalt Georgics.* NDP591.
From Snow and Rock, from Chaos. NDP349.
Louis-Ferdinand Céline,
Death on the Installment Plan. NDP330.
Journey to the End of the Night. NDP542.
Jean Cocteau, *The Holy Terrors.* NDP212.
Robert Coles, *Irony in the Mind's Life.* NDP459.
Cid Corman, *Livingdying.* NDP289.
Sun Rock Man. NDP318.
Gregory Corso, *Elegiac Feelings.* NDP299.
Herald of the Autochthonic Spirit. NDP522.
Long Live Man. NDP127.
Robert Creeley, *Memory Gardens.* NDP613.
Mirrors. NDP559.
Edward Dahlberg, *Reader.* NDP246.
Because I Was Flesh. NDP227.
Osamu Dazai, *The Setting Sun.* NDP258.
No Longer Human. NDP357.
Coleman Dowell, *Mrs. October . . .* NDP368.
Robert Duncan, *Ground Work.* NDP571.
Fictive Certainties. NDP598.
Richard Eberhart, *The Long Reach.* NDP565.
E. F. Edinger, *Melville's Moby-Dick.* NDP460.
Wm. Empson, *7 Types of Ambiguity.* NDP204.
Some Versions of Pastoral. NDP92.
Wm. Everson, *The Residual Years.* NDP263.
Lawrence Ferlinghetti, *Her.* NDP88.
A Coney Island of the Mind. NDP74.
Endless Life. NDP516.
Over All the Obscene Boundaries, NDP582.
The Secret Meaning of Things. NDP268.
Starting from San Francisco. NDP220.
Ronald Firbank, *Five Novels.* NDP581.
Three More Novels. NDP614.
F. Scott Fitzgerald, *The Crack-up.* NDP54.
Robert Fitzgerald, *Spring Shade.* NDP311.
Gustave Flaubert, *Dictionary.* NDP230.
Gandhi, *Gandhi on Non-Violence.* NDP197.
Gary, Romain. *The Life Before Us ("Madame Rosa").* NDP604.
Goethe, *Faust,* Part I. NDP70.
Henry Green. *Back.* NDP517.
Allen Grossman. *The Bright Nails Scattered. . . .* NDP615.
Martin Grzimek, *Heartstop,* NDP583.
Guigonnat, Henri. *Daemon in Lithuania.* NDP592.
Lars Gustafsson, *The Death of a Beekeeper.* NDP523.
Sigismund. NDP584.
Stories of Happy People. NDP616.

John Hawkes, *The Beetle Leg.* NDP239.
The Blood Oranges. NDP338.
The Cannibal. NDP123.
Humors of Blood & Skin. NDP577.
Second Skin. NDP146.
Samuel Hazo. *To Paris.* NDP512.
Thank a Bored Angel. NDP555.
H. D.*Collected Poems.* NDP611.
*End to Torment.*NDP476.
The Gift. NDP546.
Helen in Egypt. NDP380.
HERmione. NDP526.
Tribute to Freud. NDP572.
Robert E. Helbling, *Heinrich von Kleist,* NDP390.
William Herrick, *Love and Terror.* NDP538.
That's Life. NDP596.
Hermann Hesse, *Siddhartha.* NDP65.
Vicente Huidobro, *Selected Poetry.* NDP520.
C. Isherwood, *All the Conspirators.* NDP480.
The Berlin Stories. NDP134.
Ledo Ivo, *Snake's Nest.* NDP521.
Janouch, Gustav, *Conversations with Kafka.* NDP313.
Alfred Jarry, *Ubu Roi.* NDP105.
Robinson Jeffers, *Cawdor and Media.* DP293.
Johnson, B. S., *Christie Malry's Own Double-Entry.* NDP600
House Mother Normal. NDP617.
James Joyce, *Stephen Hero.* NDP133.
James Joyce/Finnegans Wake. NDP331.
Franz Kafka, *Amerika.* NDP117.
Bob Kaufman, *The Ancient Rain.* NDP514.
Solitudes Crowded with Loneliness. NDP199.
Kenyon Critics, *G. M. Hopkins.* NDP355.
H. von Kleist, *Prince Friedrich.*NDP462.
Elaine Kraf, *The Princess of 72nd St.* NDP494.
Shimpei Kusano, *Asking Myself/Answering Myself.* NDP566.
Laforgue, Jules, *Moral Tales.* NDP594.
P. Lal, *Great Sanskrit Plays.* NDP142.
Lautréamont, *Maldoror.* NDP207.
Irving Layton, *Selected Poems.* NDP431.
Christine Lehner, *Expecting.* NDP544.
Lenz, Siegfried, *The German Lesson.* NDP618.
Denise Levertov, *Candles in Babylon.* NDP533.
Collected Earlier. NDP475.
The Freeing of the Dust. NDP401.
Light Up The Cave. NDP525.
Life in the Forest. NDP461.
Poems 1960-1967. NDP549.
Oblique Prayers. NDP578.
Harry Levin, *James Joyce.* NDP87.
Memories of The Moderns. NDP539.
Li Ch'ing-chao, *Complete Poems.* NDP492.
Enrique Lihn, *The Dark Room.*† NDP542.
Garciá Lorca, *Five Plays.* NDP232
The Public & Play Without a Title. NDP561.
Selected Letters. NDP557
Selected Poems.† NDP114
Three Tragedies. NDP52.
Lorca, Francisco G., *In The Green Morning.* NDP610.
Michael McClure, *Fragments of Perseus.* NDP554.
Josephine: The Mouse Singer. NDP496.
Selected Poems. NDP599.
Carson McCullers, *The Member of the Wedding.* (Playscript) NDP153.
Stéphane Mallarme.† *Selected Poetry and Prose.* NDP529.
Thomas Merton, *Asian Journal.* NDP394.
Gandhi on Non-Violence. NDP197.
Literary Essays. NDP587.
News Seeds of Contemplation. ND337.
Selected Poems. NDP85.
The Way of Chuang Tzu. NDP276.
The Wisdom of the Desert. NDP295.
Zen and the Birds of Appetite. NDP261.
Henry Miller, *The Air-Conditioned Nightmare.* NDP302.
Big Sur & The Oranges. NDP161.
The Colossus of Maroussi. NDP75.
The Cosmological Eye. NDP109.

For complete listing request free catalog from
New Directons, 80 Eighth Avenue, New York 10011   † Bilingual